The MARRIAGE SPIRIT

*Finding the Passion
and Joy of
Soul-Centered Love*

DRS. EVELYN AND PAUL
MOSCHETTA

A FIRESIDE BOOK

Published by Simon & Schuster

NEW YORK LONDON TORONTO
SYDNEY SINGAPORE

FIRESIDE
Rockefeller Center
1230 Avenue of the Americas
New York, NY 10020

Copyright © 1998 by Paul Moschetta and Evelyn Moschetta
All rights reserved,
including the right of reproduction
in whole or in part in any form.

First Fireside Edition 2000
FIRESIDE and colophon are registered trademarks
of Simon & Schuster, Inc.

Designed by Irving Perkins Associates

Manufactured in the United States of America

10   9   8   7   6   5   4   3   2   1

The Library of Congress has cataloged the Simon & Schuster edition as
follows:

Moschetta, Evelyn.
     The marriage spirit : finding the passion and joy of soul-centered
love / Evelyn and Paul Moschetta.
          p.   cm.
     Includes index.
     1. Marriage.   2. Love.   I. Moschetta, Paul.   II. Title.
HQ734.M86   1998
306.81—dc21   97-40029
                                                            CIP

ISBN 0-684-83450-2
     0-684-85198-9 (Pbk)

Acknowledgments

We want to thank Lawrence Brown, media consultant, for his creative inspiration and boundless enthusiasm for our ideas. His vision and encouragement helped get us started on this project.

Our literary agent, Robert Tabian, was brilliant in helping us focus our beginning thoughts into a more coherent picture. His skill, encouragement, and wise counsel have been an immense help all along the way.

We were most fortunate to have Mary Ann Naples as our editor. She intuitively understood our message, and her creative suggestions were always on target. Her solid commitment to this book inspired our best efforts. We thank the entire team at Simon & Schuster for being so supportive and helpful.

Our children, family, and friends have given freely of their time, help, and encouragement over the last two years. Audrey and Charles Raebeck read an early proposal and shared helpful observations. A most grateful thank you to George Rubino, who spent many hours reading the manuscript and offering valuable advice. To Dara Moschetta, a special thanks for the exceptional job of editing the early manuscript. A loving thank you to our grandchildren, Rose Kathryn, James Theodore, and Alexander, who keep us laughing and ever joyful. And to all the other family, friends, and to the couples we were working with during this period, we offer our heartfelt thanks. Your support was a constant source of motivation.

We are grateful to Kurt Adler, M.D., our clinical mentor, who taught us that a true sign of mental health is the ability to merge one's own self-interest with the common interest of humanity.

To our spiritual teachers, J. Krisnamurti, Jean Klein, and Sri Nisargadatta, our deepest gratitude for helping us wake up to the truth of who and what we really are.

To all the courageous and loving couples
who shared their lives with us

Contents

Seven Steps to the Marriage Spirit

Helping couples, as a husband-wife marriage counseling team, has been our life's work. This we have done in weekly counseling sessions, on weekend workshops and retreats, and as contributing editors to the *Ladies' Home Journal* magazine and their immensely popular column *Can This Marriage Be Saved?*

Over the years we have helped partners face just about every issue that exists in marriage: infidelity, in-law problems, religious differences, money problems, child-rearing issues, prolonged unemployment, communication failures, sexual problems, physical and emotional illness, physical and emotional spouse abuse, alcoholism and drug abuse, dual-career problems, issues of power and control, and the loss of love and passion.

To deal with these issues we have taught partners to communicate better, showed them how to overcome past anger and resolve conflicts, analyzed their dreams, given them parenting skills, helped them heal their wounded inner child and guided them through the maze of confusing messages stamped on their psyches by loving but often misguided parents.

While these efforts usually helped a great deal, we felt the need for a larger perspective, one that would not only address specific problems but also give marriage a greater sense of meaning and purpose. Solving problems was essential but the next step was just as important—making sure couples did not drift into a mechanical, soulless kind of intimacy. To inspire partners to see the best in themselves and their relationships we searched for a larger vision for marriage.

This search was also a personal journey. Both our first marriages had ended in divorce and neither one of us wanted to risk repeating such a painful experience. In the early years of our present marriage of twenty-five years we were subjected to some of the same stresses other couples, especially those in second marriages, find so disruptive. Not only were we both completing our doctorates, working, and starting to build a private counseling practice, we were also raising children while attempting to integrate stepchildren and former spouses into a somewhat harmonious whole.

We have fared well. Our marriage has enriched us as individuals, has deepened our love, and was a help in carving out a satisfying family and professional life. No doubt our therapy training was a saving grace for us. Yet the need for a larger meaning to our own marriage, as well the marriages we worked with, persisted.

A NEW VISION FOR MARRIAGE

A vibrant, alive marriage has to be more than just problem-free. The concept of "good health" is a useful analogy here. Good health is much more than the absence of illness. It includes all the benefits of optimum functioning, a zest for living, and the harmony of body, mind, and spirit working together as a unified whole. Similarly, marriages, when they are strong and healthy, become powerful vehicles for personal growth and self-transcendence. They are sacred places for the generation of unselfish soul-centered love.

As you read *The Marriage Spirit* you will encounter what may be new spiritual ideas and practices. Here spiritual does not mean "religious." It refers instead to a growing awareness of your divine nature and its connection to a larger universal life force, a shared energy and intelligence that pulsate through all of us.

Our search for a broader context for marriage led us to where Western psychology and Eastern mystical teachings come together. Here we found a point of view that blends psychology and spirituality, an inspiring vision that merges the language of the psyche with the language of the soul.

While psychology encourages you to analyze your thoughts and feelings, a spiritual approach is different. The spiritual approach urges you to observe, not to analyze. It suggests that you carefully notice or "witness" how your insecure ego creates unhappiness in your life and relationships.

Through witnessing you begin to sense the larger, invisible presence in which your smaller ego self operates. This living presence has no beginning and no end. It cannot be located in time or space. It is eternal and illuminates all that appears in it. The same invisible force that rotates the planets, creates mountains, and grows flowers moves inside you. *This is your spiritual self, the self of your true divine nature. Becoming aware of this self transforms your marriage into a sacred place.*

 Becoming aware of yourselves as spiritual beings transforms your marriage into a sacred place.

Like most couples, you want a marriage in which you feel fully known, deeply loved, and profoundly valued. Only a heart-to-heart marriage can deliver this kind of soul-centered love. The heart is the symbolic center of your spiritual being. In a heart-to-heart marriage you are spiritually intimate because you open your hearts to see and touch the divine in each other.

There is a free and effortless willingness to give and receive unselfish love.

Your ego, on the other hand, closes your heart. This is the self with which you are most familiar. Your ego cares most about security, so it covets power and control. It is so consumed with itself it has difficulty seeing past its own needs and being aware of its own or anyone else's divinity. *In fact, the biggest obstacle between the marriage you desire and the marriage you have is your ego's fascination with "me, my, and mine."*

 Your ego can never give you soul-centered love. For this you need your spiritual self.

The culture we live in glorifies the ego to such an extent that you begin to believe that is all you are. Yes, your ego does play an important part in your day-to-day interactions. It helps you function and make a success of your life at work or in business. But seeing yourself and each other through the eyes of your ego is disastrous for marriage. Your ego can never give you true, unselfish love. For this you need your spiritual self.

WAKING UP SPIRITUALLY

It's crucial to understand that your marriage is actually a spiritual path. When you have the marriage spirit, waking up means you are devoted to becoming your best self, your spiritual self. From your spiritual self you can have a heart-to-heart marriage because it understands that essentially you are both one. Even though you have different bodies, different backgrounds, different views and opinions, fundamentally you are one.

Waking up to this realization makes it harder for you to see and treat each other as objects to be used. Being selfish and hurting one another becomes more difficult to do. From the perspective of your higher self, relationship problems are seen as spiritual opportunities to transcend your ego's self-centered ways of being.

Through our research and couples therapy, we discovered that there is a spiritual element present in every strong and vibrant marriage. We call that spiritual element soul-centered love.

In the following chapters we will show you how to find the passion and joy of soul-centered love through the seven steps of the marriage spirit. You will discover how to increase awareness of your higher spiritual self. This entails understanding a profound observation: *Your identity is misplaced.* You have mistakenly identified mainly with your ego self. *From this limited identity, centered on an often wounded and self-absorbed "me," you are attempting to do the impossible: share a deeply committed, genuinely caring love. It does not work.*

Spiritual intimacy enables you to use your day-to-day relationship for growing emotionally and spiritually. When you are emotionally immature and spiritually asleep you cut love off from flowing in and to you. Of course, all of us have our rough spots, the unfinished places inside us where we are selfish and uncaring. And marriage brings these out full force because you cannot hide or pretend every day of your life. Now you can learn to rise above these rough spots by calling upon your higher spiritual self. Rather than fighting and tearing down your marriage you can help one another shed beliefs and behavior that block your true divine nature from coming through.

The beliefs and behavior that diminish you spiritually come from an image you have about yourself as being less than who and what you truly are. These images, of yourself and your partner, fuel anger, mistrust, and conflict in your marriage. Seeing yourself and each other without images is essential for spiritual intimacy. We will show you how to develop imageless perception, how to observe and dissolve interfering images in the light of your spiritual self.

When you are no longer ruled by your ego's self-centered

tendencies, spiritual values become more important to you. These values are practical guidelines that help to keep you identified with your sacred self. They create a deep sense of caring in each of you for the other and ultimately for the whole human family. It is from this sacred background that soul-centered love becomes possible. With soul-centered love you will have the means by which to love each other, not the way you think the other should be loved, but rather as each of you needs to be loved.

    With soul-centered love you will have the means by which to love each other, not the way you think the other should be loved, but rather as each of you needs to be loved.

A good way to learn is by example. Toward this end we take you inside the lives of other couples. We will show you how, with the help of counseling, they developed and strengthened their spiritual intimacy. Read their stories carefully. They contain valuable advice and solutions that you may be able to apply to your own situation.

Along with each of the seven steps on the path of the marriage spirit you will find a sharing ritual. These rituals can be thought of as a ceremonial practice, a devotional service to each other and your marriage. They will answer your "how-to" questions and help you to live out the marriage spirit. They are not meant to be forced or made into a mechanical routine. Do them from your heart. They express your commitment to clearing away the obstacles created by your ego and help you remember the truth of your higher self. That truth comes through clearly as you strengthen the voice of your spiritual self. And as you become conscious of a natural, divine quality inside yourself, you begin to see the same divine quality in your partner.

It's a well-known fact that almost half of all marriages end in divorce. This isn't because people want a happy marriage less than they used to. *It's because couples haven't realized that marriage is a spiritual activity and a vehicle for personal transformation.*

No matter how bad a marriage may appear on the surface, inside there may well be a happy marriage screaming to get out. Having the marriage spirit will help you tap a reservoir of unused love. It does this by reminding you of an important fact: You have the power to consciously create a love between you that will expand your horizons, enrich your being, and inspire you to soar to heights you never thought possible.

STEP **I**

Rediscovering Each Other — Renewing Reverence

Are we not all divine? Are we not all made for a higher life?

—MOTHER TERESA

Spiritual Intimacy

Thou and I, We have well met.
O my Beloved,
Art Thou not myself?
Art Thou not the perfume of my heart?

—J. KRISHNAMURTI

To love each other with the clear mind and open heart of soul-centered love, you need your spiritual self and not your ego. Stepping behind your ego and expressing your best self, your spiritual self, will give you a marriage of never-ending love.

You have the power to transform your marriage, filling it with the special kind of love, trust, caring, and passion you have always yearned for. You can make this happen because nowhere else in your life do you have as much creative freedom as you do in this relationship. You alone determine how you treat each other. When it comes to the quality of the love you share, you as a couple are in complete control.

Being *genuinely* connected emotionally, sexually, and intellectually will not happen unless you are able to be *spiritually connected*. This requires slowing down, quieting your mind, looking inward and learning how your ego interferes with your true divine nature.

 To love each other with the clear mind and open heart of soul-centered love, you need your spiritual self and not your ego.

Couples are so used to thinking in terms of sexual and emotional intimacy that connecting with each other at a spiritual level seems unusual. In fact, many of us are little more than strangers to our inner spiritual selves. From childhood on hurts and disappointments pile up so quickly that we close off this most sensitive and caring part of us. As adults, the up-close intimacy of marriage offers a new opportunity to reconnect with ourselves and one another at this sacred level of our being.

 You alone determine how you treat each other. You have the power to transform your marriage. If you want a marriage that truly lights up your life you will have to learn about yourselves as spiritual beings.

Everyone has a spiritual self, but it is not a personal self. It is universal and impersonal. It's that part of us which stands behind our ego, aware of everything we do. Our spiritual self is the sacred presence inside us, the invisible light that animates our body, mind, and senses. The same transcendent energy that powers the entire universe pulses in and through us.

Spiritual intimacy becomes possible as you begin to realize that each of you is cut from the same sacred cloth. In *essence* you are both the same; you are one. In addition to existing as a body, mind, and senses, you exist as pure spirit. You are divine spirit in physical form. You are sacred.

Your spiritual self, free of ego and self-centeredness, expresses the sacred nonmaterial dimension of life. It is your inner source of soul-centered love and the key to personal and interpersonal well-being. Living and loving with the clear awareness this higher self provides is what all of us inwardly yearn for.

Coexisting with your higher spiritual self is your ego self, your inner psychological "me." Unlike your spiritual self, which is universal and the same in everyone, your ego self is very personal and self-centered. It is made up of all your conditioned thoughts, beliefs, and habitual ways of behaving. It has its own private logic, a kind of *survival mentality,* which it uses to make itself feel safe and secure. Its main goal is satisfying its own needs and wants, and because of this it has a tendency to be self-absorbed and selfish.

Spiritual intimacy means consciously using your marriage, the everyday give and take between you, and especially the difficult moments as opportunities to rise above your ego and express your best self, your spiritual self. At those very times when the sharp edges of your personalities clash and you retreat from each other, your commitment to spiritual intimacy calls you together in a joint effort to put your higher selves forward.

 Spiritual intimacy means consciously using your marriage, the everyday give and take between you, and especially the difficult moments as opportunities to rise above your ego and express your best self, your spiritual self.

YOUR IDENTITY IS MISPLACED

By all means, use your body to work in the world but understand what it is. The body is only an instrument to be used: you are not your body. You are the everlasting, timeless, spaceless principle which gives sentience to this body. . . . You are not in the body, the body is in you!

—NISARGADATTA

Unknowingly, many of us have taken our ego self to be our only real self and have given it complete freedom to rule our lives. We let it color our perception in terms of how we see people and events. And we allow it complete control over our behavior.

Spiritual intimacy entails a crucial realization, *that your identity, who and what you take yourself to be, is misplaced.* You identify with your body and self-image and the images "mass media" conditions you to believe you are or should be. In other words, you identify yourself with the small self of your ego mind, instead of with your larger true identity as a spiritual being.

 Unknowingly, many of us have taken our ego self to be our only real self and have given it complete freedom to rule our lives.

At first it might seem odd that most of us are so separated from our spiritual self. But remember, we live our lives in a material world, based on concrete, objective, visible reality. As small children we learn to recognize ourselves as separate from other people and objects in our environment; we learn to exert control

You identify yourself with the small self of
your ego mind, instead of with your larger
true identity as a spiritual being.

over them and use them for our purposes. In this way our vital
needs are met and physical survival is assured.

Your spiritual self is also present in childhood but it has a
different relationship with reality than does your ego. While your
ego self insists on getting heard and making its presence felt, your
spiritual self has a more sublime, surrendering quality. It observes
all that goes on in and outside of you but has less need to act on it.
While your ego self chatters constantly for attention, your spiritual self merely observes with an all-knowing wisdom and intelligence.

As an adult it is not surprising that you are more comfortable
thinking of yourself as only a body and a mind, as an emotional
and sexual being. These are the identities society conditions you
to, so your ego self gets stronger and stronger over time. Eventually, you so *over*identify yourself with your body, your roles and
images, that your spiritual essence rarely guides your existence.

As long as we see ourselves as *only* body, mind, and senses we
are on shaky ground because our ego self is extremely vulnerable
and needs constant validation. It seeks always to justify and
strengthen itself. Its needs are insatiable and it keeps us on a roller
coaster of seeking approval and avoiding rejection.

Your spiritual self, on the other hand, seeks no approval and
avoids no rejection because it is not based on a personal image. It

Despite its selfish tendencies your ego is not
your enemy. You need a stable, secure ego
to function in the everyday world.

lies deeper within you. It calls to you in a softer way and unless you turn to it and direct your attention there you will not hear it. It lets you know when you have neglected it for too long by the anxiety, emptiness, and depression that are all too familiar.

Despite its selfish tendencies your ego is not your enemy. You need a stable, secure ego to function in the everyday world. A person with a stable ego is able to balance his or her needs and wants with the needs and wants of others. Such a person is able to be cooperative, empathetic, generous, forgiving, and unselfish.

These qualities become a reality for you when your ego is guided by your spiritual self. When your ego follows the lead of your spiritual self soul-centered love flowers between you.

 When your ego follows the lead of your spiritual self soul-centered love flowers between you.

The ego and the self-centered survival mentality it operates from are more fully described in Chapter Three. For now it is enough for us to know that this selfish self constantly wants more and more control over our lives. It is capable of creating endless desires and keeps us always striving for what we think will make us secure and happy. That is why it has such a strong hold on us, even though it never succeeds. Seeing this is the beginning of freedom.

 Your spiritual self seeks no approval and avoids no rejection because it is not based on a personal image.

CONNECTING WITH YOUR SPIRITUAL SELF

Despite the strong foothold the selfish self has established we all *know* somewhere in our very being there is another invisible dimension to us, a spiritual life force that is within and around us.

All of you, at one time or another, have glimpsed your spiritual self. You sense its presence at moments when you are completely calm and totally free of fear and anxiety; when you feel a strong sense of openness, trust, and clarity toward the people and situations in your life; at those times when you unselfishly give of yourself, and in moments when you experience an overabundance of warmth and loving kindness. At these times your selfish self retreats and you connect with the sacred dimension of your being.

Critical Incidents

If you are like most people connecting with your spiritual self often occurs during moments of great beauty and joy or during times of tragedy and turmoil. It happens when some event or circumstance cracks through the routine sameness and jars you into a different awareness. It might be winning a personal victory over great odds, feeling intuitively guided to do the right thing during a difficult situation, or suffering a loss you must make peace with. Suddenly your ego self gives way, your set patterns of reacting are bypassed, and your spiritual self comes through more clearly.

NATALIE AND JOHN

Natalie and John were married for seventeen years when John was diagnosed with cancer. Natalie talks about their spiritual awakening in the face of her husband's need for life-saving surgery:

"The surgery was a family decision, the children share in all our decisions. We were all together during that period. Going through that together, knowing what we had to face, knowing that he could die, or if he didn't die his strength was gradually going to wane, was very frightening. After he had the surgery and came home, we did a lot of talking. It was the first time we made time to get down to some basic levels that we hadn't gotten down to before.

"Spiritually, for the first time we were on more level ground. I don't mean righteous stuff. He has never been a very philosophical person, he's a very caring person, but he takes things for granted. Of course I have too. While he was in the hospital and later, we began to know that life is a great deal different than it appears to be on the surface. We began talking more, reassessing where we were headed. This whole experience has opened up a great deal of ground for us. Having the time together to reassess what we wanted in our marriage, for our children, and in our life in general has strengthened us. It has been a very positive experience."

Living through a strikingly positive experience can also help you tap your spiritual self. Often such an experience has you question what is really important in your life and leads to a reassessment of values and priorities that brings your spiritual self more clearly into focus.

SAM AND JOAN

Sam and Joan rediscovered their love and a spiritual connection as a result of an unusually positive experience. A university professor, Sam had an opportunity to study in the Far East, and this set the stage for a year-long family odyssey. Neither had expected the compelling impact the trip would have on their lives and marriage.

Sam: "When we were overseas for a year, we had some good experiences together as a family. It was a good away time because it really brought our family closer together. We were adventuring out and exploring different things. But we were unprepared, any of us, for the impact it had on us as a family and as a marriage.

"We were all involved before we left. We were involved with committees and working, going off in all directions without really being aware that we hadn't been in touch with each other. I mean across the whole family. So we discovered each other, as a couple and as family members. We had a lot of time together during those twelve months going over and coming back.

"Everything just fell together. Our relationship just flourished. We stopped and were able to spend time together and rediscover each other. I say that I just kind of fell in love with her all over again.

"While we were there and coming home, we realized that we were not going to have this kind of time and how are we going to maintain our relationship without this time! We had experienced something which we really didn't want to lose. So when the pace starts to pick up we say, 'Hey, wait a minute, we are in control of this pace, and if it's going faster than we want it to, we are the ones who are going to have to slow it down.' "

Joan: "We were very caught up here before we left, in just a flurry of good things. It wasn't like it was a lot of hassle kind of stuff, I'm not saying that. We had a lot of opportunities to do interesting things and were very involved with them. I think that we realized after the fact that we were so involved in doing all those things that we really didn't have time for each other.

"When we had that year to be away, we really had time to be with each other and be with the children and really discover each other in a way that we hadn't done quite so much. And that rediscovery wasn't an intellectual kind of thing, it was a gut kind of thing.

"We were so totally removed from the culture we were in and the whole pace and lifestyle was so different. It was much more relaxed and we had time. I think that that was a very critical kind of thing. I hate to think that you would have to leave the country for that to happen, I don't know if you would have to do that or not, but there were all those things that helped us get in touch. It was more than just our relationship, although that was a very, very important part of it. It was a whole kind of personal life reevaluation. So every part of us was touched by it."

Spiritualizing the Mundane

While extraordinary circumstances can move us to a greater appreciation of life's sacred dimension, in the ordinary living of our everyday lives connecting and staying with our spiritual self happens all too infrequently. The problem is that our selfish self has taken over at center stage in our awareness. Like a small child, it creates a loud racket to make sure its needs get met. It is the constant self talk of the ego that runs on and on inside our head. It drowns out our other voice, the voice of our spiritual self.

The good news is that when you slow down, quiet your mind, and focus your attention on your spiritual voice you find your true divine nature waiting there. It smiles kindly and says, "Hello again. Where have you been? What took you so long?"

How can we use the ordinary circumstances of our lives as touch-points to remind us of our true divine nature? By meeting them with an attitude of contemplation, a willingness to reflect on them as spiritual guideposts. From this point of view everything that happens is a reminder of life's sacred dimension lying just behind the seemingly real world. How you meet each day's events will be shaped by your capacity to see them as pointers reflecting a more sacred plane of life.

ACCESSING YOUR HIGHER SELF

You can invite this contemplative attitude of your spiritual self by doing any or all of the following:

- **Meditate.** The benefits of meditation as a stress reducer are well documented. It also effectively quiets the ego mind, making room for your spiritual self to appear. (See Chapter Two.)
- **Pray.** Prayer is a way to call forth the guidance of your higher self. It creates inner space for your true divine nature to breathe.
- **Slow down.** Your ego thrives on two speeds—fast and faster. You can disconnect from it by slowing down the pace of your

life. Walk slower, talk slower, eat more slowly; make a deliberate effort to pull back on the throttle running your life.

- **Put yourself in nature.** As often as possible, surround yourself with natural beauty. Nature is not manufactured by desire. It is not a product of the thinking ego mind. Being in it connects you with the part of yourself that is beyond thought and is sacred.
- **Witness.** Learn to activate the witnessing power of your spiritual self. It will free you from the automatic responses of your selfish self. (See Chapter Four.)
- **Reexamine your values.** What is really important to you in your daily life? Does it strengthen your ego or your spiritual self?
- **Nurture your soul.** Feed your soul with inspirational readings, beautiful music, great works of art, and all endeavors that celebrate the creative spirit.

All of the above will require a focused effort and will produce wonderful results. As Evelyn Underhill beautifully states in her book *Practical Mysticism,* "It needs industry and goodwill if we would make that transition: for the process involves a veritable spring-cleaning of the soul, a turning-out and rearrangement of our mental furniture, a wide opening of closed windows, that the notes of the wild birds beyond our garden may come to us fully charged with wonder and freshness, and drown with their music the noise of the gramophone within. Those who do this, discover that they have lived in a stuffy world, whilst their inheritance was a world of morning-glory; where every tit-mouse is a celestial messenger, and every thrusting bud is charged with the full significance of life."

MARRIAGE AND SPIRITUAL AWARENESS

Many of us live out our most intimate and most important relationship from a selfish self. It blinds us to our spiritual self, which is the self we need in order to know the joy and bliss a happy marriage brings.

Creating a healthy balance between your ego and your spiritual self may seem like an impossible task. But that's usually because we tend to sleepwalk through life and marriage, *unaware of our true identity.* The essential key to living a life and a marriage which is ever harmonious and joyful is *waking up* spiritually to who and what you actually are. *The earnest desire in each of you to wake up and have your selfish self be guided by your higher self lies at the heart of spiritual intimacy.*

Expressing a spiritual awareness in your marriage dramatically changes the way you connect with each other mentally, emotionally, and sexually. Your spiritual self is the catalyst that will change your marriage from what it has been to what you want it to be now.

 Expressing a spiritual awareness in your
marriage dramatically changes the way you
connect with each other mentally,
emotionally, and sexually.

BILL AND JOY

When we first met Bill and Joy they had been married for ten years, the last year and a half without making love. They told us their marriage had deteriorated into coldness punctuated by frequent bickering. They were both tense, tightly wound individuals and this tension rippled through the whole family. Each of their sons suffered from headaches and Joy was frequently sick with stomach pains.

Bill traded stocks on Wall Street and Joan was an advertising art director. Work demands were intense, as was the stress of having to arrange for competent child care. Each day felt filled with pressures. They careened through the week, feeling frenzied and overworked, only to crash on weekends, when fights would break out between them. They were constantly on overload and blamed each other for their plight in life.

In addition, Bill and Joy were both strong-willed and stubborn about having to be right. This set up a constant power struggle in their marriage. Whatever issue came up for discussion they invariably took different sides and became locked in a battle of wills. All their energy went toward winning and getting the best of one another and this drained the passion from their sexual life. When asked about their lack of affection and lovemaking, both expressed regret and each quickly began blaming the other.

This emotional attachment to being right pushed their ego self right in the middle of their marriage. Competition simmered between them. Negativity and blame were always close by. Expressions of tenderness, appreciation, and praise were few and far between. Life's stresses created a flood of anger that was drowning their marriage. As a result Bill and Joy had never developed the capacity to step back and view their issues from the larger perspective of "us."

As we talked with them we asked if there was any time when they didn't bicker and got along well. Surprisingly, both agreed that it was when they went on camping trips. Apparently this battling couple slipped into another zone of awareness when out camping in the mountains. The whole family, they said, got along much better in this environment. Everyone chipped in to get things done smoothly. They were more accepting and considerate of one another. For Joy, it was at these times that Bill seemed to be more relaxed and pleasant. Bill experienced Joy in a lighter, more positive mood.

Bill: "After about a day or two I feel the tension has totally left me. I don't have that revved-up feeling in the pit of my stomach. The solitude and quiet calms me right down. I'm more able to think and talk at a normal pace. I feel really peaceful inside. It feels really good and I want to share that good feeling with Joy and the kids."

Joy: "I love the simplicity, I don't have a million things to take care of at once. Days don't feel crammed with a lot of things I have very little interest in doing. This is where I get to do what does interest me, like painting. I feel freed up and happy. We both get along so much better because we can slow down and be easier with each other."

We commented that the beauty and tranquility of nature can shift us out of our typical ways of thinking and acting. The awe-inspiring expansiveness of nature *opens our inner space*. This change gives our speed-oriented ego mind a rest. We slow down and become immersed in the present moment. This leads to a sharper awareness of a deeper part of ourselves.

We asked Bill and Joy to think of this change as a moving away from their ego selves to make their spiritual self more accessible to them. We pointed out that the ego self is usually so consumed with demands and pressures that it is unable to slow down. It is so busy that it has almost no free space in it. It is crowded and uncomfortable, with room mainly for its own needs and wants. The spiritual self is different. It is not pressured and hurried; it is more spacious. It has lots of room for acceptance, respect, and cooperation, attitudes their marriage was in dire need of.

We asked them what they did with the garbage they generated while camping. They described in detail how they carefully bagged their trash and carried it out with them. "Why not dump it in a stream or mountain lake?" Of course they were appalled at this suggestion. We observed that while they would never pollute the beauty of their external environment they were consistently polluting their marriage with anger and hostility.

To help Bill and Joy transfer their positive camping experiences to their everyday life, we encouraged them to consciously focus on two things—first, working together as a team and second, changing the rhythm of their lives. To become teammates they needed to seize every opportunity to help each other feel less guarded and defensive. They had to see that their need to be right came from the most insecure part of themselves and it was important to have the courage to let that go. Each needed to give the other the benefit of the doubt, show more caring, patience, and understanding, and be eager to make life easier for the other.

They could do this by taking the same qualities of acceptance, respect, and cooperation they used while camping and putting them to work in their marriage. This meant approaching every problem, every new issue and stress from the perspective of being a team. Acting like teammates would remind them that they were allies and not adversaries. It called on them to transcend their individual stubbornness and put their marriage first.

We also suggested they make slowing down and simplifying their lives a new priority. Going slow and being easy with one another was to be their new marital slogan. During the week they were to use the commute home as transition time, inwardly slowing down so that their spiritual self was more available. Stepping through the front door was to become a symbolic turning point, reminding them to switch from their ego self to their spiritual self. They agreed to making dinner, usually a chaotic affair, a special slowing-down time.

We encouraged them to make a daily practice of being on the lookout for and eliminating anything that might cause additional stress in their lives. Whenever they felt themselves slipping into a speed mode they were to take a moment by themselves, close their eyes, breathe deeply, and regain control of their inner pace.

Bill and Joy began to see how quickly and often little things pushed their power and control buttons. But instead of reacting automatically, they stayed with the vision of a higher self. They were not always successful, but more and more *as they stayed with it,* their spiritual self created a space between the impulse to argue and actually doing it. In this space a new kind of togetherness began to develop between them. Over the next several months their bickering decreased dramatically.

After five months of counseling they went away for the weekend to celebrate their eleventh wedding anniversary. Both were very tense about resuming their sexual relationship. Joy said, "I was very nervous about it. My mind kept going there and worrying.

Finally I just told myself, 'I know I can do this and make it right.' And when we did I took the lead. I wanted it to happen and I sensed that he did too, so I made the first move. It was beautiful. We both cried. And then we laughed. It was like a storm cloud bursting. Our love just came pouring out." Bill said, "It was wonderful and I love Joy for being so courageous and reaching out. It's like we're starting all over again, the feelings are so strong. When you're calm inside and really value being with each other then just looking into each other's eyes is like making love."

How many couples are living out the most important of all relationships, their marriage, with little regard for its spiritual dimension? Probably a great many. It is not surprising then that so many marriages do not last, it is not surprising that they do not grow, it is not surprising that sex rarely becomes true lovemaking, and it is not surprising that most couples yearn for a greater sense of joy in their lives. In fact, *a joyless marriage is considered to be the norm,* especially after a number of years of being together. It does not have to be this way. The marriage spirit is a path toward personal and spiritual growth, freedom, joy, and love beyond anyone's imagination or expectation.

Your spiritual self is the catalyst that will change your marriage from what it has been to what you want it to be now.

Marriage as a
Sacred Place

A successful marriage is dependent on
inviting G — d into the relationship.
—Rebbe Menachem Mendel Schneerson

It is important to
begin thinking of yourself and your marriage as divine, because as
your spiritual awareness increases your daily interactions take on a
sacred quality. More and more you come to regard your marriage
as a sacred place, a place you value, respect, and cherish.

Seeing your marriage as a sacred place has three definite benefits: First, each of you is less likely to use your relationship as a
dumping ground for stress that builds up in other areas of your
life. You consciously avoid taking frustrations and annoyances
out on each other and letting your marriage pay the price.

Second, regarding your marriage as sacred gives you extra
incentive to be more accepting. You find yourselves less interested in finding fault and blaming. Bickering becomes a thing of
the past because you wholeheartedly embrace each other and
drop attempts to change each other. You give each other complete freedom to be, while at the same time each of you accepts

the responsibility for making personal changes to create more harmony between you.

And third, when you honor the sacredness of your marriage a flow of positive reinforcement gathers energy between you. You begin to see again more of the goodness that first attracted you to each other. It is essential not to overlook the good things, the caring attitude and loving behavior, that you see in each other. That goodness stays clear and fresh when you limit the influence your ego self has in your marriage.

ALAN AND JOYCE

Alan and Joyce have been married for eight years. Joyce has felt unaccepted by Alan's parents from the very beginning. She has tolerated a distant, barely cordial relationship with them. For two years preceding the start of marriage counseling Joyce had refused to accompany Alan when he and the children visited his parents. This was a major source of disagreement and stress between them. Joyce felt Alan defended his parents and minimized the hurt she received at their hands. Alan felt Joyce overdramatized situations and believed she was trying to control his relationship with his parents. Both had dug in their heels around this issue and their egos were fully engaged in the battle.

Their different perceptions of the problem came from their mistrust of each other. Alan didn't trust Joyce's love for him and saw her as wanting to control him. Feeling angry, he closed himself off from her and could not listen closely enough to actually hear her hurt. Joyce didn't trust that Alan was making her and their marriage a top priority. She felt his parents meant more to him than she did. She too closed herself off from him and consequently could also not listen so as to hear his pain. Their mutual lack of trust kept them both in a defensive, self-absorbed mind-set.

Whenever they attempted to discuss their issues their selfish self took over. We pointed out that solutions could only come from their spiritual self and not their egos. In order to move them past their egos we asked them to stop spending energy on verbal battles that lead nowhere. Instead they needed to use the same energy to have a fundamental change in attitude toward each other. Such a change needed the presence of their higher spiritual self. We described what this spiritual self felt like subjectively—it is caring, affectionate, accepting, forgiving, and willing to focus on the best in themselves and each other. We told Alan and Joyce that this was what their ailing marriage desperately needed.

Practicing Loving Kindness

We asked Alan and Joyce if they were willing to devote some time and energy to strengthening their spiritual selves. When they agreed we urged them to immediately use their higher selves to create a haven in their marriage that was free of conflict. We instructed them to spend twenty minutes at least three times a week sharing this new place, showing each other their "best self" by practicing an attitude of loving kindness toward each other. During this time they were not to talk about problems. Instead they were to be relaxed, playful, and at ease, expressing interest in the details of each other's daily activities, thoughts, and feelings.

At their next visit Alan and Joyce said they felt great relief at not arguing and attacking each other. They welcomed having a specific time set aside that was free of the conflict caused by their egos' adversarial attitude. Over the next three months, as their spiritual selves grew stronger, their haven time expanded. They reported a growing concern for each other's well-being and felt a renewed sense of valuing each other. They were grateful for an opportunity to get back to being friends again.

Once they *consistently felt safe* with each other they became more open to hearing and understanding each other's pain. When Christmas came around Alan suggested inviting both their parents out to dinner at a restaurant and Joyce accepted the idea. The dinner went well and both felt good about the step they had taken. The emotional climate between them began to soften and they were able to display some warmth. Both remarked how they welcomed this change and the lessening of tension it produced. No longer feeling like adversaries, they resumed going out on Saturday nights together. The affection between them and sexual interest for each other began to increase. Now they were friends and lovers. All seemed to be going well.

 Once they consistently felt safe with each other they became open to hearing and understanding each other's pain.

Feeling encouraged, Joyce agreed to go with Alan and the children to his parents' home for dinner. As we talked with them about this, both were somewhat tense about the visit. Joyce was especially nervous about "being in their territory." Alan agreed that Joyce would let him know, by an agreed-upon cue, when she felt ready to leave.

When the Selfish Self Takes Over

The visit was going fine when Joyce signaled she was ready to leave. Alan was having a good time and apparently resented Joyce's wanting to leave when she did. He neglected her signal and they left forty-five minutes later. Joyce was furious. She felt betrayed by Alan and vowed, "I'm never going there again." They fought all the way home, each blaming the other.

What was remarkable about the next session, which was right on the heels of their upsetting visit, was how well Alan and Joyce were able to move beyond it. In the past this mishap would have simmered between them for days if not weeks. Now both were able to quickly assess what went wrong and make the right moves to get their relationship back on track.

As we revisited the incident with them, Alan acknowledged that his selfish self had taken over. Wanting a longer visit, he ignored Joyce's cue. Joyce, for her part, was able to see that she was not entirely a victim here. When Alan failed to come through for her, she too, quickly reverted to her selfish survival mode and wanted to punish him.

In the session Alan was the first to apologize. He said, "Well, I feel pretty stupid for causing so much upset. I guess I got greedy. We were all having a good time, the kids seemed happy, Joyce didn't seem like she was having a bad time, so I thought I'd try to stretch things out a little longer. It was a mistake. It was silly of me, I should have stuck with the agreement. Looking back it was a foolish thing to risk all our hard work over. I'm sorry for the way I acted."

Joyce was touched by Alan's simple, direct apology. After a moment or two she responded: "I'm sorry I got so angry. Maybe I was naive to think it would go without a problem. I'm sorry I said I would never go there again because I know that escalated things between us. It's not true that I'll never go to their house again. I could see your parents were making a real effort to welcome me. Let's keep moving forward, let's not slip back, we've made too much progress for that to happen." They both regretted losing touch with their spiritual selves and the harmony they were bringing to their marriage. Alan and Joyce agreed to learn from this incident, to let it go and get back to the good feelings they were having for each other.

MARRIAGE NEEDS YOUR BEST SELF

When you regard your marriage as sacred it becomes the perfect place to reclaim your lost spiritual self. Like a mirror, it reflects all of your actions and reactions. When you look closely, as we will in the following chapters, you will see the many ways that your ego self pushes aside your spiritual self. You will see how your selfish self takes over as the voice in charge of your thinking, feeling, and behaving. Right now it is difficult to see this clearly because your vision is clouded by self-limiting thoughts and beliefs and by the endless variety of fears and desires your selfish self produces. When you don't see clearly you go on automatic and act in habitual ways.

   When you regard your marriage as sacred it becomes the perfect place to reclaim your lost spiritual self.

Unfortunately, your selfish self is already well established in the center of your awareness and continually wants more and more control. It is your spiritual self that needs attention so it can shine a loving light in your lives. But your ego will not give up its domination easily. It is your commitment to holding your marriage as sacred that motivates you toward spiritual intimacy.

   It is your commitment to holding your marriage as sacred that motivates you toward spiritual intimacy.

FRANCES AND EDWARD

Frances was the vice president of a large clothing chain when a heart attack forced her premature retirement. Brash, critical, and impulsive by nature, she responded to the loss of her career with frustration and anger. Feeling displaced and useless, she dumped much of her hostility on her husband, Edward, who had retired two years earlier. When he reacted by threatening to move out they came for marriage counseling.

Edward had tolerated Frances's moodiness because of his own passive, nonassertive way of relating. He felt under pressure to please her because hers had been the high-paying, high-stress job while he had worked for a local social service agency. The increase in her anger since retirement had brought him "over the edge." Now that they were together all the time a change in their way of being together was essential.

Frances needed help to see that the ego-centered self she was used to acting from at work, and now increasingly at home, was destroying her marriage. She had so overidentified with her ego that her sense of worth was exclusively tied to the success she found at the office. Even as a child she felt that her parents' love had been based on her "doing well and being successful." Now, no longer having career success to bolster her self-esteem, she felt worthless, angry, and deeper still, afraid. *She had no awareness of herself, or Edward, as spiritual beings. And she had no awareness of her marriage as a sacred place so she felt free to vent her frustrations there.*

Edward contributed to this pattern by not holding up his end of the marriage partnership. He repeatedly would not follow through or take responsibility for the things he agreed he would handle. This "laziness," as Frances labeled it, was a constant source of frustration for her. Edward's passivity was his way of getting the upper hand and expressing anger toward Frances for, as he put it, "always criticizing me and putting me down."

Edward had trouble being up front and straightforward with Frances. He had been raised in a single-parent home with an overburdened, overworked mother who convinced him he was not adequate for much of anything. He went through life taking as little risk as possible. He did not like confrontations and was afraid of upsetting Frances and triggering her anger. He said little or nothing to her about the things she said that hurt him.

With counseling Frances and Edward began to have a fuller understanding of themselves and how they interacted. Yet Frances's anger stayed just below the surface, ready to erupt at any time, and Edward remained cautious and resentful.

Learning to Meditate

We suggested that a spiritual approach for soothing their anger and despair might be helpful. The crux of this approach meant becoming more aware of themselves spiritually. In order to do this they would have to begin to quiet their minds, and this is often best accomplished through meditation.

The sole purpose of meditation is to quiet the mind through simple awareness. It is an opportunity to let go of the things that most often preoccupy us: work, financial worry, parenting problems, all our concerns and responsibilities. It is letting go of the thoughts and feelings that agitate and disturb your consciousness. It is a time to be in stillness and connect with your inner spiritual self.

We gave Frances and Edward the following guidelines for meditating: They were instructed to sit quietly and comfortably twice a day (in the morning and evening) with their eyes closed, breathing naturally. After a minute or two we asked them to focus their attention solely on their breath. Focusing is not hard concentration, it is a gentle watching of the natural rhythm of each inhalation and exhalation. Following their breath, watching the rising and falling of their chests with each breath was their only objective.

We encouraged them to allow any thoughts or feelings that arose to come and go without any effort to control them. All that was required was watching with detachment, noting them and then letting them go. Whenever they found themselves following thoughts instead of their breath, they were to return to their breath. Any forced effort to suppress thoughts or feelings was to be avoided. Gentle awareness, noting, and letting go are all that is required.

Frances and Edward were to begin meditating in this way for twenty minutes at each sitting. When finished, they were to take a minute or two to return to normal awareness before resuming the day's activities. We reminded them that meditation is a life-long practice, not something you push to get right at each sitting.

If they went slowly and stayed with it their rewards would be great.

Meditating helped Frances and Edward become more aware of the thoughts and feelings that ran through their minds. They saw how often complaints and blame occupied them and how difficult it was to just note them and then let them go. Gradually, however, they began to have more and more success in interrupting the automatic responses of their ego selves.

In the quiet moments meditation provided they began to develop a new awareness of themselves. Frances began to see herself as more than just her job and the power and status she attached to it. Edward saw himself as more than just a passive victim and began taking more adult responsibility for his actions in the marriage. He began to assert himself by being more direct about his feelings and not playing the part of victim.

 The sole purpose of meditation is to quiet the mind through simple awareness. It is a time to be in stillness and connect with your inner spiritual self.

To help Frances deal with her feelings of being depleted by the loss of her job we urged her to start a daily "gratitude log." Here she was to enter everything that she was grateful for in her life at present: her health, her loving husband, their ability to retire comfortably, her dog Willy. Writing in the journal each night made her recall that as a child she had often prayed to comfort herself during difficult times. We encouraged her to resume this practice.

Prayer is a way of asking for guidance, clarity, courage, and wisdom in difficult and joyous moments. It is not pleading for spiritual favors from above. It is turning inward to communicate with and listen for the divine living presence within. It is an expression of thankfulness and gratitude and a powerful way of restoring spiritual energy. Through prayer we humbly open our hearts so the light of divine being will shine in us.

With the daily practice of meditation and prayer, Frances began to feel more calm, and her angry outbursts diminished. She stopped dwelling on the past. The tender, softer side of her began emerging more often. Now the good things about her present life drew her attention. Ed began to feel less on guard and moved closer to her. Together they were more relaxed and able to work through how they planned to create their future.

 Prayer is a way of asking for guidance, clarity, courage, and wisdom. It is not pleading for spiritual favors from above. It is turning inward to communicate with and listen for the divine living presence within.

SWITCHING CHANNELS IN YOUR MIND

Marriage is one of the best places to develop your spiritual self because when you live intimately with each other day after day you get to see yourself as you really are instead of as you imagine yourself to be. Your divine self may show up one moment while your less-than-gracious selfish self makes an appearance in the next. Paul is no stranger to this situation:

"I'm always surprised when suddenly I hear myself barking at Evelyn. It catches me off guard because it's not my usual manner. But there I am barking away because I've gotten frustrated about one thing or another. I'm not very patient when little, unexpected things go wrong. That's when I hear myself, as if the voice didn't belong to me, snapping, being harsh, and just plain taking advantage of her kind nature.

"She doesn't bark back, though, and that's good because it leaves me standing there, my words still hanging in the air, feeling, 'Oh, no—how could I have said that?' But it is me, not the me I'm most proud of, but me nonetheless. I apologize and love her all the more for giving me the space, without blame, to see my rough edges that still need polishing."

When our selfish self does show up in our awareness we can choose to replace it with our higher spiritual self. We are all familiar with the TV remote control. It is a good visual to remind you to switch channels in your mind. For example, if you are like most people, you just "channel surf" through marriage. When you go on automatic and mindlessly get stuck on a "dumb show," thinking angry, negative thoughts about your partner, you have tuned into your selfish self.

At that very moment you could "click" into your sacred self, asking for guidance on how to handle the particular situation or negative mood you are experiencing. Let go, give the remote over and let your higher self "click" in and do the rest. When you see yourself stuck in your selfish self, at that point, immediately switch channels to your sacred unselfish self.

So while each of us may have tendencies to idealize our behavior, the truth of who we are at any moment is displayed in the day-to-day living of our marriage.

RENEWING REVERENCE

When you love someone, in reality you love the ultimate in them.
You love the divine in them.

—JEAN KLEIN

Making your marriage a sacred place where spiritual intimacy thrives calls for *bringing back reverence*. Reverence is part of the falling-in-love experience. It appears when you are filled with adoration, devotion, passion, and even awe for the one you love. With reverence it feels totally natural to honor, respect, even worship your beloved. And of course, the wonderful thing about reverence is that it re-creates itself in the lover. Feeling so much love for another triggers intense love feelings in yourself.

 Making your marriage a sacred place where spiritual intimacy thrives calls for *bringing back reverence.*

The beauty and goodness you see in your partner intuitively touches the same qualities in yourself, they connect you with your own inner divinity. You then feel happy, optimistic, joyful, the world becomes a wonderful place to be. However miserable you may have felt before, the exchange of feelings of reverence leaves you feeling confident, secure, open to others, and seeing the best in them and the situations that arise in your life.

With reverence it feels totally natural to honor, respect, even worship your beloved.

We long, as spiritual beings, for reverence because the great passion that goes with it pulls us away from our selfish self and puts us back in touch with our spiritual self. In love you are pulled away from your selfish self by the spiritual magnetism of your partner. That magnetic power is the special passion of reverence. It is a *passion for the person,* for the goodness he or she reflects. It is this passionate reverence for another that ignites your own inner goodness and brings you closer to your spiritual self. We'll have more to say about this kind of passion in Chapter Fifteen.

Reverence starts to wane when your selfish self shows up. Your selfish self, your "me-me-me" begins to grab control over what you think, feel, and act. As time passes, disappointments pile up, anger and hurt accumulate; the adoration, devotion, and passion of reverence begin to fade.

You can keep reverence alive by learning how your ego self operates. When you stay spiritually awake and observe how and when your ego influences your thoughts and feelings you prevent it from dulling your passion.

Crucial in this effort is your conscious choosing capacity, your conscious ability to make choices and decisions. Choosing is the most powerful thing we do as humans. If you have a dog or a cat as a pet take a good look at it for a moment. What separates you from it is your capacity to reason and make choices. Animals react instinctively, humans choose.

 We long, as spiritual beings, for reverence because the great passion that goes with it pulls us away from our selfish self and puts us back in touch with our spiritual self.

Renewing reverence, keeping its flame of passion alive between you, is a choice. It is a conscious decision you make. It is deciding that your marriage is indeed sacred and you want to honor it as such. Each time you consciously devote energy to renewing reverence for each other you strengthen spiritual intimacy.

Without reverence marriage is inevitably a shallow affair, a functional arrangement for the meeting of custodial needs. For the latter, your ego will suffice. It can easily consume a lifetime creating one desire after another. To renew reverence you must be willing to transcend your ego and embrace your true divine nature.

Now we would like you to exercise your choosing power by deciding to earnestly devote yourself to the ritual that follows.

STEP I RITUAL

REDISCOVERING EACH OTHER— RENEWING REVERENCE

Research has shown that *set and setting* exert a powerful influence on the result of any ritual. "Set" refers to your frame of mind as you enter the experience. For best results, you should be relaxed, free of preoccupation, and able to devote your full attention to the present. "Setting" refers to the physical surroundings: A quiet and comfortable atmosphere free of intrusions is most essential. Ensure that small children are asleep and turn off the phone, television, and personal computer. Set aside enough time, approximately forty-five minutes, to complete the process.

This is a ritual for you to do together as a couple. It is preferable that it be done away from home in a setting of natural beauty of which you are especially fond. If this is not possible, it can be done in the most beautiful room in your home or in an area of your home where you can easily create an atmosphere of beauty and serenity. Some soft music, some flowers, and scented candles will help create the setting you need. Also it will help relax you.

Read the following story and directions through completely before actually doing the ritual. This will give you an overall sense of what is required. Some couples find it helpful to read the directions into a tape recorder and then play them back. In this way each of you will be hearing the directions at the same time and will be free to concentrate on them. If you do use a tape recorder for the directions be sure to record them in a slow, soft voice.

JAMES AND ROSE

Married for ten years, James and Rose first met as brokers in a large real-estate firm. They came for marriage counseling because, as Rose put it, "All we do is fight." James said, "I'm starting to dread coming home at night." Both agreed that when they were first married they had been best friends and lovers. "We could talk about anything and everything, and always had fun together. Because we were in the same field, we also shared all the ups and downs of our careers together," Rose said. "Now that Rose is home with the children we don't have that," James added. "And, frankly, rehashing my day's work at night is often the last thing I feel like doing."

Rose grew up with three sisters in a middle-class family. Her parents believed that praise led to arrogance and conceit. "None of us got any praise because my parents thought it was wrong. They felt if they made one of us feel special the others would feel hurt and that would be unfair. No matter what I did: Being really good, getting straight A's, always working hard, it was never a big deal because that's what was expected."

James grew up in a working-class family. His father was a building superintendent and his mother took in sewing work at home. James always felt a sense of shame about his family's lack of material success. He grew up surrounded by cousins whose fathers had better jobs. As a youngster he was competitive and excelled as a student and as an athlete. Throughout high school and college he won academic honors while playing three sports. He was a driven competitor.

While doing the ritual, Rose revisited the time before they were married: "We were working together in a large real-estate firm. James and I had been dating and I felt I was falling in love with him. One day, as I was on my way toward his office to tell him about an important memo I just received, I saw him talking in what I thought was a very intimate way with a very attractive woman who just starting working with us. I felt sick to my stomach, quickly turned around and headed right back to my office. I knew he didn't see me and felt relieved about that.

"A short while later, just before he was to go into a *very* important meeting, he called to confirm a dinner date we had for that evening. I remember responding in a cold and distant way. When he asked me what was wrong I told him nothing was wrong. He would not accept that. He told me he could hear something was not right in the way I was acting toward him. I stubbornly stood my ground and insisted nothing was wrong, told him I'd see him later, and hung up the phone.

"I remember it like it was yesterday. Within a half-hour James burst open my office door, slammed it behind him, pulled a chair right up to my face, and made me look straight at him. 'I love you,' he told me. 'I know something is wrong with you and I'm not going back to that meeting until you tell me what is going on.' I felt weak from the intensity and sincerity in his voice; that I was so important to him just opened my heart. I loved him more at that moment than I ever loved anyone before in my life. For me that was the most romantic moment in our life together."

Looking directly into James's eyes, Rose continued: "I want you to know that even with all our current problems I do love you very much. You are very important to me because I still consider you my best friend. I do admire and respect the advances you have made in your career. I respect the fact you were able to get ahead without cheating anyone or stepping over anyone. I admire that you are an honest person, a sensitive person who does care about other people and their feelings. I do appreciate all you've done for our family, the good lifestyle you've provided us with, the fact that you work very hard to make sure we're all comfortable.

"You are very precious to me and I'm sorry I don't let you know that often enough. I do feel a deep sense of gratitude having you in my life and without you even knowing it I do thank God for you."

It was now James's turn to recall his memory: "It sounds pretty gross but what came to me was when we were in Mexico together and I got the mother of all stomach viruses. I didn't stop throwing up for about three days and got badly dehydrated. Rose had to call in a doctor, and he wanted to put me in a hospital, but I refused. So they set up an IV in the room to get some fluids into me.

"Rose was terrific. She took care of me, cleaned up my slop, never left my side the whole time. It was a real nightmare, even the IV infiltrated and my arm blew up, but she stayed cool and calm and loving. For me it was very hard to have her see me that way, out of control and pretty helpless. I kept wondering if it would make her see me in a different light, but it didn't. Later, I realized that that was a worry coming from my own need to be on top in every situation. But Rose never blinked. I knew then that she really wanted me in her life in a serious way. It made my love for her shoot way up there."

James then slid closer to Rose on the couch, took her hands, and said: "And I love you a hundred times more now than I did then. You're smart, beautiful, you're the best mother Andrew and Kimberly could ever have. I admire your intelligence, how you keep reading and learning about new ways for us to be better parents. I love you for being so caring, always making sure I remember my family's birthdays. I respect you for being so caring toward your parents and your sisters. You've taught me how to be a better son and brother. Because of you I feel I've become a better person.

"Taking you for granted is the last thing I ever would want to do, and I'm sorry that I have. You are very important to me, I do love you, and I am so very very grateful that you are in my life and are willing to share your life with me."

DIRECTIONS

Relax and close your eyes. Take slow, deep breaths, in, then out, in and out. With each breath, become aware of any physical tension or tightness you are feeling in your shoulders, in the neck area, or anywhere else you usually localize stress. Wherever you feel tension, direct your awareness there. Breathe slowly through it and focus on letting it go. Do the same with any interfering thoughts or issues that may be on your mind. Just let them go. Breathing in calmness, breathing out tension and stress. Breathing in calmness, breathing out tension and stress. Allow yourself to relax, slowly breathing calmness in and tension out.

Now, with your eyes still closed, revisit a time before you were married, when you were at the height of your new interest as lovers. In your mind's eye, visualize a scene where you remember feeling especially happy, thrilled, and in love, a time that stands out from all the rest as special because of the warmth, passion, and love in it. See this scene now in your mind's eye, as if it is the beginning of a movie that is unfolding before you.

Take in the details of the scene, the sights, sounds, and scents of where you are. Now, staying in the scene, see yourself and your partner. Actually see yourself, your expressions, and hear what you are saying. Become aware of your feelings. *Let the movie run so you see the entire event.* Allow yourself to be there as fully as possible.

Become aware of the impressions that stand out most vividly. Become aware of what made this time so special that you have stored it in your memory bank. Let your whole being, body, mind, and soul drink in this recollection. Feel your heart open up, watch as it fills up with reverence. Take your time, go slowly.

Open your eyes and join hands, look directly at each other. Take turns telling each other what you remember about this most romantic of times. Then come back to the present. Tell each other about the love you feel. Tell each other why you value each other, why you are important to each other, and why you admire and respect each other. Describe the gratitude you feel about being able to share your life with your partner.

Now you are ready to proceed on your own.

The Rediscovering Each Other—Renewing Reverence Ritual should be practiced once every three months. Coming from the heart, it is a spiritual antidote to the frenzied lifestyle in which most couples are caught. It is a structured opportunity you create. It orders your priorities, reminding you of what is really important in your lives. It imbues your everyday interactions with rekindled love and appreciation, and it helps open your heart, calling forth your spiritual self.

Becoming Your Best Self — Your Spiritual Self

Two people have been living in you all of your life. One is the ego, garrulous, demanding, hysterical, calculating; the other is the hidden spiritual being, whose still voice of wisdom you have only rarely heard or attended to.

—SOGYAL RINPOCHE

CHAPTER THREE

Survival Is Not Living

The ego is like an iceberg. Ninety percent of it is underwater.
As we observe it, the submerged begins to move into the light of
observation, and melts in the light of
awareness.

—MEHER BABA

The best way of seeing divine light is
to put out your own little candle.

—ENGLISH PROVERB

LINDA AND JASON

Jason called to set up an appointment. He said he and Linda were "drifting further and further apart." During their first session Jason complained of Linda's constant spending and her demands for more and more things. He resented the financial pressure she put on him. Arguing about this, he said, placed a tremendous strain on their marriage.

Linda said Jason is "like an absentee husband. He's never really here for me. He works all the time and when he is home he is so preoccupied with worrying about himself and watching his sports that I might as well be alone. He wants to have all his pleasures while denying me mine."

Over the last year and a half Linda and Jason had been living more like roommates than husband and wife. Sex was almost nonexistent, and when it did happen it was more of a physical relief than making love. They spent little time together other than what was needed to take care of household chores and meet parenting responsibilities. They had few friends, and had stopped playing together as a couple.

Jason grew up with an abusive, alcoholic father who never missed an opportunity to criticize him. "Whatever I did it was never enough, and believe me I was a pretty good kid. I was never in trouble, always worked hard, had good grades—it didn't matter. He always had a putdown or a nasty comment. I couldn't wait to leave home."

Jason approached his adult years with an ego full of doubts and insecurities. He lacked confidence and overcompensated by being a perfectionist. While he always performed well he worried endlessly about being good enough. Afraid of rejection, he was driven to be perfect and to be liked at all costs. He put so much energy into coping with the day-to-day world that there was very little left for Linda and his marriage. Linda's overspending threatened the tight sense of order Jason needed to feel safe and secure.

Linda grew up being pampered by affluent parents whose sole mission was to make sure she had the best of everything. They constantly sent Linda the message "you're special and better than anyone else." As Linda put it, "My mother was weak, she spoiled me constantly. She couldn't control me so I always got my way. My father was never home so he showed his love by buying me things."

Linda's inner sense of security is based on the things she can acquire. Her ego self insists on protecting itself and expanding its importance through having and getting more. The more she has, the safer and more loved she feels. She is very competitive and envies anyone who has more than she does. Now a mother with two small children, Linda is unable to go to a neighbor's, friend's, or relative's home without feeling jealous, comparing what they have to what she has. Consequently, she always needs the "biggest swing set, the better fence, the best kitchen, the best clothes."

Underneath all this wanting is a terrible fear of inadequacy. Both Linda and Jason lack self-confidence and self-esteem. They look outside themselves for stability, acceptance, and love. The alternating waves of fear and desire they experience are typical of a survival mentality.

STUCK IN SURVIVAL

Your ego-centered, selfish self is concerned first and foremost with surviving, with physical safety and emotional security. It fosters a state of mind we call a *survival mentality*. Within this mind-set your ego is almost exclusively preoccupied with self-protection, self-interest, and self-expansion. It is inherently restless and insecure. Meditation masters refer to this restless ego as "monkey mind" because it is always jumping from one thought to another. It is constantly moving, looking back, looking ahead, rarely ever stopping to stay calmly in the present moment.

The major concern of your selfish self is "me, my, mine." The extent of this preoccupation varies from person to person, but the underlying pattern is always the same, a consuming preoccupation with protecting itself against hurt, with ensuring that its interests are served, and with expanding its self-importance.

Living from a survival mentality means being motivated mainly by fear, it means getting is more important than giving and being right more important than cooperating. Power and control are what matter most. A great deal of energy and attention go into getting, being, and having "more." This mind-set makes it difficult for us to see past our own needs, wants, and desires.

Living from a survival mentality means
being motivated mainly by fear, it means
getting is more important than giving and
being right more important than
cooperating. Power and control are what
matter most.

Loving from the "me, me, me" doesn't work; it leads to competition, power struggles, mistrust, clinging dependency, possessiveness, and clever mind games played for manipulation and control. With a survival mentality marriage becomes short on passion and romance and long on frustration and disappointment.

Eastern mystical teachings tell us that your ego was intended to be an instrument through which your spiritual self could express itself, bringing clarity, compassion, and wisdom into the *practical* world of everyday living. However, when it acts on its own without the benefit of your spiritual self it is like a lost child, frightened and confused, frantically running around trying to find security for itself. And like an upset child it creates a loud racket in your consciousness. It demands all your attention, wanting you to think, feel, and act in "me-first" ways. Going through life with only your ego in control means you will cope and survive, but you will not truly live. Survival is not living.

      Going through life with only your ego in
control means you will cope and survive,
but you will not truly live. Survival
is not living.

Before you can be spiritual lovers you must prevent your selfish selves from coming between you. You must become skilled at recognizing all the different forms, shapes, and expressions your selfish self masquerades as.

TRAITS OF A SURVIVAL MENTALITY

A survival mentality is a particular way of looking at the world, ourselves, and other people. At the center of this mind-set is our self-absorbed ego. In everyday life we can usually count on this insecure selfish self to show up in the following ways:

The Selfish Self Is

- Obsessively concerned with safety, security, and superiority.
- Constantly criticizing, judging, fault finding, and blaming.
- Consistently negative and pessimistic.

The Selfish Self Needs

- To be right.
- To be perfect.
- To win over others.
- To be in control.

The Selfish Self in Action

- Expects to be pampered.
- Holds on to anger and hurt.
- Is unforgiving.
- Uses "poor me" in order to win and have control.
- Is as harsh and condemning toward itself as it is toward others.
- Is highly materialistic, caring more about things than about people.
- Has an insatiable desire for "more": more money, power, control, more things.
- Lives a life full of contradictions.

In the following pages we will explore the various ways this selfish self shows up in and between you so that you can become an expert on how it operates. In Chapter Four you will be introduced to the spiritual practice that tames the ego's tendency to monopolize your attention and awareness.

FEAR AND DESIRE

Your survival-oriented ego is a storehouse of fear—fear of illness, fear of death, fear of failing, fear of not being good enough, fear of not having enough, or fear that if you were fully known you would not be deeply loved. There is the fear of being lonely and the fear of getting close to people. Fear and insecurity are common in a reality created by a survival mentality. *It is this survival mind-set that keeps all of us, to varying degrees, outwardly and inwardly insecure.*

Living with so many fears makes escapes feel like a necessity. These escapes take a variety of forms: overeating, overspending, overworking, overshopping, indiscriminate sex, losing oneself in front of the TV or computer, and alcohol and drug abuse ranging anywhere from the misuse of prescription drugs to habitual pot smoking and the use of cocaine. We pursue such escapes because they provide an illusory relief from anxiety. In marriage all they really do is create one more arena where partners are pitted against each other.

Living from a survival consciousness also keeps us stuck in the endless pursuit of desire. The difficulty here is that what your selfish self desires never seems to bring genuine happiness any closer. A survival mentality keeps us always wanting, wishing, yearning, hoping. Whether it's wanting recognition, wanting money, wanting approval, or wanting things, we are always wanting. When we don't get what we want we become anxious, depressed, and angry. We feel either cheated or inadequate. Getting our self-centered desires satisfied brings only flashes of happiness. The majority of us find only brief episodes of true joy in life. We may fill our lives with every conceivable kind of pleasure, but real joy seems to come only in flashes.

 Getting our self-centered desires satisfied brings only flashes of happiness.

In a survival mentality, desire and pleasure take on an exaggerated importance because they bring our ego relief from anxiety and boredom. Desire and pleasure pull us along while fear and anxiety nip at our heels.

 Desire and pleasure pull us along while fear and anxiety nip at our heels.

ATTACHMENT

The way of the selfish self is not only the way of fear and desire, it is the way of *attaching* to things and people for security. Your selfish self seeks happiness by pursuing and trying to attach to objects (whether people or things) that it imagines will bring fulfillment. Attachment is a form of dependency and a major cause of suffering, because if you lose what you've become attached to for pleasure or security, the pain can be unbearable.

The dependent part of you puts up a fierce struggle against letting go of its cravings. It is so accustomed to grabbing, grasping, clinging, and holding on to that it does not want to let go, it is actually afraid to let go. The more insecure it feels the more tightly it attaches. The focus of attachment could be a husband, a wife, children, parents, friends, money, position and status, a house, a car, furniture, or a favorite form of entertainment.

Attachment is not love. In marriage it can become clinging dependency, possessiveness, jealousy, selfishness, or neglect. In the early stages of relationships many couples confuse attachment with love. While initially it may seem like unselfishness, a willingness to please, and even devoted attention, with time the basic insecurity that underlies attachment begins to surface. Eventually one partner comes to feel that he or she has value and importance only for the security he or she provides.

 Attachment is not love. In marriage it can become clinging dependency, possessiveness, jealousy, selfishness, or neglect.

KATHRYN AND JAKE

Kathryn and Jake have been married for two years. They dated for a year and a half before marrying. Kathryn was attracted to Jake because "his values are in the right place and we think alike on a lot of issues. Also, I knew I could trust him." Jake said he was drawn to Kathryn because "she's a beautiful person, we hit it off right from the start, she showed me a lot of attention and that counted a lot with me."

Unfortunately, tension has already developed in this young marriage. Jake feels he is no longer as important to Kathryn as he once was. "When we were engaged we were always together, doing things, talking, having a good time. Now she thinks more about her friends than she does about me."

Kathryn said she felt sad and confused over the distance that was growing between them. She said she was beginning to realize that she might not be able to give Jake the amount of attention he needed without feeling controlled and cut off from the other people in her life. When she and Jake went out to parties and community events, she said, he usually kept to himself and did not make much of an effort to mix with others. In fact, he got angry if he felt Kathryn spent too much time talking with friends.

More and more Kathryn finds herself worrying about Jake's possessiveness, wanting her all to himself, and about his jealous reaction when she spends some time with her family or friends. Kathryn feels that Jake's love for her is really all about himself. Much to Jake's credit, he was able to hear Kathryn's concerns without becoming overly defensive.

At one point in our sessions we asked him if the uneasy, insecure feeling he was having with Kathryn was an old or a new feeling. He told us it was a very old feeling and clearly remembered the same kind of uneasiness as a small child. He said neither of his parents made him feel especially loved or wanted. In the mind of a small boy this experience was translated to mean "I must not be lovable." The ego that came to that conclusion still acts from it today. The doubt about his own lovableness makes Jake cling to Kathryn in a possessive, dependent way. Kathryn experiences this clinging attachment as control rather than love.

WITHDRAWAL

Another common problem in survival-mentality marriages is withdrawal, deliberately holding back a part of yourself for protection. Your self-protective ego views closeness as a precarious situation, one that continually raises fears of being swallowed up and losing one's individuality. You don't fully give all of yourself because your ego believes that closeness and individuality are mutually exclusive. For that self-absorbed part of you, being emotionally close is too threatening.

   Holding back in marriage leads eventually
to emotional distance and mistrust.

The ego's basic insecurity dictates that we play it safe and only give ourselves partially. This is why many marriage partners think that holding back is necessary to safeguard their individuality. Such a belief is in keeping with the pervasive insecurity of a survival consciousness. These partners equate being fully open, interested, and involved with their partner as weak, vulnerable, and dangerous.

RACHEL AND PETER

Rachel and Peter have been married for fifteen years. Peter is a contractor who builds custom homes. He is low-keyed and soft-spoken. Rachel, perky and energetic, works part-time as a substitute schoolteacher. Rachel says she is hurt and angry because Peter keeps secrets from her, makes decisions without consulting her, and often will talk things over with his father before she hears about them.

Rachel: "I have a 90–10 marriage, I give 90 percent and Peter gives 10 percent. He takes and takes but gives back very little. It gets me fed up, and when I'm fed up everything goes, the love, the sex, everything, you name it."

At first Peter said Rachel was exaggerating. He said that he helped out around the house much more than any of the neighbors. Rachel quickly shot back that she wasn't talking about how much Peter did around the house. She agreed he did more than his share. It was his not sharing in other ways that had her so hurt.

"I never know what's on your mind, what you're feeling about things, what you're thinking about. When I ask you about anything, vacations, our retirement, the kids' futures, you barely give me an answer. You're in your own little world and you let me in when you want something." Rachel's frustration was clearly evident. She threw up her hands and gave Peter an annoyed look.

"See, this is what happens all the time, she doesn't want to talk, she wants to fight," Peter said. He went on to tell how his parents had spent their whole marriage bickering. His mother always had the final say and his father usually felt defeated. Peter had watched this go on and identified strongly with his father as a victim of an overbearing, controlling wife.

He confided in the session that he believed that if he did share more of his thoughts with Rachel she would "just use it to argue me down on things. She's a strong-willed person, she can't help that. She complains now that I don't talk, but maybe that's better than fighting all the time." Peter's ego self learned early on that the only way to be safe in a marriage is to not get close. This conclusion led to his guarded, defensive posture with Rachel.

Actually, withdrawing and holding back for protection only reinforces feeling unsafe. Holding back in marriage leads eventually to emotional distance and mistrust. When we hold back a part of ourselves and don't reveal ourselves fully, an honest soul-to-soul spiritual connection never develops between us. Boredom and a sense of loneliness become prevalent. Original feelings of closeness, sharing, and sexual passion then begin to diminish. Healthy individuality is created in marriage when we share ourselves deeply and fully with each other, not by hiding or moving away.

COMPETITION

Competition is another important problem a survival mentality creates in marriage. Partners compete with each other either overtly or subtly over who has the power and control. They play a continual game of who is one up and who is one down. Every interaction, whatever the situation or issue, becomes a battleground over who is going to win and who is going to lose. When there is competition in a marriage, envy and resentment are sure to follow.

Competition creates an adversarial climate, as each of us is continually guarding against a possible defeat. In an atmosphere of competition, minor statements of disagreement are often taken as personal rejection or attacks, which lead to retaliation. Having the "edge" or advantage over each other becomes an unspoken goal.

In an atmosphere of competition, minor
statements of disagreement are often taken
as personal rejection or attacks, which
lead to retaliation.

AMANDA AND LYLE

Amanda runs the mortgage department of a major bank. Her
husband, Lyle, is president of a large electronics firm. Both have
control-oriented personalities. Consequently, each expects to get
his or her way in situations. Marriage, which requires a great deal
of cooperation, has been very difficult for them. While both are
devoted to their only child, Brian, every child-rearing decision
becomes a new battleground for control.

Amanda's and Lyle's need to be in control is so strong it
dominates their every interaction. Each is afraid the other will
gain a position of power. Each weighs and measures every advantage the other gets. Even though they have achieved a great deal
and have the potential for a wonderful life, they are unhappy
people. They cannot relax with each other, put down their
guard, and feel safe. Their marriage is a cold, unforgiving territory watched over by a suspicious and mistrusting ego.

Your selfish ego competes because it is basically insecure: It
uses power and control as a way of feeling safe. Winning over
others, being one up, getting one's own way all make it feel
secure. Your ego self would like to control all of life. Knowing it
cannot, it seeks control whenever and wherever it can.

BREAKING FREE

So much of what we think, feel, and do comes from a survival
mentality that it is not difficult to see why so many marriages end
badly. Relationships lived from this limited mind-set are a buffer

against being completely alone and living an isolated, lonely life. They help ensure basic survival. Beyond that they offer very little genuine love and caring because going past yourself and putting your partner first is not possible from a survival mentality. That is why most survival-mentality marriages end badly. They begin on a high and slide into boredom, bickering, and blaming. When partners do avoid divorce they often end up among the resigned, passionless, "staying together because we are too afraid to sepa-rate" couples we are all too familiar with.

Happy couples, "in-love" couples, couples who passionately desire each other (long-term, not just in the beginning), couples whose trust is unquestioned and who feel grateful and blessed to be sharing a life are married at the spiritual self level of their being. They are sharing a spiritual intimacy, consciously discov-ering and connecting with the divine in themselves and each other. Their marriages are bombproof, they stand the test of time and don't come apart no matter what life presents to them.

The kind of love we truly yearn for comes only from a *spiritual connection* with the one person on the planet with whom you are intimately sharing your life. Connecting at this level is the real reason to be married. It's *the* reason that makes all the other reasons come alive. You can begin right now by *earnestly deciding* to move yourselves and your marriage out of a survival mentality.

Witnessing: Getting Your Ego out of the Way

There is in you the core of being which
is beyond analysis, beyond the
mind. . . . It is simple, open, clear and
kind, beautiful and joyous. . . . Know
yourself to be the changeless witness of
the changeful mind.

Mind is interested in what happens,
while awareness is interested in the
mind itself. The child is after the toy,
but the mother watches the child, not
the toy.

—NISARGADATTA

Only your spiritual
self has the ability to witness your selfish self and free you from a
survival mentality. This is how you get your ego out of the way.
Witnessing is being silently aware of what is going on inside you,
of all that happens in your mind and through your senses. From
the witness stance, you merely want *to look*, watching the move-

ment of your thoughts, feelings, and sensations rising up and passing along on the surface of your consciousness. Witnessing means seeing the workings of your ego self and not acting on them.

You are always talking to yourself. But you rarely, if ever, focus on this inner dialogue as an outside observer. Watch your mind. Observe what goes on inside yourself, the thoughts that pass by, one after another. Then you will get a firsthand view of your ego mind at work.

Witnessing is an alert watchfulness. It is an attitude of watching the watcher. The watcher is your self-centered ego, that part of you which continually makes judgments, conclusions, and interpretations of all that it sees and experiences.

Witnessing comes from your spiritual self. It is a special kind of awareness because it is free of any judgments, choices, or opinions. It is simply a watching of your inner reactions and responses carefully, without any self-blame or self-glorification. Judging of any kind means that your ego self is back on the scene.

Through witnessing you get to know your ego self as it really is in each present moment. The neutral observation of witnessing highlights the contradictions between how you see yourself and how you actually behave. Being aware of these differences opens the possibility for change.

As I mentioned earlier, when frustrated by little things going wrong I would get annoyed and cranky. It happens less frequently now because Evelyn and I have spoken about it and I am very aware of my tendency to react this way. Sometimes it still comes up.

For example, working out of two different offices and having a weekend home in a third location means we live a rather nomadic lifestyle. Recently Evelyn, after getting ready to start an evening of work, left her travel bag and suitcase on the bedroom floor, blocking a direct path to the bathroom. She turned off the lights before she left. Sometime later I found myself groping my way toward the bathroom in complete darkness. I stumbled over the bags and almost did a swan dive into the toilet bowl.

Cursing, I got up and turned on the bathroom light. My blaming ego immediately sprang into action: "Goddamn it, how could she be so careless, she never thinks about anything she does. I could have broken my neck because of her. Just wait! I'm going to let her have it but good. I'm going to leave these bags right here so I can show her this mess."

There was a sense of self-righteousness that went along with this inner tantrum. As the thoughts and feelings passed through my mind, my witnessing self observed the whole scenario. I let witnessing take over, allowing me distance from the emotions. In that distance I could consciously choose not to have the angry outburst be my response. A calm feeling took over and instead of waiting to surprise Evelyn with the "evidence" of her misdeed, I moved the bags and later said, "Evelyn, let's both remember not to leave our bags where we can fall over them. I came in before in the dark and tripped. So let's make sure we also always leave the bathroom light on." That was it. No blaming, no judging, no feeling one up because I made her one down. Just a smooth and easy statement of the facts, which left us still feeling as close and warm as before.

When you can clearly see the facts about a person or situation right actions will follow. Right actions leave no trace of regret, guilt, or shame. Witnessing and right action go together because witnessing helps you to interrupt your tendency to react impulsively with destructive anger, criticism, inappropriate guilt, and anxiety. Your spiritual self, because it is not motivated by desire or fear, can see facts clearly. When your self-centered ego is guided by your spiritual self right action follows.

   Only your spiritual self has the ability to witness your selfish self and free you from
a survival mentality.

AWARENESS MOMENT TO MOMENT IS KEY

The witnessing attitude is a new way of looking. With a survival mentality your insecure ego works mostly by analyzing events and situations. As an analyzer it wants to answer a question or solve a problem, to get to the bottom of things, to determine right from wrong, or to reach a decision or draw a conclusion. This way of analyzing is important in the practical side of your life, but it is not very useful in creating intimacy.

So often when couples come to see us for marriage counseling they spend several sessions acting like lawyers arguing a case. Each partner uses a lot of energy analyzing their situation and making a strong case against the other. They are determined to prove their view of the problem is the correct one. Our effort is to help them understand that there is a better way for them to look at their situation. As long as your analyzing ego is in control you will tend to see your partner's shortcomings and not your own.

 Witnessing is pure *in-the-moment awareness*.
It happens now, in each new moment,
without any analyzing.

When the thinking mind of your ego analyzes a present situation, it is usually looking back at the past or ahead to the future. Witnessing, on the other hand, is pure *in-the-moment awareness*. It happens now, in each new moment, without any analyzing. It is the in-the-moment awareness of witnessing that helps you immediately see your thoughts, feelings, and reactions as they begin to arise. For most of us, because analyzing is so common, understanding comes after the fact. For example, we usually become aware of our inner tensions and conflicts after they have firmly taken hold disguised as a headache, a sudden change in mood, or a way of behaving that is uncharacteristically negative and un-cooperative.

Through witnessing, when you observe rather than analyze, you begin to see how and when your survival-oriented self shows up and that it has a characteristic pattern or style. Your ego self may consistently appear as meek, apologetic, and needing approval. Or it may take the form of smug superiority, sarcasm, and conceit. Knowing what your general pattern is helps you be more success-ful at interrupting your ego self before it makes a mess of things.

ENDING AUTOMATIC PATTERNS

You develop witnessing awareness as you begin to *watch* for the fears, hurts, angers, and anxieties that cause you to get all tied up inside. Gradually you'll learn to observe yourself, to see when and how you cause your own unhappiness. For example, without a witnessing attitude, as soon as you feel the slightest "pinch" of fear, let's say of being controlled or manipulated, you may do something negative as a defense, such as getting nasty, being sarcastic, or attacking. These reactions only create more conflict between you and your partner. By witnessing you *carefully observe* the negative thoughts and feelings that start working inside your mind without acting on them.

Through witnessing you don't allow your ego self to automat-ically take over and create more pain. In fact, you see more clearly not only the attack you may or may not have received, but also what you may be doing (if anything) to invite or prolong that hurt or attack. In other words, you become acutely aware of when you are feeling controlled and manipulated and when you are doing the controlling and manipulating.

This kind of self-awareness is new for most of us. Usually, we don't give much attention to what passes through our conscious-ness. This frequently leaves us feeling overwhelmed, because an unwatched mind has no way of regulating how fast it is going.

Giving attention to our mind's flow enables us to begin slowing down our thoughts, feelings, and behavior to a more manageable pace. Then in-the-moment awareness is more possible and we are less likely to go on automatic and repeat patterns that cause us pain and unhappiness.

 Through witnessing you don't allow your
ego self to automatically take over and
create more pain.

I know that between Paul and myself our selfish selves tend to surface at times of stress. When I feel under pressure I become anxious and immediately want to eliminate what is causing the stress. I want to move quickly, find a solution, complete the task, or solve the problem. For my anxious ego, sooner is much better than later. Often, I fail to see that what I need to ease my stress may be different from what Paul may be needing in the same situation.

Paul needs to move more slowly when under stress. He likes to consider the situation, look it over, think about it, and then act. For example, while writing this book, we each dealt with deadlines differently. Each of us worked independently on a topic and then we came together at an agreed-upon time to collaborate on what we had written. This agreed-upon time was our self-imposed deadline. I always have a strong need to finish on time or, preferably, before the deadline.

Recently, I had finished my writing. Our deadline was Monday morning and it was now early afternoon on Saturday. Paul said he was going to spend the day getting a haircut, going to the hardware store, and then doing some yard work. I saw the anxious ego start thinking, "Why isn't he choosing to use this precious time to work on our chapter? If we worked all day today maybe we could be finished by tonight. Why is he choosing now to get a haircut and do the yard work? Doesn't he realize our deadline is approaching, we need every spare minute we have. No, I don't want him to spend the day this way. Because of him we won't finish on time. I must show him, convince him he shouldn't do this, this is foolishness and a waste of important and productive time."

I saw myself begin to be annoyed at him and the situation. Witnessing helped me see that I felt as if I were being controlled, when actually, I was about to do the controlling. Seeing all this, I did not try to get Paul to change his plans. I was able to see that he wanted a break from writing and going out for a while was what he needed to do.

It is your higher self and not your ego that is capable of this kind of observing awareness. The ability of your spiritual self to witness the contents of your consciousness, the continuing movie of your mind, is your saving grace. The detached awareness of witnessing enables you to see and break through the automatic thinking, feeling, and acting patterns of your ego. These automatic patterns are ways the insecure part of you attempts to control for security. They produce fear and anger. More than anything else it is fear and anger, stirred up by the ego, that cause distance in a marriage. Interrupting these patterns is essential, and your spiritual self, as witness, makes this possible.

 The ability of your spiritual self to witness
the contents of your consciousness, the
continuing movie of your mind, is
your saving grace.

MARTY AND DENISE

Marty and Denise have been married for nine years and have twin boys three years old. Both say they would like to have another child, but since the twins arrived their marriage has been in a state of siege. Both carry an intense anger, which is always there just beneath the surface. A year before the twins were born Marty left his job as a New York City police officer and purchased a fast-food restaurant. Being in business for himself was his special dream, and he invested every penny he had in the project. Denise, he said, was behind him "100 percent."

Neither of them was prepared for the stress the new business and the twins would put on their marriage. The stress continues and has split them apart emotionally and sexually. "I think all the time of being a single parent," Denise says. "At least then I'd be in control of my life and maybe have some fun. Now, I might as well be a single parent but I'm not in control and I have no fun."

Attack, Counterattack

Denise complained that Marty was constantly away at the business and his every waking moment was consumed with worry about how well it was doing. "When the twins were born he was late coming back to the hospital to see them, stayed for an hour, barely paid attention to me, and rushed back to the restaurant. He said his manager had just quit, but it's always something. Our whole life is invested in that place, it's always between us. Marty is unhappy because I don't want to have sex with him but if I don't feel special, which I don't, why should I?"

Marty could hardly contain himself while Denise was talking. "To hear her talk you'd think I was off playing golf, but I'm not, I'm working hard for us and the twins, to make sure we have a secure future. Sure the business hasn't taken off the way I would have liked, but it pays the bills and that's what counts. Denise is never satisfied, she always wants more. Since the twins were born she's been a mother and not a lover. All I hear are complaints. She constantly puts me and the business down. Listening to her you would think we were in the poorhouse, but she spends money like there is no tomorrow. So which is it?" Denise shot back, "He resents my spending money on the kids because he wants to use it for the restaurant. I'll be damned if my kids are going to do without while he hoards it all for himself."

It is this kind of attack, counterattack communication that has been destroying Marty and Denise's marriage. Before coming for help this negative dialogue would leave them slamming doors and cursing one another. This was their self-centered egos at work, condemning, judging, blaming, justifying, and defending. Both were genuinely concerned about their marriage, but when the selfish self orchestrates a negative, self-serving argument good intentions do not go very far.

A Turning Point

Marty and Denise were close to a point of no return. Their anger had been piling up too fast for too long. While neither of them wanted to divorce, they saw their marriage spinning dangerously out of control. Feeling desperate, they had come for help. We strongly encouraged them to view their decision to get help as a turning point. We helped them see that this decision cut through their resentment and bitterness. It did not come from their selfish selves, it came from the larger wisdom of their spiritual selves.

Each clearly saw that coming for help put their marriage and family first and their individual need to be right second. Both said they felt greatly relieved just sharing their problems. They knew they had done the right thing. For a couple who had been constantly battling this was a small success. Their spiritual selves had served them well.

Gradually, with our coaching, Marty and Denise began to differentiate between the voices of their ego selves and the voices of their sacred selves. We explained that whenever they heard inner thoughts of anger, hatred, resentment, thoughts that blamed and attacked the other, their ego was in control. Whenever they felt an inner urging for kindness, patience, and caring, when they remembered the bigger picture to which they made a commitment, their marriage and children, when they felt a need to still the mind and wish for their hearts to open, this, we said, was the voice of their sacred self.

We emphasized that this approach required an important change in how they viewed their marriage. From here on they would have to regard their marriage as a sacred place, deserving great respect and reverence. Only then would they be able to give it the healing attention it needed. We made it clear that a conscious choice was required on their part. They could, at any time, consciously decide to revere their marriage by allowing their spiritual selves to play a larger part in how they treated each other.

Witnessing the Selfish Self

Learning how to recognize and limit the intrusion of the selfish self into their daily interactions became a new path for Marty and Denise to travel in their marriage. Limiting the influence of a survival-oriented ego creates free space in which the sacred self naturally appears. We encouraged them to observe their inner selves, to practice stepping back and using their in-the-moment witnessing awareness to observe their ego minds at work.

Once they began to look, they saw how often their insecure egos intruded in ways that would distance them emotionally. For example, when Marty came an hour late for a big Memorial Day barbecue they had planned, Denise, while waiting for him, saw herself begin thinking, "I can never depend on him, he only thinks about himself, he doesn't care about me. That selfish bastard did it again, I didn't even ask him to help me, I did it all myself. The least he could do is come on time."

Denise saw herself begin to feel hurt and angry. She saw her thoughts go on and on berating Marty for taking advantage of her. But this time her sacred self witnessed all these thoughts and feelings move through her consciousness. As she had learned, Denise did not deny her feelings, dwell on them, or act them out. Instead she allowed them to rise up and pass away. When Marty did arrive he immediately looked for Denise's reaction. Seeing she was not angry, he went over, kissed her, and apologized for being late and disappointing her. Denise felt the sincerity in his words and returned his affection. They both said later they "had a great day together."

Becoming more in tune with their witnessing ability also helped Marty and Denise stop fighting about money. Marty could never get Denise to cooperate in preparing a monthly budget for them to follow. When Denise would overdraw their checking account Marty would go "ballistic." Denise would fight back and they could spend a week barely talking to each other.

The next time Marty got a notice from the bank that their account was overdrawn, he made a conscious effort to stay in the witnessing attitude and observe his ego reacting. He remembered thinking, "She's so spoiled she doesn't have an ounce of self-discipline. How could she do this? She knows money is tight. Doesn't she care at all about the pressure I'm under? That's it! I'm getting a separate checking account and cutting up the credit cards." Marty even "saw" his heart start to beat faster as his anger and adrenaline started rolling. Usually at this point he would pick up the phone and start blasting Denise, but he didn't.

He remembered to step back and got some distance from his hot emotions. From this detached posture he felt in better control. When he did speak to Denise it was not from a blaming and attacking frame of mind. He was more calm and presented it in a matter-of-fact way. Denise did not respond with defensiveness, and instead they both talked about money for the first time without a fight. "Do I still think she overspends? Sure," Marty said, "but now, since I don't get into telling about her being irresponsible maybe we'll get somewhere."

Your spiritual self, because it knows no pretense and no deception, helps you to be real with each other. It cracks through the routine numbness your ego self creates between you, it fosters deep honesty and sincere interest in the details of each other's joys and pains, and it ignites passion through openhearted caring, which leaves no doubt that you are a top priority in each other's life.

Your spiritual self, because it knows no
pretense and no deception, helps you to be
real with each other.

STEP II RITUAL

BECOMING YOUR BEST SELF —
YOUR SPIRITUAL SELF

The purpose of this ritual is to help you practice (a) witnessing
the workings of your ego and (b) shifting identity to your spiritual self. The first part of the ritual is done on your own, the latter
part will be done together as a couple. The ritual covers an entire
week: Begin it on a Monday and use Wednesday and Friday to
complete it.

MONDAY

On Monday have as a conscious intention taking the witnessing
stance as often as possible throughout the day. Carry a small
notebook with you so you can note down how and when your
ego self shows up. This means you will be on the lookout (being
"choicelessly aware") for any negative, pessimistic, blaming, criticizing, judging, or condemning thoughts or feelings that appear
in your awareness. This is your selfish self in action. It might show
up as feelings of inadequacy or of superiority after comparing
yourself to someone else. It might surface as worry, anxious
anticipation, or as envy, jealousy, and compulsive desire.

Your selfish self could also take the form of exaggerated self-importance, boasting, being grandiose, or fishing for compliments. It could present itself as "kindness" whose real motive is self-serving in some way. Whatever form it takes, your challenge is to notice when and how it appears in your awareness.

  Witnessing means seeing the workings of your selfish self and not acting on them.

Remember when you take the stance of the witness just observe, *do not analyze.* As soon as you realize you are being negative, making a judgment, are being critical, condemning, or angry, just note it and let it go. Or if you happen to be in a particular mood (perhaps just upon waking up in the morning), feeling anxious, sad, or irritable, just observe it, make note of it in your notebook. Do not put energy into analyzing "why?" just note the thought or feeling and then immediately turn your attention away from it. The purpose of this part of the ritual is to see when and how your selfish self appears without putting any effort into changing what you see.

Also, be aware of not blaming or criticizing because of what you observe. When you blame or criticize yourself you are no longer witnessing. At that point it is your ego that is watching. Each time you are successful catching your selfish self at work make a note of what form it took, what the thoughts and feelings were. If the whole day passes and you make no notice, write that down also. These notebook entries are important because they will help you share your experience with your partner later on.

In watching yourself you will need courage to accept what you see, because it may not be a pleasant sight. Because your ego does not want to be exposed and tamed, it may create even stronger thoughts of fear, anger, hatred, and longing just to keep you in its grip. Keep witnessing, in silence, without any blaming or discouraging thoughts. Do not act on any fear, anger, doubt, or desire for the entire time you are engaged in this ritual. See the thoughts and let them pass by. Do not go into them by dwelling or analyzing. Just notice them, record them in your notebook, and let them go.

WEDNESDAY

On Wednesday you will continue witnessing but now after noting your reactions begin to practice switching your attention away from your ego self and to your spiritual self.

Using Affirmations

In this early stage it is helpful to use an affirmation when making this switch. Affirmations are carefully structured thoughts designed to replace old, negative, self-limiting tapes that run inside you. They are *positive* statements you make to yourself that declare and confirm your spiritual essence. Affirmations are always stated in the present tense. They engage your creative imagining power to manifest a new reality about yourself, your partner, and your marriage.

After letting go of any ego-centered thoughts or feelings, use the following affirmation to help you switch your identity. Say it slowly and silently to yourself: "I am compassionate awareness, which sees all that appears and disappears and yet remains unchanged."

Write the affirmation down in your notebook under the Wednesday heading so it will be available for you to use in the moment. Each time on Wednesday that you witness your selfish self in operation, after writing down the form it took, practice switching to your spiritual self with the use of this affirmation.

Remember, you are not merely your body and your mind, rather you are using both for the manifestation and expression of your sacred self. You have nothing to lose. If you doubt the presence of your sacred self, that's all right. But just for a while,

---

   Affirmation: "I am compassionate awareness, which sees all that appears and disappears and yet remains unchanged."

---

agree to suspend that doubt and act *as if* the existence of your sacred self is a reality. Keep an open mind and for now have faith and trust in the existence of this higher self.

   The highest purpose you can share as a couple is helping each other look inward and know your true spiritual self.

FRIDAY

On Friday come together as a couple at a time and place where interruptions are least likely. Take turns sharing what each of you has noticed in the previous days of witnessing. As each of you listens to what the other says, *be sure to witness your reactions.* Avoid making comparisons or judgments about each other's experience. In this way you will be creating a safe place for each of you to practice overcoming a survival mentality and growing closer to your inner spirituality.

OSCAR AND LORI

Oscar and Lori were in counseling for eight months because of their loud, angry fights, which were frightening their four-year-old daughter. They shared with each other what each of them noticed about themselves in this witnessing ritual. Here is what they had to say.

Oscar: "I know there were a lot of times when I was lost in my thoughts and forgot to take notice of them. But there were enough times when I did remember and it gave me a lot to think about in terms of understanding myself.

"When I looked over my notes what surprised me most was how often I sounded angry. I sounded like someone with a chip on his shoulder. That's not how I see myself at all. But so often, whether it was about myself or other people just passing by, I saw myself being critical and finding something wrong with them just to make myself feel good. This started me thinking about my own feelings of adequacy or inadequacy and how they influence what I do and say.

"The other trend I noticed was how much worrying I do about the future. So many times I saw myself having imaginary conversations with clients over deals I have pending with them, and worrying about how they will turn out.

"The third category, so to speak, was how much of the time I slipped into fantasy. It was a real eye-opener to see how much time I spent in one mental escape after another. By the way, I did repeat the affirmation. It felt awkward at first, but it helped me switch away from myself."

Lori: "What I noticed more than anything else was my 'poor me' syndrome. I couldn't believe how often I felt sorry for myself. In one situation after another, whether it was at work, with friends, or in stuff that went on with my mother and sister, or even with you, Oscar, I always seemed to take it to a place where I'd end up feeling sorry for myself. So that was something of a shocker, I never saw it so clearly. It's something I want to change because my life is really pretty good and I have very little to be sorry about.

"Also, I saw myself comparing myself to almost every other woman I saw. I heard myself say, 'She's thinner, she's prettier, she's more confident,' and so on. I never realized I was so competitive with other women. I really loved repeating the affirmation, it helped me feel stronger and more confident, I also felt myself be more loving."

Remember, this ritual is to help you witness the workings of your ego mind so that you can shift your identity to your spiritual self. The more you observe your ego at work the less it will control you. With this discovery you are able to break through the ego's exclusive hold on your thoughts and feelings.

The highest purpose you can share as a couple is helping each other look inward and know your true spiritual selves. Your higher self will incorporate your self-absorbed ego as a pointer for a larger sacred intelligence that is just as effective yet less selfish and disruptive. It is through the discovery and acceptance of your sacred self that you begin to love each other without your ego getting in the way.

STEP **III**

Seeing Each Other Without Judgment — Imageless Perception

Surely to understand is to see the truth of something directly, without any barrier of words, prejudices or motives.

—J. KRISHNAMURTI

CHAPTER FIVE

Dropping Images: Seeing Each Other New

The real voyage of discovery consists
not in seeking new landscapes but in
having new eyes.

—MARCEL PROUST

Memory is a good servant, but a
bad master.

—NISARGADATTA

SARAH AND MICHAEL

Sarah works for a large marketing firm. She is married to Michael, who owns a small business. Their four-year marriage was thrown into a crisis when Michael discovered Sarah's affair with a colleague in her firm. Sarah spent the first two months in therapy alone. Michael refused to come in with her. He was hiding his pain behind a façade of masculine pride and self-righteousness. "Sarah had the affair. It's her problem, not mine." Sarah began working through the guilt and self-loathing at her betrayal of the trust between them. Eventually, at our urging, Michael joined the sessions.

Sarah told us: "Right after we got married everything changed. He became Mr. Responsibility. It was like he was consumed and obsessed with his business. I work too and my job is also demanding but I still made time for us to have fun and to make love. Before we were married he would tell me how beautiful I was, he was so romantic, he would look at me like he longed for me. We got married and it was all over. I know it's no excuse for what I did. I feel so sick about this."

Michael felt emotionally crushed by Sarah's affair. He said, "The one thing I had always felt sure of was that we would be faithful to each other, and now that's gone." He felt confused and kept repeating, "This makes no sense to me. I cannot understand why this happened."

We encouraged Sarah to look beneath her feelings of guilt so she could discover what else her pain might be telling her. Michael's presence in the sessions was an important catalyst that helped her do this. His demeanor was exceedingly cold and unforgiving. Michael's "looking down" at her in the sessions helped Sarah get in touch with a strong feeling of being inferior to him. She realized now this feeling had always been there.

While Michael tended to be reserved and self-conscious, Sarah was much more the free spirit. Growing up, Sarah believed that her strong desires and carefree personality made her a bad person. As a child she had developed a self-image of being "not as good as." She felt not as good as her all-sacrificing mother, who allowed herself little pleasure or joy. And she saw herself as not as good as her self-righteous father, who preached the virtues of discipline and self-denial. Now in her marriage she felt she was back to being "not as good as." Sarah's image of Michael was that of a critical, disapproving parent.

Michael's image of Sarah was that she was immature and selfish, concerned mainly with "playing and having a good time." He felt Sarah was not able to appreciate how hard it was for him to get a new business off the ground, "I know she works hard too, but her job is pretty secure, mine is not." Sarah could see that at times Michael was right. She did procrastinate on important things and was impatient with Michael for working so much, especially when it meant giving up some fun together. Yet she was angry at Michael for his judgmental attitude. He seemed quick to blame or correct her. For a long time, Sarah felt Michael had been sending her the message that he was "a better person," and inside herself she had begun to agree with him.

Michael's self-image also played a role in their problems. He acknowledged that because of his own insecurities he did "hold myself above Sarah." This contributed to his feeling superior and judging her. Michael had an image of himself as being very adult and very responsible. He came across as tight and controlled, which he believed was a sign of maturity. This image made it difficult for him to relax, have fun, and be at ease with himself and with Sarah.

By having an affair Sarah had violated her own standards of personal integrity. Her "rebelling" had damaged the trust and sacredness of their marriage, and she was clear about this. Now she and Michael were realizing that the same trust and sacredness was also damaged by the images they carried about themselves and each other.

MAKING IMAGES

Images play an important role in your everyday life. You couldn't survive without them. You use them in learning to speak, to drive a car, to do your work, to shop, and so forth. Images are put together from all the information your brain receives from your senses. Your brain organizes and records this information as images. Whether it is a tree, another person, or an onrushing train, your eye and brain work together to provide a mental picture so you can orient yourself to the object in an appropriate way.

Images enable you to make order out of the vast amount of data your senses take in at every moment. By using images, the brain, like a computer, can store a tremendous amount of information and experience and have it ready for recall in a simple, shorthand way.

At this level the image-making process goes on automatically, without any conscious awareness on your part. A few weeks ago Paul and I went to hear a talk given by a well-known author, a woman we had never seen before. As she started to speak I witnessed my ego self thinking, "Oh, she's just like Aunt Ellie, the way she looks, the way she speaks, how she carries herself." Since I am very fond of my aunt, in this situation I was creating a *positive* image of this author, but it was an image nevertheless. I put a familiar image from the past onto a new, unfamiliar person. At that moment I no longer saw the person in front of me in a clear, unbiased way. The image of my aunt came in and influenced how I saw the author.

However, you can *consciously* use the image-making process to serve your creative imagination. That is when your image-making ability taps the universal energy of your spiritual self and a life-enhancing creative imagination is born. From creative imagination comes great works of art, from cathedrals, symphonies, paintings, and literature to a new recipe for cheesecake—all come from a conscious intention to use images to manifest an inner creative vision.

SELF-IMAGES

Fighting against the marriage spirit are the images *you have about yourselves.* Self-images are the masks we wear for security and self-protection. Look around anywhere and you will see people who purposely set out to fit the latest version of being glamorous, seductive, successful, intellectual, rebellious, politically correct, or whatever.

Self-images are the outer and inner pictures we carry forward from childhood. For most of us it is our outer body image that gets the lion's share of our attention. Who doesn't have a list of physical changes we imagine would make us look and feel better?

The media constantly bombard us with "new and better ways" to look, think, and act. All of us are continually under pressure to create and present an acceptable external image.

This outer image is only part of the story. Your inner image expresses all the beliefs and conclusions you hold about yourself. Self-images are mental pictures your ego creates. These images determine not only how vulnerable you are to the pressures of mass media, but how you behave in all your relationships, especially your most intimate ones. They express how you think and feel about yourself and other people. Your internal image is a kind of subjective, thumbnail sketch of how you see yourself.

For example, a twenty-one-year-old woman has her first child, a son. She is frightened and unsure of being a mother. Little more than a teenager herself, she has the sole responsibility for raising the child. Her husband, also a very young man, struggles financially. Although he loves her and the child, he is uninvolved as a husband and father. Because she had been raised in a very strict, authoritarian household, the young mother wants her son to have the freedom she never had. She decides to raise her child in a more permissive fashion.

She does this by setting very few limits and without realizing it pampers him, giving in too often to his wants and demands. She also tends to be overprotective, thinking this is the best way to ensure that the child will be safe and healthy. This young mother forms an image of herself as "a good mother" and believes that the proof of being a good mother is having a child who is happy and cooperative.

The child, having been pampered, is defiant and uncooperative. He has an image of himself that says, "I should get what I want, when I want it, and without having to do anything." Having been overprotected, he lacks confidence and tells himself, "I'm not capable, I can't do things by myself, therefore things should be done for me."

Faced with her son's "naughty" behavior, the young mother feels herself a failure. Her image as a good mother has been damaged, and she responds to the child from her hurt image. The child experiences an unhappy or perhaps even angry mother and creates an additional image of himself as "not good" or "unlovable." Of course, mother is not the only influence here, the child's father and grandparents, siblings, teachers, and friends are all acting and reacting with him and also help shape his developing self-image.

The son grows into adulthood carrying a "not good and unlovable" image that says, "I should get what I want when I want it, people should take care of me, and I do not have to concern myself with other people's needs." In his close relationships he hears any request made of him as a demand because he feels overwhelmed by a world he feels inadequate to handle on his own. He may have a hard time trusting women, and when he marries he will act in ways that keep his wife emotionally distant from him. To ensure being seen as "good and likable," he may, at times, be pleasant and agreeable. However, when his expectation of being catered to is not fulfilled by his wife he may act like a "bully." He is careful not to get too close for fear of being "found out as being unlovable."

Another example of how self-images develop might involve a father with an image of himself as a "man's man" with clear-cut ideas on how to treat boys and few notions about being with girls. With his son he does "guy things," with his daughter he is distant and awkward, overly protective yet uninvolved. The daughter creates an image of herself as "inferior" and an image of men that says, "They will protect you but not get close to you."

Depending on her experience with other important people close to her, as well as life circumstances, she may go into adulthood seeing herself as "generally not good enough and certainly not as important as a man."

She will probably choose a husband who is a good provider but not capable of a loving closeness. In fact, the only man she may be attracted to and want love from is one who is incapable of truly loving her. She may feel "without a man I am nothing," and no matter how much she may succeed in life on her own, she will not be able to feel complete unless a man is there protecting her.

Having an image of yourself and believing it to be true is one of the greatest causes of pain and unhappiness. Positive images are no exception, because no matter what particular positive image you may have developed about yourself someone is bound to come along and put a pin in that image.

For example, if you have an image of yourself as "brilliant," someone will eventually show you how his or her intelligence is superior. Or if you have an image of yourself as "beautiful" someone more beautiful will come along, and either you or someone else will compare you to that person and the image you have about yourself will be hurt.

It's essential to realize that all emotional images, positive or negative, exist only in your mind. They are real only if you believe them. They keep you caught in the web of hope and disappointment, using up precious life energy in unnecessary suffering.

 Having an image of yourself and believing
it to be true is one of the greatest causes
of pain and unhappiness.

IMAGES OF EACH OTHER

Most couples begin their marriages seeing each other fresh and new. But over time partners disappoint each other and cause each other hurt and pain. When these disappointments, hurts, and pains go unresolved they begin to pile up and take on a life of their own. They become the images we carry of each other. They unexpectedly come up in conversation or in fights. These images are the barriers to seeing and hearing each other clearly. They lead to hurt, distance us emotionally, and dull our passion for each other. Here are some examples of images at work:

According to Lenny, "Wendy is not happy unless she's got something to bitch about. I come home, walk up the driveway, and nine times out of ten I'll hear her screaming about something." Wendy, on the other hand, says, "Lenny is Dr. Jekyll and Mr. Hyde. He wants his family to think he's Mr. Wonderful, but with me he's a real smart-ass. Whenever we go out he drinks too much and starts coming on to every woman in the place."

Mark tells Sofia during a session, "You're like a black cloud that moves in and out of my life. You're negative and pessimistic about everything. Nothing good ever happens to you." Sofia responds, "And maybe, Mark, you've been pampered and spoiled all your life so thinking about someone else is just too much for you. You want one of those Stepford wives, a robot who'll just please you all the time and make no demands."

"He's a mean critical parent, and is never satisfied with anything I do," says Jennifer of her husband, Bob. "Jennifer," says Bob, "is a teenager who never grew up. Jennifer cares about Jennifer and not much else. She takes and takes but doesn't give back."

Alex and Martha recently separated for two months but now they are back together. Alex says of Martha, "She's like the boss who is out to nail you. Nothing gets by her and everything has to be her way or no way." According to Martha, Alex is "one of those used-car salesman you can't trust. I can never get a straight answer out of him, I never get the sense that I can depend on what he says. He's always copping out and making excuses for himself."

These husbands and wives all have something in common. They have developed emotional images of each other. As we said earlier, these images are made up from all the accumulated hurts, angers, and disappointments that were never fully resolved and healed.

If I have an image about you, can I see you clearly, as you actually are in the current moment? If I have an image about myself, does that image color how I see, think, and feel about

> ❧ When disappointments, hurts, and pains go
> unresolved they begin to pile up and take
> on a life of their own. They become the
> images you have of each other.

myself and you in different situations? In our marriage when I have an image about you and an image about myself and you have an image of me and an image of yourself, who is married—our images?

If you and your partner have a fight in the morning that goes unresolved you will most likely spend the rest of the day reinforcing your respective images of each other. If you were impatient with your partner's indecisiveness and she or he got angry at your abusive tone, you strengthen your image of him or her as "wishy-washy" and she or he adds to her or his image of you as "a rude bully."

When you get together at the end of the day, those are the images that meet each other. Images prevent you from seeing and knowing each other fresh, without a bias from the past. While each moment is obviously new, your ego places an old picture of how you experience each other on that new moment. Image-to-image relating is a telltale sign of the ego self at work. When you look at each other with an evaluation, with a motive, with a judgment or a conclusion, you are looking through an image.

> ❧ Image-to-image relating is a telltale sign of
> the ego self at work. When you look at each
> other with an evaluation, with a motive,
> with a judgment or a conclusion, you are
> looking through an image.

It is important to underscore that *the facts and issues involved in the argument are real*. The feelings behind those facts, the accumulated hurts, angers, and disappointments, are what we carry over as images. From those incomplete and unresolved feelings we create the permanent emotional images we have of each other. If we left our argument with only the facts on our minds, we would simply have an issue that had yet to be worked out. And most issues between couples can be worked out, but only when we deal with facts, not with images.

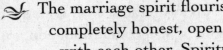 Most issues between couples can be worked out, but only when we deal with facts, not with images.

Whenever images interfere between you, connecting soul to soul becomes impossible. When the past intrudes into the present, you no longer relate to each other heart to heart, but rather your negative images relate to each other. And the more you react and respond through these images the more disconnected you become from each other.

The marriage spirit flourishes when you are completely honest, open, and fully present with each other. Spiritual intimacy is not possible when images exist. So it is essential that you learn how images develop and what you can do to prevent them from coming between you as a couple.

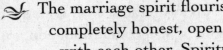 The marriage spirit flourishes when you are completely honest, open, and fully present with each other. Spiritual intimacy is not possible when images exist.

As a couple, accumulated emotional images prevent you from having a true spiritual connection. How can your hearts open when images keep you from seeing the divine in each other? It's not surprising, then, that image–to–image relating frequently leads to the bitter complaint, *"How can you love me, you don't even know who I am,"* or *"You've got me so figured out you won't let me be new."*

THE BEAUTY IN BEING GENUINE

When you have no mental pictures about yourself you can be genuine. Being genuine means you come to your partner with no pretense, no "airs," with nothing phony and with nothing hidden. There are no mind games going on. Being genuine means being sincere, earnest, candid, direct. You are honest, straightforward, open. There is a relaxed ease as you express yourself. You are not self-conscious nor do you have anything preoccupying you. When you are not self-absorbed you have no agenda.

ᴥ One of the most powerful things *you* can do to keep your heart open is to be vigilantly aware of the images you have about yourself and your partner and let them go. Without an image the sacred in you touches the sacred in your partner.

When you encounter the sacred in your partner it calls out the sacred in you. Love begets love. No matter how strong an image you may have about yourself, when your partner has no image about you it calms and relaxes you. You sense no attitude of judgment or evaluation, and you feel safe, your defenses fall, you put down your mask and allow yourself to be real. When there are no images operating in your marriage the ego softens, relaxes its role as "lookout," and begins to make its way back home, merging into its spiritual self.

One of the most powerful things *you* can do to keep your heart open is to be vigilantly aware of the images you have about yourself and your partner and let them go. Without an image the sacred in you touches the sacred in your partner.

Imageless Perception: Living in the Now

> If your thoughts are active, and your activities rushed, then you cannot be fully alive and conscious in the moment. Only if your thoughts are quiet and your heart at peace, can you be fully attentive and aware of the unfolding moment.
>
> —A SPIRITUAL WARRIOR

Remember Michael and Sarah, the couple we spoke about in the previous chapter? Without realizing it they had allowed their images of themselves and each other to sidetrack their marriage. To get back to loving each other they had to prevent these images from coming between them.

To help them do this we instructed Sarah to be vigilant about witnessing herself as inferior to Michael. She was encouraged to consistently be on the lookout for the ways in which this "less than" self-image crept into her awareness. When it did, she was to bathe it in the light of her spiritual self. She would do this by withdrawing attention from the image, not dwelling on it, and denying it the energy it needed to survive. If Michael said or did something to provoke this "less than" image, she was to point it out to him immediately, and without blame.

Michael was also instructed to be aware of those times he felt insecure and his image of "being better than" took over. At those times Michael was to witness making himself feel big (because he really felt so small) by putting Sarah down.

We encouraged Michael and Sarah to stay in the present, coming together as if for the very first time. We asked them to cultivate and practice "imageless perception," seeing each other without judgments or conclusions of any kind. In this way they would be interrupting images as soon as they appeared in their witnessing awareness. Only then could they work together to keep their souls touching. Sarah and Michael, with acceptance and forgiveness, decided to move forward in their marriage. Now they had a way, with help at first, to rebuild their trust and honor their marriage as a sacred place.

IMAGELESS PERCEPTION

Contrary to what you have been led to believe, love is not blind. Love has a special way of looking we call *imageless perception*. It is seeing each other through the eyes of your spiritual self.

With imageless perception you look without preconceived ideas or images of each other. It is looking with a nonjudgmental "I." This kind of looking keeps the marriage spirit alive and your hearts open.

Imageless perception means that when you look at each other there are no images in the way, no mental pictures from the past going through your mind. You see each other fresh in each new moment. This way of looking is full of energy and unrestricted attention because it is not distorted by images.

On the other hand, when you look with your ego self you don't see clearly because past images, whether they are positive or negative, get in the way. As long as there are images of any kind, *direct,* unbiased perception is impossible. Any image puts you in a box, labeling and categorizing you. Looking with your ego self means you are seeing the present with the eyes of the past.

❧   Looking with your ego self means you are seeing the present with the eyes of the past. Imageless perception means you are looking without images, seeing each other fresh in each new moment.

As we said earlier, your spiritual self, because it has no motives, no desires, and no fears, sees the facts about a person or situation clearly, as they actually are. It does not superimpose anything on a person or situation. Because your spiritual self lives in the eternal, ever-present now, what it looks at it sees with full attention, fresh, clear, and new, moment to moment.

For example, when waking up in the morning, or coming home from a day's work, or coming back from being away on a trip, you don't look at your small child or at your dog or cat thinking, "She was good yesterday so I will be happy to see her today," or, "He misbehaved before so I'm not going to be happy to see him now." Whether the last time you were together was *positive or negative* that first seeing, *if no prior image interferes,* is filled with an innocent, welcoming joy. There is a wonder and excitement at being in the new moment with them *because no accumulated images are operating.* Seeing from this perspective connects you with them spiritually.

Imageless perception does not mean seeing the world through rose-colored glasses. Your spiritual self sees *the fact* of an abusive or dangerous person or situation immediately. Without hesitation it knows the best way to respond. It is your ego self that convinces you to go along with things and people that are not good for you because it has you thinking, "If I don't stay in this relationship who else will want me?" or, "This could be an opportunity of a lifetime." All the while your spiritual self is really aware, paying attention, pointing you toward the facts you need to see. Too often we let its wisdom go to waste.

LIVING IN THE NOW

You get to imageless perception by living in the now. Living in the now means being fully present, image-free in the current moment. If you are no longer in the past, because the past is gone, and you are not in the future, because it hasn't happened yet, then where are you? You are in each new moment as it unfolds in your awareness.

This requires being centered in your spiritual self. The chatter generated by your ego has been eliminated. Your awareness is amplified, your attention is unrestricted and at full strength. You are calm, without any stress whatsoever. You know a complete ease of being, an effortless awareness of what is. From this state of being, all your actions are right actions. You have stepped out of the everyday rut of ordinary, automatic, action-reaction, mechanical living.

 Living in the spiritual now means being fully present, image-free in the current moment.

Living in the spiritual *now* does not mean that we do not use the past to help us plan for the future. There is a big difference between planning and projecting.

Projecting means taking past events, and the feelings associated with them (usually fears, worries, insecurities, wishes, hopes, and fantasies), and placing them onto an imaginary future as if they were real. The need to plan, however, is always a part of life—

planning the house you want to buy, the vacations you take, college for the kids, your retirement, and so on. But ideally such planning will be a rational activity your mind undertakes using as many facts as are at your disposal. This kind of rational use of facts to plan your lives (to whatever extent they can be planned) does not deplete spiritual energy.

Your spiritual energy is wasted when your ego clings to the past with regret, sadness, and hurt. And your spiritual energy is also lost when your ego self projects ahead, looking to the future with worry and dread. Looking back and projecting ahead stirs up an inner dialogue filled with sorrow and regret as well as fear and insecurity. Also stirred up are feelings of self-pity and self-doubt, of anger and bitterness. These emotions are what deplete your spiritual energy and give life to the image-making process. And when your mind is full of images, your marriage suffers.

  Your spiritual energy is wasted when your
ego clings to the past with regret, sadness,
and hurt. And your spiritual energy is also
lost when your ego self projects ahead,
looking to the future with worry and dread.

HOLDING ON TO NOW

Paul recently had to battle a host of old images: While I was writing an early draft of this book, my doctor called with the results of my annual physical. He said there was a jump in my PSA level from 3.0 to 5.8. I knew that a jump in PSA was an early warning sign for prostate cancer. He wanted me to come in and repeat the test. I did and it came back higher, 6.2. "Look," he said in a reassuring way, "PSA is only one indicator. Everything else is fine, but we should get a biopsy to be sure." He referred me to a urologist to schedule a biopsy. The earliest appointment was ten days away.

In the meantime, I continued working and writing as usual. I am generally not prone to worrying about things, especially my physical health. But as the days passed I became increasingly anxious. A sick feeling in my stomach was becoming more constant. Whenever my mind was idle waves of fear came over me. A kind of low-level panic was being fueled by images from my past, which now came roaring back with a vengeance. My mind was resurrecting scenes long ago put to rest.

When I was eleven years old my mother died of cancer. My father, two sisters, and I struggled along, but it was a terrible time for all of us. Now that old sadness was back. My mind was reliving all the fear, grief, and sorrow of those painful years. I was consumed by sadness for myself, for Evelyn, for our children and grandchildren. Now they would suffer the same kind of loss I had endured. I knew what was in store for them. I was reacting as if I were already dead and going through the grief and mourning with them. These were the images feeding my anxiety and sense of dread.

Evelyn, watching me become more and more withdrawn, insisted I talk about what was going on inside me. As I talked about what I was thinking and feeling, I felt less anxious. Also I became more aware of the thoughts and feelings as they were beginning to form in my mind. Witnessing them as they started to take shape helped me interrupt them. I saw that when I was not bringing in the past or projecting ahead about what might happen, my emotions did not run out of control.

At those times when I wasn't distracted by my work or some task or activity I focused my energy and awareness on staying in the current moment, in the spiritual *now*. As soon as I saw my mind wandering away I pulled myself back. This helped ease my anxiety. I also used my creative imagination to help me stay calm by practicing the technique of visualization.

Using Visualization

Staying in the spiritual now is difficult to do when you are filled with fears and anxieties. Visualization can be used to ease tensions and anxieties and bring about a deep sense of inner peace and comfort. Visualization is using the mind's power of imagination in a conscious way to create circumstances you want to manifest in your life. With visualization you purposely create a vision of yourself already possessing some quality you want to develop or a goal you want to achieve. Athletes, for example, frequently use visualization to improve their skills. They repeatedly imagine themselves, in great detail, playing the perfect game. Sick patients use visualization to help their bodies fight disease. In their minds they create a vivid scene in which healthy cells successfully fight off sick ones.

In my mind's eye I created and entered into a serene environment where I felt calm, relaxed, and happy. Whenever my anxiety seemed to be getting the upper hand I sought the tranquility which came with the special, safe "inner environment" I consciously created. The more time I spent there, the more vivid the feelings of peace and well-being became. And the more secure I felt the better I was able to stay with the facts of the situation. If it turned out I did have prostate cancer I was certainly catching it early. I knew there were effective treatments for it. A close friend had recently gone through such treatment and was now feeling fine.

My thoughts and images of death, grief, and mourning were not based on current facts. Staying with the facts of the situation in the spiritual *now* pulled the plug on the images that were making me anxious. By the time the biopsy appointment came I had shifted emotionally to a calm place. I was in control and my fears were not controlling me. As it turned out, the biopsy was negative.

Your life takes place in the present moment, *now,* not in the dead past or unborn future. As long as your ego is constantly chattering inside you it creates a steady stream of mental pictures

Whenever you witness your mind projecting into the future or dwelling on the past, shine all of your awareness, like a spotlight, directly on it. In the spotlight of consciously focused awareness the chattering stops.

about the past or future. With these images moving through your thoughts your mind is rarely quiet.

Whenever you witness your mind projecting into the future or dwelling on the past, shine all of your awareness, like a spotlight, directly on it. In the spotlight of your consciously focused attention the chattering stops. What happens to you when you silently watch your thoughts moving? They stop. Try it and you will see.

Consciously focusing attention on your images allows you to choose whether or not to give them the mental energy they need to survive. When there is no energy put into thoughts and words, pictures of the past or the future wither away and imageless perception comes into being. The way to stay in the spiritual *now* is to be aware of when thoughts are pulling you back to the past

 The way to stay in the spiritual *now* is to be aware of when thoughts are pulling you back to the past or projecting you ahead into the future. Know that when you dwell on the past you create depression; when you project into the future you create fear and anxiety.

or projecting you ahead into the future. Know that when you dwell on the past you create depression; when you project into the future you create fear and anxiety.

LISA AND HARRY

When they came for counseling, Lisa and Harry had been married for five years and had a three-year-old daughter, Meg. Both beamed when they spoke about Meg, yet it was clear that not much else was going well in this young marriage. Despite being together for only five years, Harry and Lisa felt deeply disappointed about their marriage. Each had doubts about whether they were right for each other. For the last two years they had been arguing more frequently. The negative images they had developed about each other were very clear. Lisa saw Harry as "selfish and afraid of being close." Harry's image of Lisa was that "she's never satisfied, she always wants more."

Lisa had left her teaching job where she was well liked and respected to be with Meg. She was happy about that decision but angry and "turned off" to Harry because she felt so disappointed by his lack of interest and affection for her. She described Harry as "selfish" and interested only in his work and hobbies. He fell asleep most evenings in the den and usually spent the night there. Sex was something that "just happens four or five times a year." She said, "He doesn't have a clue about who I am and what my life is like. He's content to just work and go out once in a while." She vouched for him being a good father, but as a husband Harry had let her down "big time."

The only thing that Lisa said that Harry agreed with concerned their lack of sex. According to Harry, Lisa was "impossible to please, the kind of person who doesn't know how to be happy." He put great pride in his efforts to work hard and be successful. He was "anything but selfish." He complained that Lisa had shown very little interest in or appreciation of his efforts. He felt constantly under attack and wished Lisa would "cut me some slack by being less angry and pessimistic."

We told Lisa and Harry that their marriage was in trouble partly because they had neglected each other by giving so much of themselves to their new roles; Lisa as a new mother and Harry as provider. Both felt exhausted at the end of the day. They had neglected to give conscious attention to the quality of their togetherness. Their marriage had drifted into a mechanical performance of routine behavior and fixed images of each other.

If they wanted things to change the first thing each would have to do was to develop a new attitude of reverence toward their young relationship. This would mean seeing their marriage as a sacred place and giving it the kind of devoted attention, caring, and adoration something sacred deserves.

During our sessions together we pointed out that it was essential for them to acknowledge as well as understand the hurt they each felt. Lisa felt hurt by Harry's neglect and Harry was similarly effected by Lisa's lack of appreciation. It was this hurt and disappointment that caused their anger with each other.

We made it clear that acting from this disappointment kept them stuck in negative images of each other. Because of these negative images they were continually hurting and being hurt by each other. They had to leave the past behind and begin honoring their marriage as sacred in the present. This would begin to get them unstuck.

The Me Insists on Reliving the Past

Counseling helped Lisa and Harry learn how to leave the past behind. They began to see that *they could choose the kind of marriage they wanted*. Their marriage could be a place where their past repeated itself or it could be a place where they learned together how to *grow up and create love*. We helped them see that their egos insisted on reliving the past, while it was their higher spiritual selves that were needed to create love in the present.

This view of marriage helped both of them see how they were, without realizing it, reliving their individual pasts in their shared present. As a child, Lisa had felt ignored by her workaholic father, who was never at home, and an overly dependent mother, who could barely take care of herself. She created an image of herself as "not lovable enough to be cared about." Now in her marriage that same image was getting reinforced by Harry's lack of interest in her.

Harry, too, saw how Lisa could easily become a reincarnation of his own parents. Both were overprotective perfectionists. Harry, an only child, created an image of himself as "not adequate" and an image of being loved as "being smothered." He felt that Lisa's needs would, if he let them, also smother him.

How Lisa Needed to Be Loved

Harry was encouraged, despite his fears, to see how Lisa needed to be loved. While he had indeed been a good provider, he was at best a part-time husband. Too much of his energy was taken up with a survival mentality and needing to prove himself "strong enough to succeed." Work had become his top priority. He became aware of how he also brought in the past by placing Lisa in the same category as his parents. He was afraid that if he gave her the attention she wanted, she would swallow him up. This fear gave him just cause to distance himself through work.

We helped him to see that this distancing behavior fueled Lisa's image of him as selfish and uncaring. Lisa was, in fact, suffering from a deficiency of nurturing. She needed more emotional involvement on his part and more expressions of physical and verbal affection from him. He made a commitment to become a lover to her both inside and, most important, outside the bedroom.

How Harry Needed to Be Loved

Lisa also had to be clear about how Harry needed to be loved. During our session Harry spoke about how important it was for him to be appreciated by her. He said he needed to feel she admired him and respected his efforts to accomplish and achieve for himself and the family. We encouraged Lisa to give Harry this kind of caring as much as possible.

In order to do this Lisa was cautioned to watch her tendency to contaminate their marriage by bringing in hurts from the past. She was also reminded not to project ahead by worrying about the future. All her energy was to go into remaining *present-centered*. She came to understand that her spiritual self, unlike her ego, does not accumulate images from the past. It lives each moment fresh. Staying centered in the present helped Lisa make a strong effort to give Harry the kind of love, support, and recognition he needed.

Minding Your Own Business

We emphasized to Lisa and Harry (as we do with every couple we work with) the importance of "minding your own business." When they come for marriage counseling, husbands and wives are convinced that it is their partner who is causing problems in their relationship. Each one is sure that the other holds the key to their happiness. They are experts in how their partner should change.

We tell each husband and wife to mind their own business; to focus on what they must change in themselves. Being an expert on yourself, rather than on your partner, is what counts. Minding your own business means being open to hearing how your partner experiences you, as controlling, critical, insensitive, cold, distant, arrogant, or whatever and accepting it as true instead of arguing about it. This does not mean you agree that his or her view is *absolutely true*. It means you can accept that there is enough truth in your partner's experience that you will honor it as valid.

Lisa had to mind her own business by staying in the present and not allowing past hurts to consume her. She needed to make more of an effort to let Harry know she admired and appreciated him.

Minding his own business for Harry meant making sure he did not hide out emotionally from Lisa. He needed to avoid distancing himself by showing her more affection outside the bedroom.

Each was to focus only on his or her own actions, rather than on what his or her partner was or was not doing. Their goal was to not allow the past to interfere with angry or negative thoughts and behavior. If this did happen an apology was to be immediately given. An apology would remind both of their commitment to become more loving. It would send a clear message that safeguarding their closeness was indeed a mutual top priority.

Undoing Fixed Images

Because of their fixed images of each other we suggested they use their creative imaginations to develop an affirmation that would help free them from this stuck position. As discussed earlier, an affirmation is a carefully created thought designed to engage the spiritual self. It helps change the tone and content of our inner self-dialogue.

We suggested to Harry and Lisa that upon first waking, they take the few minutes it would require to deliberately place in their consciousness the following affirmation, which they came up with: "My spiritual self, my real self, is guiding my words and deeds, keeping our marriage a sacred place." They were to meditate on this idea, focusing on what a sacred place means to them. This practice would help them to witness, daily, their words and deeds, making sure they did not put energy into their fixed images of each other.

After five months of working together in counseling, Lisa and Harry are feeling more connected and closer as a couple. Lisa: "It's like every day we're cleaning out the space between us! We've gotten so good now at catching the 'me' always trying to bring in a lot of negative stuff. It's amazing that when you really pay attention, you see how much negative thinking your mind does. It's been so helpful to think of our marriage as a sacred place.

"We're not as defensive as we used to be. We're changing. I feel a new excitement between us, an opening up inside. I'm touching something inside me I never paid attention to, the part in me that sees the good in things. In choosing to focus on the good between us I'm finding so much good in myself."

Harry sees it this way: "I finally realized that she was on my side and that we're working together. I guess I never really saw Lisa, but only who I thought Lisa was. I guess that's why I didn't trust her love and I kept myself separate. But I've gotten better at interrupting those kind of thoughts. I feel now we're becoming one. Becoming one doesn't sound so good, because it sounds like you're giving up all your independence. I worried a lot about that, but you don't lose anything. You are yourself, she is herself, and yet at the same time there's a third thing there and that third thing, the marriage, becomes more and more important. I can't tell you the gratitude I feel having Lisa in my life."

As you learn to shift your inner identity away from your ego and stay in the spiritual *now* with imageless perception, you begin to live your marriage as a sacred place. You become more loving to each other. There is a heartfelt gratitude for the good fortune of being in a marriage with a loved partner, sharing a conscious effort to wake up. Marriage now is joyous; fun and laughter are the norm. Freedom, individuality, and togetherness blend in a magnificent melody of the soul. You feel in communion with each other.

COMMUNION CREATES COMMUNICATION

When couples sit with us and explain why they decided to come for marriage counseling they usually say, "We can't communicate with each other," and they are right. This is because they are not in communion. True communication cannot happen unless you are first able to be in communion with each other.

One of the great benefits of living in the spiritual *now* is that it puts you in communion. Being in communion means being in sync with each other. Your mental, emotional, and spiritual energies meet in the same place, at the same time, with the same intensity. Your awareness is fully focused in the present moment and your attention is open and full. There are no intruding messages running across your mind, no preoccupation distracts you. Your are clear, calm, and quiet, so you easily and effortless take each other in. You are able to come together to share thoughts and feelings easily. You hear each other clearly because you feel connected to each other heart to heart, soul to soul. When in communion you are enveloped in the presence of your spiritual self.

    One of the great benefits of living in the spiritual *now* is that it puts you in communion. True communication cannot happen unless you are first able to be in communion with each other.

Good communication, especially about important issues, flows easily between you when you are in communion. From this place you each approach the conversation with only *one* intention, to fully understand each other. Both your egos are absent and there are no hidden agendas. *You do not need to win, or convince, or control.* What becomes most important is understanding each other.

What interests you most is being clear about what both of you are saying. You just want to understand and think together. With this kind of communion your spiritual connectedness grows stronger. Sharing your thoughts and feelings is both a comfort and a joy.

The subjective feeling when you are in communion is a calm alertness. The moment is ripe for anything to unfold: humor, a creative thought, the sharing of something beautiful, a serious feeling, or a concern that has surfaced and needs to be given attention. True communication, talking, and sharing about more than just the routine custodial details of daily life rests on your ability to commune together in the image-free moment of *now*.

There is nothing you can do, achieve, or buy that will outshine the peace, joy, and happiness of being in communion with the partner you love.

Remembering the true purpose of your life together, waking up to your spiritual nature, is what helps keep you on track. There is nothing you can do, achieve, or buy that will outshine the peace, joy, and happiness of being in communion with the partner you love.

STEP III RITUAL

SEEING EACH OTHER WITHOUT JUDGMENT: IMAGELESS PERCEPTION

This ritual has four related parts to help you practice imageless perception and living in the spiritual *now.* Do them in the order in which they appear. Give yourself sufficient time for each part. Do the individual components on your own and share them with each other later.

Part 1: Self-Inquiry Questionnaire

Becoming aware of the emotional images that influence your lives is part of the marriage spirit. We have designed the Self-Inquiry Questionnaire to help you discover the images you have about yourself, other people close to you, and the world in general. The following questions are offered for your thoughtful consideration. Write the answers in your journal for future reviewing. Others have found rereading the answers every three to six months very helpful and illuminating. Look for any changes in your answers. See if the images you have about yourself have dissolved, or if you have acquired new images in their place.

1. Do you have an image about yourself? What are the different ways you see yourself? Include as many images as you can come up with.
2. What beliefs, opinions, and conclusions do you hold about yourself?
3. How do these beliefs, opinions, and conclusions influence your relationships?
4. What belief do you have about yourself that you would not want anyone else to know?
5. In your everyday life how do you protect or enhance the images you have about yourself? For example: If your image is "I am not good enough," you may use being perfect (or as close to it as you can get) to cover and protect your inner sense of not being good enough from being found out.
6. What purpose does the image you carry about yourself serve? For example: You may hold on to the "not good enough" image in order to have a built-in excuse for not taking risks to do more with your life.
7. What cues show you your images may be operating? For example: Whenever you are feeling insecure, are blaming yourself, feeling superior or inferior, or comparing yourself to someone else, it is likely that an image is operating within you.
8. What images do you have about your partner?
9. What images do you believe your partner has about you?
10. How do the images you have about your partner influence the way you treat him or her?

11. If you did not have images of your partner, how would your treatment of him or her be different?

Part 2: Early Recollections

The clearer we are about our self-images the better our chance to be free of them. Another way to access emotional images of ourselves is through early recollections. An early recollection is an event or incident you can personally recall and not something that was told to you. Most people begin to remember events at around three years of age, though some remember earlier, and for others it's later.

What is your earliest recollection? Recall the incident with as much detail as possible. Write it in your journal as though you were telling it to someone else. After you have written down the story of your early recollection ask yourself the following questions:

1. What was *the most vivid moment* in the incident I just recalled?
2. What was I *feeling in that most vivid moment?*
3. What conclusion did I come to about myself or others from this early recollection?
4. What part of my personality today is shaped by the image I created at an early age?

For example, Evelyn recalls: I remember two incidents that occurred when I was three years old.

Incident one: My mother and I had come to America, having escaped from Vienna, Austria, during the holocaust of World War II. Of our whole family, those who were not killed had fled and were living all over the world. My father had escaped to England. Mother and I came to New York to live with my grandfather (who, while on business in America, stayed in order to survive). Mother and Grandfather had to work, so I was put into a nursery school or what today would be equivalent to a day-care center. I could not speak or understand English. I remember crying about being left. The teacher then gave me a big pot of spaghetti and told me to feed the children at my table.

Most vivid moment: Scooping the spaghetti onto the children's plates.

Feeling: Feeling strong and happy.

Image created and conclusions made: I am strong when I am feeding others. The way I will be safe in the world, especially a world I do not understand, is by giving to and pleasing others. In this way I have control and feel safe.

I have learned to let go of the image of myself as needing to please in order to feel safe. I also understand that interest in others cannot be self-centered, because the interest then is only to enhance one's own self-image and not to enhance the people themselves. Also, I still, at times, have to be vigilantly aware of the image of myself as not feeling safe unless I am in control. An interesting consequence of this early life incident is an intense desire for understanding my self, others, and life itself.

Incident two: Again I was about three years old, it was in that same nursery school. We had taken a boat ride around Manhattan. We came off the boat ramp and all the parents were there to pick up the children. Nobody was there for me. I had waited for what seemed a very long time when suddenly I saw my grandfather come running toward me.

Most vivid moment: Standing afraid and alone, Grandfather running toward me.

Feeling: First feeling was fear of being abandoned. Second feeling was relief and intense love from my grandfather.

Image created and conclusions made: I am alone and need to be rescued. Men are rescuers. When a man loves you, he rescues you.

I am thankful that, as the result of a lot of inner work and a strong and loving marriage, I have been able to let go of the image of myself as needing to be rescued, of men as having to be rescuers, and of measuring the love of a man by how good a job he does of rescuing me.

Part 3: Living in the Spiritual *Now*

This part of the ritual needs to be done outdoors, in a park nearby, at the beach, or in the mountains. Any natural place close to you that has not been commercialized or overdeveloped and is quiet will do. First make sure you are as relaxed as possible, that you have no pressing issue or concern taking up mental energy. Take a few moments to sit quietly, breathe deeply, and let your body and mind shift into a relaxed, calm space. Let whatever specific issues are on your mind go (you can come back to them later) and breathe deeply and slowly in and out. Do not rush your breath, slowly inhale and slowly exhale, letting the tensions go.

When you feel calm and centered begin slowly walking. Be aware of your body as it carries you forward. *Feel* yourself walking, bring your awareness and attention fully focused on each slow, deliberate step. If you find your mind wandering bring it back, focusing on each careful step and each relaxed breath you take. Walk slowly, you are not going anywhere. Let yourself be here. Let any thoughts that come up go right out of your mind. Watch them come and let them go.

Now begin to look at the natural surrounding you find yourself in. Practice observing without any movement of thought in your mind. Practice seeing whatever your eyes fall upon *without naming or labeling,* without any mental associations to whatever you see. If these do come up let them go. You are walking and observing only, not thinking. You are on a walk of pure, in-the-moment perception, without the movement of thoughts.

There is no need to identify or name what you see. Just practice seeing things as they are. Can you see them as if for the first time? Do it. Observe without naming what you see. Practice silent observation, no internal or external verbalizing. Have all of your attention devoted to looking. Take in the details of what you see, giving no energy to either liking or disliking. Just observe with full, devoted attention. When no words are going on in your mind as you look, you are seeing with imageless perception. Stay with what you are looking at until you feel the essence of the object. You will begin to feel yourself filled with what you are observing, communing with it and connecting with it spiritually.

Paul recalls taking such a walk: "It was mid-June in the Catskill Mountains. I had been sitting quietly, following my breath as a way to quiet my mind and relax my body. When I felt calm and at ease inside I began walking down a tree-bordered dirt road. It was about six in the evening. There was no wind at all. The sky was bright blue. All around it was absolutely quiet. There was no external noise, no people, no dogs barking, no machinery running, not even birds chirping. The silence felt pulsating and alive, the only sound present was of the living, breathing earth I stood upon.

"I walked slowly, deliberately placing each step, feeling my weight shift from one leg to the other. As thoughts came I let them go. They held no interest for me. I was fully absorbed in the walking. After some time, I no longer had the sense that 'I' was walking, there was just walking. Looking around I made an effort to see without thinking about what I saw, to just stay with the seeing. I began to feel the silence around me in a different way. It was around me and within me. I was part of it and it was part of me, with no sense of separation or difference."

As a brief daily practice for living in the spiritual *now* try the following: No matter where you are, at home, on the job, in your car, with family and friends, as soon as there is an awareness of your thoughts projecting something onto the future, or reliving an incident of the past, immediately pull yourself back into the *now*. Sometimes, it may help to say to yourself, *"I am now!"* This practice is effortless and results in a feeling of calmness.

Part 4: Being in Communion

As a couple, seeing through the eyes of your spiritual selves means taking each other in with an open heart and devoted attention. We would like you now to create an opportunity to meet and come together in the sacred realm beyond your ego. Find a comfortable place where you can face each other, hold hands, and look into each other's eyes. Allow yourselves to look at each other as though you were meeting each other for the very first time. See if you can look at each other *without* mentally referring to each other as "my husband" or "my wife."

Take each other in just as you did the objects of nature. Do not name or label anything about one another. Look at your partner, taking in his or her whole being without any comments whatsoever. Again, there is no talking, no verbalizing either internal or external. There is no liking or disliking, no comparison, no judgment, no conclusions. Be careful not to get lost in distractions. As you see thoughts cross your mind, observe them with all your conscious awareness. They will dissolve under your benevolent scrutiny. Continue giving full and devoted attention to your partner. Take each other in with a silent mind. Stay in the *now.* Give full, complete, and devoted attention. When you sense a shared, warm affection enveloping you, express it in simple loving terms.

STEP **IV**

Defusing Anger

*God wants nothing of you but the gift of
a peaceful heart.*

—MEISTER ECKHART

Accumulated Anger Kills Love

At the center of non-violence stands
the principle of love.

—Martin L. King, Jr.

Ilene and Karl

Ilene and Karl have been married for fifteen years and have four children. Karl called to arrange an appointment, saying his marriage was "hanging by a thread." In fact, he wasn't sure Ilene would agree to come in. "We've been angry for so long she doesn't believe it can change." Two days later Ilene called. She would come in with Karl but wanted us to know how hopeless she felt. "I have to be honest with you. There's not much love left between us."

When we met with them for the first session Karl said their life together was "pretty empty." Beneath their anger and frustration each had the same question. "Can our marriage be saved?"

Ilene began by saying: "I don't understand what went wrong with us, we have everything any couple could hope for. Four wonderful children, a beautiful home, friends, close family, and enough financially to live comfortably and do almost anything we would want to do."

Karl: "I told you five years ago I wasn't happy and your response was that you were happy so I must have a problem and I should go see someone and get some help. That did it for me. I got so angry I just shut down. It's like I turned a switch off inside me."

Ilene responded: "I try and talk to him, he just won't let me in. And he's got all these restrictions. I can't ask questions, I've got to make statements, then when I make statements, he says, 'What do you want me to do about it?' I just think he doesn't like me."

Karl: "She just won't hear my needs. I want to do things with her, I want a companion, I want to be able to talk to her about things, other than just the kids. We live two separate lives. She won't do anything with me, she won't work out with me, or go dancing, or play tennis. She just wants to go to a movie, which I hate to do, or go to dinner with friends. I can't talk to her about anything; right away she gets defensive."

Ilene: "Well, you never have anything positive to say to me. All you do is put me down. Why would I want to do things with you, so you can abuse me? I've put up with it for years because I was afraid you'd leave, but I can't take it anymore."

Karl: "Well, I've got years of hurt and anger in me."

Ilene: "Well, I feel plenty hurt and angry too. You come home from work like a bull. I feel like I'm walking on eggshells. I get a headache just knowing you're coming home."

Karl: "And when I walk in you're usually screaming at the kids, hysterical about one thing or another."

Ilene: "Well, maybe if I could count on you to give me some help with them I wouldn't have to yell, but all you know how to do is bully them. When was the last time you gave them or me some kindness? That's what I want, some kindness, some interest and attention."

Karl: "Well, you'll never get it by being bitchy. Did it ever occur to you that I want the same thing? I want some attention too."

Ilene: "Then show me that's what you want by treating me like I was important to you, not just someone else you can boss around."

Accumulated anger kills love. When the pain of being together begins to outweigh the pleasure, each new layer of anger brings you closer to a point of no return. Accumulated anger that is not resolved goes underground and poisons your marriage. It kills love by destroying trust and creating hurt, blame, and guilt. No matter how strong your love is initially, a steady diet of anger and bitterness can close your hearts to each other permanently. So, as a couple, it is essential that you understand anger and how to deal with it in your marriage.

When spiritual intimacy is strong between you, you "carefront" the anger in your relationship. Carefronting means expressing and working through angry feelings in a way that does not damage your basic trust and love for each other. When carefronting anger you extend patience, kindness, even affection in the face of disagreements and the frustration and disappointment that goes with them. This is totally different from *confronting* each other with anger in a way that hurts you and your marriage.

Carefronting allows you to express anger in a nonblameful, nonattacking way. It helps you make the best use of your conflicts by using them as raw material for growing, both psychologically and spiritually. This kind of togetherness lights up every aspect of your life; you are better at work and better with children, family, and friends.

Carefronting anger depends on your ability to have your ego and spiritual self in balance and working smoothly together. The problem is that your ego doesn't want to cooperate with your spiritual self, it wants to be in charge. It looks for ways to keep you preoccupied with it. While you're traveling the path of spiritual intimacy, your selfish self tries to pull you back and gain control by throwing up a storm of negative emotions. Chief among these emotions is anger, and in the hands of your ego it can ruin your marriage.

MISHANDLING ANGER

When your ego self operates on its own, cut off from your spiritual self, it usually mishandles anger in one of four ways:

• **Venting:** Some of us feel fully entitled to vent our anger at will. This is an explosive, overemotional, blast everything and everybody way of coping. We justify this venting by telling ourselves that holding on to anger is known to be harmful. But explosive venting is just as destructive because venting has a way of escalating our original angry feelings. When this happens our initial anger gets magnified many times over. Blowing up sets off a chain reaction of emotion, which feeds on itself. Whether we mean it or not, venting usually leads to expressions of anger that attack and belittle our partner.

Venting anger conditions us to be "hot-tempered," it reinforces "fighting" as a way to handle stress and solve problems. And venting has hurtful results not only because harmful things get said (and often regretted), but also because the sheer volume and intensity of the expressed anger pushes our partner far away emotionally. When the storm dies down, a huge void is left between us and getting reconnected can be slow and painful.

• **Holding on:** A second way we may abuse anger is by holding on to it for excessively long periods. Some of us nurse our anger, we become preoccupied with it, brooding over it for days or weeks. Sometimes we forget what it was that got us angry to begin with, but we continue being angry anyway. Holding on to our anger this way ensures that we always have some stored anger tucked away, ready to be added to whatever new frustration or disappointment comes along.

Storing grievances is a way of using anger to create distance when one of us feels threatened by "too much" closeness. Holding on to anger can also lead to all sorts of physical problems, from migraine headaches to ulcers. The ego then makes good use of these by seeing them as further proof of our "suffering" and victimization.

• **Denying:** Some of us are so afraid of angry feelings that we deny ever being angry at all. We may be conscious of our anger momentarily, but we immediately banish it to the outskirts of our awareness. Instead of being direct about how we're feeling, we have our anger come out in other ways, like seemingly innocent teasing or biting sarcasm, or in behavior designed to induce guilt or envy.

• **Projecting:** The fourth way we are likely to misuse our angry feelings is to project them onto someone else. We take our own hostile and aggressive feelings, push them outside our self, and attribute them to our husband or wife. We make our partner the persecutor and ourself the victim. This is the blame game we play when we can't admit our own faults and refuse to accept responsibility for our behavior. In reality we own the anger but rather than see and face it in ourselves we dump it off, making it their problem.

All of the above are ways the ego uses anger to maintain control. Venting belittles others, puts them down. It is an attempt to make them feel small. Nursing our anger, holding on to it in silent suffering, is an attempt to get the upper hand by making the other feel guilty. Denying anger and having it come out in disguised ways such as teasing or sarcasm catches our partner off

---

Carefronting allows you to express anger in a nonblameful, nonattacking way. It helps you make the best use of your conflicts by using them as raw material for growing, both psychologically and spiritually.

---

guard, giving us the advantage. Projecting our anger makes someone else the "bad guy," the perpetrator, while we get to be the victim or martyr.

UNDERSTANDING ANGER

Most of us probably did not grow up in families in which expressing our anger was made easy and safe. Most likely we didn't see anger being expressed in a mature, sensitive way. We may have been told that anger is something we shouldn't have. We were allowed to have feelings of happiness and pleasure, but we were given the message that anger is wrong. This way of thinking forges a connection between anger and the feelings of guilt and shame. For some, being angry isn't possible without also feeling guilty and ashamed.

You may have a difficult time with your anger because when the feelings move through you, you become flooded over, swept away on a rising tide of emotion. While reading and thinking about this takes time, it actually happens in a split second. Before you realize it you've gone on automatic, dealing with your anger in whatever way you've become accustomed to, even if it hurts your marriage.

Anger expresses itself in a combination of attitudes and behavior. The most common are annoyance, frustration, impatience, resentment, hostility, animosity, indignation, rage, sarcasm, irritability, sulking, pouting, ignoring, exploding, withdrawing, and hurtful teasing, and being unreliable, undependable, rude, and "uptight." And it's your anger acting when you provoke, aggravate, agitate, hassle, and are offensive.

Anger is a secondary feeling. Beneath anger is pain—the pain of hurt, fear, guilt, and frustrated desire. But anger, unlike the other feelings, has an element of power associated with it. Being angry often carries with it a feeling of strength and aggression. Most of us don't feel strong when we are hurt, afraid, guilty, or frustrated in our desires. In fact, these are emotions that have us

In the presence of your spiritual self, anger
is handled with attention and awareness
and then defused as a negative force in
your marriage.

feeling especially vulnerable. The "me" associates hurt, fear, guilt, and frustration with being weak and chooses instead to ally itself with anger. Anger is the ego's favorite choice because power gives the illusion of security and control, which your ego self craves.

To limit the potential negative effects of anger you have to take it out of the hands of your ego. It's your spiritual self that must be involved when anger moves through you. In the presence of your spiritual self, anger is handled with attention and awareness and then defused as a negative force in your marriage.

Anger as a Spiritual Warning Signal

Your sacred self helps you understand anger as a spiritual warning signal that tells you:

• **You have lost sight of your conscious intention to have your marriage be a sacred place.** When you are not consciously treating your marriage as a sacred place, you unconsciously turn it into a dumping ground for all your negative thoughts and emotions.

• **You have forgotten your true divine nature.** You have fallen into believing that all you really are is your ego, your selfish self. You've lost contact with your higher self and have become caught up in your anger. You feel cut off, alone, and defensive. You need to find a way back, past the obstacle of anger, to your spiritual self.

• **You have temporarily lost faith in the divine guidance within you.** It is the wisdom of your higher spiritual self that brings clarity to your problems, be they real or imagined. When anger moves through you, you are heavily conditioned to look outside yourself, blaming and judging others. You forget to call upon your sacred self for guidance at the very times you need it most.

 ✒ Anger is a secondary feeling. Beneath anger
is pain — the pain of hurt, fear, guilt,
and frustrated desire.

When you understand anger as a spiritual warning signal you don't allow your ego to use it as a tool for manipulation and control. As a couple you use your new understanding of anger to make the following agreements:

1. Give each other permission to be angry. That is, you agree that you won't judge, blame, or make each other wrong for feeling angry. You promise to continually check your awareness and stay spiritually focused in the present moment. This means no anger will accumulate between you because you have promised to tell each other *immediately* when you sense anger moving through you. George and Dara have a strong sense of the marriage spirit. During a marriage enrichment workshop George shared with other couples how he and Dara handle their anger.

"We never let our negative feelings about each other just sit there; we never let anger stay and fester. She is very good at handling anger. I was not. I used to clam up and get all closed up, but she immediately would insist that we deal with it and that is good.

"Anger is never allowed to accumulate because then it comes

out backward. It comes out in all other ways and ruins the relationship, sabotages the relationship. The only way to prevent that is by facing the anger, letting it come and stare you in the face, and then dealing with the issues behind it. It's getting to those issues that's really important."

2. Make a pact that you will not attack each other, verbally or physically, when you are angry. This is of utmost importance—you must make this pledge to each other and keep it. In this way you will consciously honor your mutual intention to keep your marriage a sacred place. When you do that you will not contaminate it with hostile, negative energy. Don't use anger as an opportunity to say things that you know will hurt each other. Always safeguard each other's self-esteem no matter how angry you may get. When you come through for each other in these ways, you can hear anger without getting defensive. Philip and Lucille, another workshop couple, also talked about anger.

"I always know Lucille really cares for me, because she never tries to tear me down. In my family almost all of my brothers and sisters are light complexioned, they're very light, and my brothers used to always notice that it gets to me when they call me black, they really liked to stick it to me . When I married my wife I told her about that, and I don't care how mad she got at me, she never used that one thing that she knows would upset and hurt me. She never uses anything no matter how mad she gets that she knows would hurt me or tear me down."

3. Agree that any anger in your marriage *belongs to both of you*. Together you jointly create the fabric of your marriage. If one of you is in emotional pain the other cannot be separate from it. This means that when one of you is angry the other can't simply dismiss it by saying, "It's your problem, deal with it." You agree that you will actively help each other when anger arises. You will make a point of reminding each other to trust your inner divine guidance and have faith that as long as you stay open and cooperate with each other, healthy solutions will come into focus.

"I am much more able now to disagree with Philip and still be caring. I think our children helped me see that it is possible to be displeased and still hold and love and care. We are not always able to solve our disagreements right away, but because we've agreed anger between us belongs to both of us, what we basically have been able to do is sort of say, 'I'm unhappy about this and don't agree about this, and I want to make an appointment to discuss it. Let's have breakfast together or whatever, but in the meantime, let's go ahead and act on what we basically really do feel for each other.' I can sleep close to him, touch him, hold him, knowing that we still have to resolve something. It is possible to be caring for each other even though there are unresolved issues between us."

With these agreements in place you are ready to learn how to handle your anger in a way that is not destructive to your marriage.

 If one of you is in emotional pain the other cannot be separate from it. This means that when one of you is angry the other can't simply dismiss it by saying, "It's your problem, deal with it."

DEFUSING ANGER

The first thing you need to do is learn how to manage the intense emotional component of anger. The solution here is to be on very close terms with your anger, to be friends with it, so to speak. This means dropping old ideas or beliefs you have about anger itself being "bad" or destructive. As we said earlier, old, accumulated anger that hasn't been dealt with and successfully resolved is harmful to your marriage. Anger that is used by the ego to dominate and control is destructive. But *present-moment anger*, as it arises, is an emotion much like fear or joy or surprise. What is crucial is how you express it.

When you stay rooted in your sacred self, by not allowing your ego to come in and take over, anger will naturally pass through you. In the focused awareness of your higher self, witnessing takes place. You will note the anger arise, you will observe its movement. Just observing allows the feelings to move through you easily and freely. If you allow your selfish self to take hold it will latch on to the anger and push you out of the present. It will bring in the past, by having you revert to your old familiar way of being angry, by either venting, holding on, denying, or project- ing. You'll be out of the spiritual *now*, having lost the opportunity to release your anger in a natural, healing way.

Remember, anger arising in the present is not your enemy— be on good terms with it. *What is crucial is how you express it.* By following these steps you'll be able to express your anger in a straightforward, uncomplicated way, much like conveying any other type of information about yourself to your partner:

1. Activate the witnessing ability of your spiritual self by just observing the anger with detached interest. Don't put mental energy into analyzing it.
2. Watch the fiery feeling as it moves in you but *do not name it to yourself as anger.*
3. Focus all your energy on watching it. Your mind will want to wander off. Bring it back. Breathe deeply through the anger, keep taking deep breaths as a way to help the emo- tion pass through you.
4. Allow the emotion to rise up in and through you. Allow it to blossom and then wither. It will pass right through you like a cold chill.

You want your anger to move through you freely and cleanly. You prevent this from happening when you lose your awareness and allow your ego self to take over. Witnessing anger means closely observing it with *interested detachment*. Even though you are watching it closely, your detached stance ensures that when it moves within you, you will not feel compelled to act on it. There is no judgment about it, no condemnation of it, no comments about it at all. You let it arise and bloom fully inside yourself and then allow it to pass right through you.

 Remember, anger arising in the present is not your enemy. Be on good terms with it. What is crucial is how you express it.

It is when you fail to witness anger that you treat it as something to *act on* rather than to *be with*. Being with your anger means allowing the physical and emotional response *that is anger* to run its course without interfering with it, without pushing it out at others or down inside yourself.

MYRA AND SETH

Myra and Seth have been separated for five months and want to put their marriage back together. But each time they get close, fighting pushes them apart. Angry battles were the major reason for their separation. Recently, Seth reported making new progress: "We were talking on the phone, and everything seemed okay. All of a sudden she starts telling me that she's been looking at our tax returns and she has a lot of questions about where all the money is being spent. She starts implying, in a vague round-about way, that maybe I've been hiding money from her. All this comes out of left field. It's the same old story with her, suddenly her claws come out and I react instinctively.

"Usually I would get so infuriated I would start cursing her out and hang up. But this time I didn't. I saw the rage well up in me but I didn't say a word. I could feel myself getting flushed. Believe me, I was really steamed. But I didn't react, I kept taking deep breaths. It became like an experiment, I wanted to see if I could avoid exploding. I knew what would happen if I did. I wanted to see what doing it differently would be like.

"She was going on and on about the taxes, but I was focused on what was going on inside me. Finally, she says, 'Are you there?' That was a turning point. I knew then that I had weathered the storm and that we were on new ground. I told her that whatever questions she had would be answered by me or by our accountant. I told her I didn't want to talk about it on the phone. I wasn't angry, I was calm. She said that would be fine with her. I could tell she was stunned. And then there was this awkward silence because usually at this point we would be screaming at each other. Since we weren't, there was this long gap in the conversation. So I changed the subject and asked her about my son. Everything was smooth from that point on.

"When I hung up I felt happy and relieved. I was happy that I didn't blow up. I saw myself want to do it but didn't. That made me feel good. Usually, after blowing up at her I'd feel guilty and she would stay angry for days. So it was a relief not to go through that. And I'm glad that I didn't do more damage to our marriage even though I felt she was accusing me of stealing our money."

HOLDING UP THE SACRED MIRROR

So far you've learned how your ego typically misuses anger and you've made new agreements to treat anger as a spiritual warning that your ego is back in control. You have also learned how to deal with the strong emotions that usually go with anger. Now you must be able to put these new agreements and information to work in your marriage.

While your intention is to have your higher self carefront anger, you may not always be up to the challenge. Old habits die hard. Your selfish self looks for every opportunity to grab the spotlight in your awareness. So your efforts to carefront anger may not always be successful. The "down times" come when one of you loses focus and reverts to an old, self-centered way of being angry.

This is a powerful moment of choice for the other partner. How you react will probably determine whether the two of you will quickly get over this slip or if it will turn into a bigger problem. It is very easy when faced with a partner's slip-up for your own ego to seize the moment by counterattacking, blaming, and making your partner wrong. This will only trigger defensiveness and lead to more anger. The way to avoid this "tit for tat" response is to hold up the sacred mirror.

Instead of counterattacking or blaming when your partner slips up you reflect to your partner the fact that he or she has forgotten to use anger as a spiritual warning signal. You "hold up a mirror" by reflecting that your partner's ego and not his or her sacred self has just acted out anger.

 The "down times" come when one of you loses focus and reverts to an old, self-centered way of being angry. This is a powerful moment of choice. How you react will probably determine whether the two of you will quickly get over this slip or if it will turn into a bigger problem.

Holding up the sacred mirror requires putting your ego self aside, allowing your spiritual self to show your partner his or her *in-the-moment* anger. Because it is your spiritual self and not your "me" holding up the mirror, there is only a statement of fact. For example, "Paul, right now is one of the times when I feel you being angry and sarcastic." Or, "Evelyn, this is when I feel you being angry and refusing to listen." There is no blame, no attack, no faultfinding, no bringing in past angers, no making the other wrong. There is simply a reflecting of a fact, in the same way and with the same tone of voice as if you were pointing to the weather and saying, "It's starting to rain." When the issue is presented this way there will be little, if any, defensiveness in your partner. He or she will be able to see him- or herself and recognize how he or she just acted.

When your partner holds up the sacred mirror to you, see it as an act of love on behalf of your marriage. Your response also needs to be an act of love. If you feel yourself get more annoyed because you've been "corrected," witness this reaction. See it for what it is, more self-centeredness. Let it go, don't take it seriously. Lighten up, see that your partner has just courageously done the right thing by you and your marriage, and simply say, "You're right, I'm sorry. Let's talk."

As a couple we can also use holding up the sacred mirror to work on other aspects of ourselves that need our attention. As we grow and evolve all of us are works in progress rather than finished products. There are always some sharp edges to our personalities, which need smoothing so we can fit together better as a couple. Living intimately brings these sharp edges into full view.

It is hard for most of us to see ourselves objectively. That's where the sacred mirror can help. Here's an example: Evelyn believes that I have to have my own way in situations and that if I don't get it I become sulky and "in a mood." I don't think it's true. I see myself differently. The next time we face a choice and I'm pushing hard for my way, not being flexible, and sulking about alternatives Evelyn will say, holding up the sacred mirror, "Paul, this is one of the times, right now, when I'm experiencing you as having to get your way. You're tuning me out and are not open to looking at other choices."

Now the ball is squarely in my court. I am faced with honestly looking at myself, at my actual behavior, not how I think I am. What shall I do? My options are to courageously look at myself and see if Evelyn's feedback is accurate. If it is, I acknowledge it, apologize, and push past my ego to see if I can adopt a more flexible approach. Maybe Evelyn is right and I do want my own way more than I am aware of. A new area of personal growth is now open for me.

My second option is to refuse to look honestly, become defensive, and debate the accuracy of Evelyn's observations. This way of responding will damage the trust between us. It leads to a dead end. Having the marriage spirit means I'm committed to doing what's best for my marriage, so my choice is clear. I'm open to seeing what my day-to-day relationship with the one person who is closest to me can tell me about myself.

 When your partner holds up the sacred mirror to you, see it as an act of love on behalf of your marriage. Your response also needs to be an act of love.

We also encourage couples to use the sacred mirror as a way of injecting humor into situations that might otherwise be tense. The ability to laugh at ourselves is precious. Seeing the silly side to so many of our petty angers and annoyances helps us avoid taking ourselves too seriously. Laughing at ourselves is the best kind of humor.

Evelyn and I humorously hold up the sacred mirror to each other with special cue words. For example, if we run errands before we start working, she sometimes gets impatient and starts complaining about my moving too slowly. If she overdoes it I'll say something like, "Darling, you're getting on my nerves." "Darling" is our special, funny cue word. It's funny to us because we say it in a lilting, exaggeratedly affectionate way. When either one of us uses it the other knows it's time to check our behavior, to slow down and be more aware of what's happening between us.

We urge couples to find some playful cue words that will be a mirror in which they can see upcoming annoyances. The tone of these cue words is loving and playful, yet serious. They are a good way of nipping annoyances in the bud, before they become angry feelings and get out of control. They help prevent the accumulation of hurt and anger. If you had a piece of glass or a splinter in your finger, you wouldn't let it sit there, you would remove it as soon as possible. It's the same with anger: Remove it before it deepens and becomes infected.

Holding up the sacred mirror is one of the most effective ways to honor your marriage as a sacred place. At the very moment when things are about to go wrong, when your ego selves are about to pollute your sacred place with a lot of "me"-centered, lower-self, acting-out behavior the marriage spirit will move in one of you. Your spiritual self will make its presence felt and one of you will wake up and remember that nothing is more important than keeping your marriage healthy and holy. This is your unselfish true divine nature shining through. The more you welcome and express it the stronger it becomes as a life-guiding presence.

GROWING BEYOND ANGER

Once you are no longer held hostage by angry feelings, anger itself can be a doorway to discovering important things about yourself. The more you allow yourself to witness your anger the more you'll be able to grow by discovering what's beyond it. Witnessing invites the presence of your higher spiritual self. It gives you clarity, and with clarity you are able to drop old images (ideas and beliefs) that dull your vision of who and what you are. Here are some examples:

SCOTT AND LYDIA

When Brian was born, Lydia left her job running the nursing department at a large teaching hospital to be with him full-time. But after two years her husband Scott said, "I can't take it anymore." What he couldn't take was coming home every night and finding Lydia in an angry, sullen mood. Usually there was some surface reason for her anger, but Scott insisted they were excuses. Gradually he persuaded Lydia that they needed help to find out what was really going on between them.

At first it was a struggle for Lydia to look inside herself. With help she was able see what more her anger might be saying to her. What she realized was that staying home was making her miserable. While she loved Brian and enjoyed caring for him, she often felt bored and unchallenged. The more she filled her day with things to do the more frustrated she became. She didn't want to look at the conflict that was going on inside her. She wanted to be a "good mother" but didn't feel happy doing it. She felt stuck. Anger was the surface level of her confusion and frustration.

By looking into her anger Lydia learned how difficult it was for her to be honest with herself; she saw how she resisted seeing what her real feelings were. She was living from an image of what a good mother would do and what she thought others expected her to do. Looking beneath her anger helped bring these issues to light and freed her from her self-imposed unhappiness. Once she and Scott focused on her real feelings of frustration and lack of fulfillment a solution was easily worked out. Scott's mother, who was retired, agreed to baby-sit while Lydia went back to work part-time.

RANDY AND MARILYN

After many failed attempts to get Randy to look at his anger, Marilyn told him she wanted a separation. She couldn't tolerate his constant sulking and pouting. That's when Randy called to make an appointment. He described growing up in a fatherless home with a mother and three older sisters. All of them catered to him as the baby in the family. Whenever things didn't go his way pouting brought immediate help. Now, as an adult, the same angry pouting brought criticism from Marilyn, who refused to be controlled by it.

Facing a separation, Randy forced himself to look at what other feelings were in his anger. What surfaced was his deep sense of personal inadequacy. For the first time in his life Randy described his severe lack of self-confidence and strong self-doubt about his ability to meet the challenges of being a husband, father, and provider. Sulking was the only way he knew to handle difficult, upsetting emotions. Sulking had always brought comfort and relief. Until now. Now he had to learn a new way to express and deal with the anxiety he felt. Finding ways to build his self-esteem and confidence became a new focus for him. This effort, unlike his sulking, Marilyn could respect.

JUDY AND MALCOM

Judy and Malcom both have large extended families, and Malcom goes out of his way to do special favors and be helpful to everyone. But not everyone is as giving and considerate as Malcom. At those times his anger gets out of control. Any perceived slight or lack of recognition will send him into a rage for hours. What's more, according to Judy, Malcom will "want to write the person off entirely. He'll refuse to see them or speak to them and they don't even know that something's wrong."

Malcom discovered that beneath his anger was the deep hurt of believing himself unlovable in the eyes of others. From this sense of unworthiness he saw how he "overcompensated," doing more for everyone else than they could ever do for him. This was how he tried to prove his lovability. When it failed, when someone he was good to didn't make a similar effort, he was enraged. To Malcom's private logic it felt as though they were saying, "You're not good enough for our love."

By following his anger to its underlying cause Malcom discovered that the great disappointment he felt about others mirrored the disappointment he felt about himself. He finally understood that feeling taken for granted and enraged were inevitable as long as he expected others to make him feel lovable.

VERA AND JIM

It was a second marriage for Vera and Jim. She had no children, he had three. Ever since their marriage three years ago, Vera had been physically ill and emotionally "tormented." Whenever Jim's children came to visit, whenever they called him or he called them, whenever he had to speak to his ex-wife concerning them, Vera became enraged. She found many reasons for her anger—loss of privacy, money spent on the children that took away from her and Jim, anger over the children's being "cold and uncaring" to her—all seemingly rational reasons for getting annoyed. However, the depth of Vera's reactions, rage, hostility, and fighting with Jim made it clear to them both that something else was going on.

In exploring the purpose her anger was serving, Vera discovered that by holding on to the anger she could also hold on to her victim image, blaming others for what was happening in her life. Not wanting to take responsibility for herself, Vera wanted Jim to take care of her "the way he takes care of his children." Vera didn't want to grow up, and she was angry about the possibility that she might have to.

Jim, on the other hand, wanted an adult woman to share his life, not another child. Vera's anger had precipitated a crisis that brought her face to face with her real issue: the false belief that she was not good enough or strong enough to face life as an adult woman.

When you are no longer afraid of anger, when you don't feel ashamed of it or feel overwhelmed and controlled by it, you are able to witness it like any other human emotion. The detached witnessing of anger helps you look beneath it to the deeper feelings that triggered it in the first place. Here are some questions to guide you in exploring beneath your anger:

- What is *in* my anger? What are the thoughts and feelings contained in this anger? Do I feel justified in having this anger?
- What does the anger leave me feeling *about myself*?
- What might I be afraid of?
- What might I be hurt by?
- What might I be feeling guilty about?
- What desire do I have that is being frustrated?
- What do I see in my partner that angers me yet reflects the same thing I wish *not* to see in myself?
- What purpose does my anger serve? (Your immediate response may be "nothing," but look again and repeat the question.) If I didn't have this anger, what would I be doing differently in this particular situation?

Once you have carefully and patiently answered each of the above questions you will have a better understanding of what is motivating your ego to anger and what is either driving you to hold on to it or preventing you from resolving and letting it go.

CHAPTER EIGHT

Staying Connected While Solving Conflicts

The ideas of "me" and "mine" are at
the root of all conflict.

—NISARGADATTA

Conflicts usually result from a clash of styles and a clash of needs. Earlier we mentioned that Paul and I have different styles when dealing with stressful situations. My style is to act as quickly as possible to remove the stress. Paul's style is to go more slowly. He takes more time to look the situation over carefully before deciding what action to take.

Couples may have different styles in a variety of areas. Take meeting new people, for example. One of you may immediately want to "get together," while the other may be more reticent and need time to warm up. Styles may be different when it comes to spending and saving money. How much contact do you have with extended family? Frequent visits or an occasional get-together? A big area of style difference is how you express feelings. One of you may be bubbly and enthusiastic while the other is more reserved.

What is important is that you clearly understand your different styles and avoid making judgments about each other's way of being. A difference in styles can come together to enrich your relationship. Certainly that's the best way to view it. And you can look at it that way as long as you are not rigidly locked into having to be right, and as long you can accept your partner's difference without making him or her wrong.

 Conflicts usually result from a clash of styles and a clash of needs.

Paul and I discovered that our writing styles were different as we worked on this book. My style was to do a first rough draft, finishing the chapters and getting all the content down before going back to write a final version. Paul's preference was to get each chapter complete before moving on to the next one. We avoided a deadlock by finding a way to combine both of our preferences, a new way that would suit both of us. We came together by rough finishing each chapter first and then, while Paul continued to work on the final draft, I started making notes on the next chapter.

CLASH OF NEEDS

Conflicts also come about when one of you has a strong need that conflicts with a corresponding need of the other. For example, you may have a strong need to be with friends while your partner prefers the two of you spend the time alone. Or you may have a need for frequent lovemaking while your partner's need is less frequent. You both like to vacation, but one of you wants to sit on a beach while the other wants to sightsee and shop. On weekends you need time alone to catch up on chores, but your partner needs your help with the kids. All these differences set the stage for conflict.

When conflicts come up between you each of you must feel heard and understood. It is essential to see that your partner is not locked blindly into his or her view and can put him- or herself in your shoes and see the situation from your point of view. When each of you is able to make this effort you create an atmosphere of good faith and cooperation, which immediately softens your conflict, making it feel less adversarial.

But cooperation and good faith are not likely when your selfish self is on the scene. It wants to have its own way. Immediate gratification makes it feel secure. If your ego takes over when a clash of needs occurs there is a good chance your emotions will run amuck and your ability to communicate will evaporate. When this happens you end up angry without even clearly understanding what each other's needs are in a particular situation.

   Cooperation and good faith are not likely
when your selfish self is on the scene. It
wants to have its own way.

You can prevent this scenario from unfolding when you remember to understand your anger as a spiritual warning signal. It reminds you that a situation is at hand that requires the participation of your higher spiritual self, not your ego. Your higher self is capable of good faith and cooperation. It honors the agreements you made about handling your anger. And your higher spiritual self knows how to find a solution you will both be happy with. It does this naturally and easily because its basic nature is peace and happiness. It has no need to win or be in control. It's your best resource in a conflict. All you need to do is remember to call upon it. Ask yourself, "What would my higher self do in this situation?"

Your higher spiritual self knows how to find
a solution you will both be happy with. It
has no need to win or be in control. It's
your best resource in a conflict.

FACING CONFLICTS AS A TEAM

Having the marriage spirit means we've made a conscious commitment not to use our relationship as a dumping ground for the
stresses that develop in everyday life. This shared intention, to
keep our marriage sacred, makes us a team. And as with any
team, if the players are angry, calling each other names, and out to
show each other up their chances of winning are slim. As game
time approaches the players must find a way to close ranks, pull
together, heal their differences, and make the success of the team
their first priority.

 Ask yourself, "What would my higher self
do in this situation?"

As a married couple we're a team dedicated to expressing the
everlasting love of the marriage spirit. That's what's best for us
individually and for our marriage. As spiritual teammates we
don't allow the selfish impulses of our egos to get in the way of
our love. We don't allow bickering, hostility, or anger to preoccupy and distract us. We see clearly that our individual well-being
is inseparable from the well-being of our team and its larger
vision.

As spiritual lovers working together we have come to understand that in every conversation we have, in every task we

undertake, in every project we attempt together, *process is more important than content*.

We stop being good teammates when we give more attention to the content rather than the process going on between us. Content refers to "what," while process refers to "how." For example, when facing a conflict over a clash of needs, content has to do with *what* the conflict is about—I want to buy a sports car and you want a sedan. Process has to do with *how* we go about discussing it. If you are talking over each other, not really listening, shouting to get yourselves heard, your process is a mess. Most likely nothing will get accomplished at the content (buying a car) level.

There is absolutely no point in continuing to argue over content while your process is in chaos. Ineffective process sabotages your efforts to find a solution, and the issue goes unresolved. The more unresolved issues we have in our marriage the greater the tension is between us. This tension leads to more conflicts.

 As spiritual lovers we have come to understand that in every conversation we have, in every task we undertake, in every project we attempt together, *process is more important than content*.

LISTENING WHILE SHELVING YOUR EGO

So often in our office, when couples sit across from us and attempt to talk through a conflict, they quickly end up arguing. What starts as a well-meaning conversation suddenly looks and sounds like two lawyers arguing a case. Each is more interested in scoring points than in hearing what the other has to say.

When you are talking through a conflict of needs, rising feelings of frustration, annoyance, or anger indicate an out-of-control process. Your ego selves have slipped into arguing over who is right and who is wrong. This arguing is a cue to witness the frustration and annoyance. Use it as a spiritual warning signal to STOP THE ACTION. Hold up your hands in a "T" shape and say, "Time out. We're not getting anywhere, let's cool off."

Take a few minutes to calm and center yourself. Some deep breaths will help. Make a conscious effort to go within and shift your awareness away from your ego. Trust the higher wisdom of your spiritual self. Relax, be open and receptive to hearing what your partner has to say.

Now you are ready to start talking again. This time take turns: One of you will listen while the other speaks first. Listening— truly listening—requires that you give full attention to what is being said. Partial attention is half-listening, while another part of you is thinking about what you're going to say when your turn comes. This does not count. Only listening with full attention, nothing else on your mind, counts.

Give all your attention, all your energy to listening. For this your ego must be out of the way. Shelve it. Then listen so you can hear the facts and the feelings behind the facts in what your partner is saying. When you have captured the thoughts and feelings your partner is conveying, you've successfully put yourself in his or her shoes for the moment.

As the speaker, after you've expressed your needs in the situation, ask your partner *"What did you hear me say?"* This is a very

 Give all your attention, all your energy to listening. For this your ego must be out of the way. Shelve it. Then listen so you can hear the facts and the feelings behind the facts in what your partner is saying.

important question because it keeps your conversation focused and on track. It ensures that each of you fully understands the other's position. Use this question as frequently as necessary in your conversation. It will save time by eliminating misunderstandings and the confusion they cause.

 As spiritual teammates we don't allow the selfish impulses of our egos to get in the way of our love.

When answering the question as the listener you should start with the phrase *"What I heard you say was . . ."* Repeating the words reinforces using the question. Now reflect, as completely and accurately as possible, your understanding of what your partner's position is on the subject. Your partner will then confirm that you have understood his or her message or give clarification until a complete understanding is arrived at. Proceed no further until you agree a complete understanding is at hand.

Now switch roles, giving the listener an opportunity to explain his or her position. Once again use the *"What did you hear?"* question to arrive at a complete understanding. Once you have heard each other out and have a full picture of each other's needs you are ready to brainstorm together to find solutions.

LIVABLE SOLUTIONS

Usually the solutions to your conflicts will fall into three general categories. These are *Capitulation, Compromise, and Coexistence.* ★

★ Early in our careers we had the good fortune to know and study with David and Vera Mace, pioneers in the field of marriage counseling and founders of The Association of Couples for Marriage Enrichment. We owe our understanding of anger's crucial role in marriage and the three C's of conflict resolution to the Maces.

Capitulation means giving in, giving a gift to your partner by giving in to what he or she asks and needs of you. There are times when capitulation is possible because you know your partner feels much more strongly about whatever it is you are in conflict about than you do. So you give in and present a gift to him or her. In a competitive relationship, capitulation might be unthinkable. In a love relationship it is a kind and gracious act, one that ensures similar acts on your behalf from your partner.

When Evelyn and I were building our second office, the architect came up with two plans. Plan A, which I favored, called for new construction of the office and waiting room area. Plan B, Evelyn's choice, put the waiting area in a different location using already existing space. Each plan worked well. Given all the changes necessary for each plan the cost would be nearly the same in both cases. Evelyn's plan created more windows, bringing in more light, which was very important to her. She strongly wanted Plan B. While I preferred Plan A I did not feel strongly about it. I gave in and we did Plan B. We both are thoroughly happy with it.

 Capitulation means giving in, it means giving a gift to your partner by giving in to what he or she asks and needs of you.

Compromise is a second healthy alternative to conflict. In arriving at a fair compromise you both, without pressure or deception, make concessions until you comfortably agree. Compromise means neither one of you feels like a loser. You are both ready to give something up until you find a solution you are both happy with.

For many years Paul and I produced and cohosted a weekly public access television program called *Love and Marriage*. Each week we struggled to find compromises over content and format issues: What topic would the program cover, what key points would we make during the program, would there be guests, which one of us would open, close, do interviews, and take phone calls?

Because the final product had us "on air," visible to a great many people, it was crucial that we both felt comfortable with what we were doing. Neither of us wanted to be there feeling forced or coerced. Each week we were challenged to cooperate and find compromises for each decision we saw differently. What helped us do this was being committed to the fact that we both needed to be happy with the result. When you are looking for a compromise that works for both of you, put your energy into helping each other feel happy rather than pushing for your own view. The solutions will come.

 Compromise is a second healthy alternative
to conflict. In arriving at a fair compromise
you both, without pressure or deception,
make concessions until you comfortably
agree.

Coexistence comes into play when, despite your best efforts, neither capitulation nor compromise are possible. At these times it is crucial not to use power to push or convince your partner into a solution he or she feels is not right for him/her. Since you both see that there is no other option open to you at this time, you opt to coexist with the situation, to live with it peacefully, with all the facts out in the open and fully understood between you. Periodically you look at the situation again. Allowing some time to pass may make a solution more possible. For the present, coexistence with kindness and understanding is your chosen path. With coexistence the quality of your togetherness is kept sacred, above the particular issue that has you temporarily at odds.

Right now Evelyn and I work out of two offices, one in the city, the other an hour away in the country. Our life would be much simpler (less traveling, less maintenance, not having to have two sets of office supplies and furniture) if we could settle in one place. But we can't agree where that would be. Each location has certain advantages one of us feels strongly about and neither of us feels we can give in. And a compromise (finding a third location? Heaven forbid!) feels impossible. So, we coexist, traveling between locations. Periodically we reevaluate our thoughts on the subject. Perhaps time will create some external change that makes a decision more possible. Or one of us will change our view, making compromise or capitulation more possible. Until then, we coexist and carry on, without resenting each other for the duplication in our lives.

> Coexistence comes into play when, despite your best efforts, neither capitulation nor compromise are possible. At these times it is crucial not to use power to push or convince your partner into a solution he or she feels is not right for him/her.

The following steps will help you resolve conflicts:

1. Agree, without being angry, that you have a conflict of needs.
2. Talk about the issue without any intention of convincing each other of anything.
3. Take turns talking and listening. State clearly the *facts* about the issue at hand. Before going any further make sure you each agree on the facts as stated.
4. After stating the facts, take turns presenting your thoughts and feelings about those facts.

5. Reexamine the facts, this time keeping in focus each of your needs surrounding those facts.
6. In order to get some distance from the conflict, ask each other, *If you were totally free of any personal needs,* in this situation what would the facts alone be pointing to as the solution to this issue?
7. Finally, take turns presenting your ideas about how to solve the problem in a fair and equitable way given each of your needs.

Each of you must feel you've been heard, that your needs have been taken into consideration, and that the conflict has been solved to your satisfaction. Be sure to use capitulation, compromise, and coexistence as needed. *Remember, you are not enemies. You are a loving team. Conquer the conflict between you as a loving team.*

ACCEPTANCE

Anger teaches us the necessity for acceptance. Probably the most difficult thing for all of us to accept is that in life there is no *absolute security.* Our bodies, our lives, the world we live in, the entire universe, all are constantly moving and changing. Nothing is static, nothing stands still. Life, our very existence, has change and uncertainty built right into it.

Despite these facts most of us yearn for a sense of permanence and security. In fact, it is when our security has been threatened, whether actually or only in our minds, that we get most angry. Acceptance helps us stop fighting against life's natural currents. It's a willingness to take life as it is without it fitting it into our personal wishes and desires. Paradoxically, the more we allow acceptance to guide our way of meeting life's uncertainties, the more that very acceptance offers a stability we can trust. Accepting "what is" as graciously and creativity as possible carries us away from our ego and strengthens our connection to the sacred ground of our being, our true divine nature.

It is when our security has been threatened that we get most angry. The more we allow acceptance to guide our way of meeting life's uncertainties, the more that very acceptance offers a stability we can trust.

SURRENDER

Surrender means letting go of your "me," easing your attachment to your body and ego self and cultivating an awareness that your true being is in the realm of spirit, a transcendent living presence, and not in the body-mind. Surrender to your sacred self. Trust that it will guide you in clarity and wisdom.

Make it a daily practice to sit quietly for twenty minutes in the morning and before you go to bed at night. Quiet your mind by letting your thoughts go as soon as they appear. Allow your body to relax as fully as possible. Go to that place in your awareness which is behind the mind. Seek the light that makes all the images, thoughts, and beliefs possible. Make it a place you're comfortable with and return to it often. Doing this will help you take your ego self, with all its angers, likes and dislikes, doubts, fears, wants, and desires less seriously.

Your personal self is so involved with "me, my, and mine" that it can't see the possibility of a larger reality to your being. It's your impersonal sacred self, your true divine nature, that awaits once you surrender.

 Surrender means letting go of your "me."

FORGIVENESS

Forgiveness is not for the forgiven but for the sake of the forgiver.

—ANONYMOUS

Anger and conflict bring us inevitably to forgiveness. Anger, resentment, bitterness all carry the seed of forgiveness within them. Forgiveness anchors one end of a continuum with hatred at the other. They are connected, not separate, just as we are connected to those we hate. As long as we harbor hate our "enemies" are forever with us. They live in the anger we carry toward them. And that anger has us living under a dark cloud of negativity, with little chance of knowing the sunshine of peace and harmony.

Just as surely as carrying anger poisons our memory of those we wish ill, it will poison us as well. Self-hatred, self-condemnation, self-criticism, and the depression that follows them all flow from anger carried within. If we are good at judging, blaming, and criticizing others it's foolish to think we'll spare ourselves the same scorn. Without forgiveness we risk making ourselves sick in body, mind, and spirit.

Forgiveness is not something we push ourselves to do for others, and it is not a pardon we grudgingly grant. Forgiveness is for ourselves. It's freeing ourselves from the burden of anger, from its little pinches to its massive aches. Forgiveness is the healing flame that burns away the poisons.

 Forgiveness is not something we push ourselves to do for others, and it is not a pardon we grudgingly grant. Forgiveness is for ourselves. It's freeing ourselves from the burden of anger.

Your ego self cannot offer forgiveness. What you can do is call upon your spiritual self for forgiveness to move through you. This means there must first exist within you a *willingness* to embrace forgiveness. It is a willingness to free *yourself* of anger and hate. When you free yourself of strong negative emotions, you are cleansing the mind and soul, opening a window to let in fresh air and sunshine. The willingness to forgive is the utmost expression of love for yourself and for your partner. It is a spiritual awakening to compassion. Practicing forgiveness is making a statement about what you really want your life to be. It's a way of saying loudly, NO MORE PAIN, no more doom and gloom, no more heartache.

STEP IV RITUAL

DEFUSING ANGER

Part 1

In your marriage every time an anger goes unresolved it hardens into a brick of hostility and sits there between you. Over time these "bricks" pile up and without knowing it you've built a wall right in the middle of your marriage. Eventually this wall gets so high you can barely reach out and touch each other. The first part of this ritual is designed for those of you who may be currently caught in an anger crisis. Go back and reread the case of Ilene and Karl, which began Chapter Seven. We told Ilene and Karl that their marriage was on the critical list and in intensive care. They needed to act with a sense of urgency, just as they would with a critically sick child. Here are the instructions we gave them. Go over them carefully and begin imple-

menting them in your own marriage. If you follow them seriously you will take a big step toward getting out of crisis and
into solution.

1. There must be a complete end to violence of any kind
   between you. Verbal abuse is violence. There is to be no
   yelling, screaming, cursing, name calling, insulting. No
   threatening to leave, no attacking of any kind, no putting
   down, no hostile silent treatment.
2. You must adopt an "as if" mind-set and act from it. You are
   to behave as if you highly respected each other, treating
   each other with utmost kindness and consideration. Treat
   each other as you would a dear old friend who came to visit
   for a week.
3. Immediately start "minding your own business," that is,
   focus all your attention on yourself and not on what your
   partner is or is not doing. Whenever you find yourself
   thinking a critical, negative thought about your partner, ask
   yourself, "What else could *I* be doing to help my marriage
   get well?"
4. From this moment on live in the spiritual *now.* No bringing
   up the past. For right now, at this critical time, thoughts of
   the past or the future are irrelevant to your current situation. If either one of you forgets your higher self and acts
   angry, unfriendly, rude, or uncaring the other will still
   carry on positively by holding up the sacred mirror. You
   will say, *"This is one of the times that I experience you as being
   angry and hurtful."* The other will not debate the point but
   take it as a reminder to get back on track caring for your
   recovering marriage.
5. Each of you needs to remember *it is not enough to love your
   partner the way* you *think he or she should be loved, you've got to
   love him or her the way he or she needs to be loved.*
6. Whenever either of you feels anger start to rise, witness it.
   Do not get involved with the thoughts and feelings, just
   witness and let them pass. Use the questions presented in

the previous chapter to help you explore the deeper feelings behind your anger.

7. Make it a top priority to focus on what is good between you. Spend two hours each weekend doing something together you both enjoy. This is an essential beginning step in becoming friends again.

8. Creating some quiet and peaceful time between you is of utmost importance. In every spare moment you have, remember that your marriage is a sacred place, show it the reverence it deserves in your every word, gesture, and deed.

9. Whenever possible, without force or coercion, show each other affection and reinforce any positive feelings as they come up.

Part 2: The Healing Forgiveness Dialogue

In most marriages there is some unresolved anger that takes away from love and caring. It may have to do with something that happened a long time ago, something that has been put on a back burner and that you hardly ever talk about. Or it may have to do with something more recent, some activity causing pain and unpleasantness between you.

Until now you've not been able to talk about it in a way that was helpful and healing. So the incident, the memory, the event remains a painful episode in your history as a couple. We want to help you talk about it now in a way that will be beneficial and healing. The fact that unresolved anger can cause so much trouble is what makes this ritual very important. Set aside an hour without interruptions to do it seriously.

Once you have set aside at least an hour and are sitting comfortably together, take each other's hand. Holding hands will remind you that you are sharing a painful issue so you can strengthen your love and togetherness. Approach this dialogue as if it were to be your last talk together. There will be no "later" and no tomorrow. There is only NOW. Open your heart so you can take in each other's thoughts and feelings in a loving way.

Please follow these directions carefully:

1. Each of you is to go within and recall an anger which you feel is still unfinished. It doesn't matter if it is something you've discussed before or an issue you have never spoken about. What matters is that it feels like a piece of unfinished business between you. Each of you may be thinking of the same episode or each of you may have a different story. That doesn't matter either. What matters now is having a dialogue that heals and brings closure to it.

2. Take turns listening to the other's story.

3. Talk about the incident in question, not only about your anger but *also about how you felt hurt and what still hurts you about it today. It's the hurt that needs healing, not the anger.* Remember to talk *only* about yourself, *your* thoughts and feelings. Do not analyze the motives or behavior of your partner. Stay focused on yourself, *expressing your anger and hurt with kind intentions. Do not attack or blame.*

4. When it is your turn to listen, do it without your "me" getting in the way. Say nothing while your partner is talking. Just listen. Listen so as to really hear what is being said, *both the facts and the feelings behind the facts.*

5. If you find yourself internally commenting about what you are hearing, witness it and end it. If your mind wanders bring it back as soon as you notice you've lost attention.

6. When your partner finishes say: "Let me tell you what I heard you say." Convey your fullest understanding of what you've heard. Then ask your partner "Have I understood you?" Listen again to any clarifications he or she may make.

7. Once you've been able to put yourself in your partner's shoes by wholeheartedly listening, have your partner verify that he or she feels you have understood. Now make a sincere, heartfelt apology. Apologize for the pain caused by your words and deeds. Do not justify your behavior, do not make excuses, only give a genuine apology.

8. After each of you has told your story and you have ex-

changed sincere apologies, give each other the gift of for-giveness. Tell each other you are forgiven and that each of you has forever finished with the hurt that was shared. Reassure each other that there is no longer an obstacle of hurt or anger between you.

End your healing forgiveness dialogue by telling each other how happy and grateful you feel to have each other in your lives. Let your love and affection for each other flow into whatever expression you feel comfortable with.

Repeat this part of the ritual often. Looking into each other's eyes, voicing and feeling the love between you, is powerful medicine. Taken on a regular basis its effects are enormous.

Creating Marriage's Strongest Bond — Unquestioned Trust

One who cultivates the higher self will soon find that the lower self follows in accord. That is how a man becomes a great man.

—MENCIUS

Unquestioned Trust

It should be the effort of each to ease
and enrich the life of the other. In this
way each is safe. Each feels that he
is worthwhile; each feels that he
is needed.

—ALFRED ADLER

CAROL AND WAYNE

Wayne and Carol have been married for eight years. They have a
seven-year-old son. Wayne made the appointment for counseling
after Carol received a phone call from a woman with whom he
had a year-long affair. At the start of the session Carol attempted
to describe her reaction. Through tears and sobs she said, "When
I got the call I just felt devastated, it was the last thing I expected.
I just couldn't believe it was happening. I was numb, the hurt and
anger were there, but my first reaction was numbness.

"I tried to call Wayne at the office but he was out. I left a
message for him to call back. The waiting was horrible. Part of
me wanted to believe it was some prank call. But a larger part
knew that my world had just been turned upside down. When

Wayne called back he didn't want to talk on the phone so he came right home.

"We stayed up all night talking, actually we've hardly had any sleep all week since this happened. Wayne says it's all over, that's why she called, she's angry and wants to hurt him. He says it didn't mean anything, he says we should forget it and move on with our lives. How can he say it didn't mean anything? It went on for a whole year. Whenever I try to talk to him about it he gets defensive. This only frightens me more. How can I trust that it's really over and that it won't happen again. The worst thing is not being able to trust him."

Wayne responded, "I don't know what else to do. I've tried to tell Carol how sorry I am. I don't want to cause her any more pain. I don't want our marriage to end, I love Carol, I'll do whatever it takes to get over this. She's been saying she wants me to leave, I don't want to move out but if it will help I will."

MOVING FROM INSECURITY TO SECURITY

In marriage unquestioned trust means giving your heart to each other for safekeeping with *absolute* confidence that it will not be broken. Unquestioned trust is a level of trust that is indisputable. It is a trust you have complete faith in and do not question. It is the same kind of trust you have in the sun rising and setting, in your heart beating and lungs breathing. Sharing the marriage spirit means the quality of your trust *has to be* unquestioned.

     In marriage unquestioned trust means giving your heart to each other for safekeeping with *absolute* confidence that it will not be broken.

Unquestioned trust is the bridge that carries you from insecurity to security. Even though in the big picture of life there is no guaranteed security, your marriage is one of the few places where you can create it. As we said earlier, you and only you are in control of how you treat each other. Each day, through your words and deeds, you can consciously choose to create unquestioned trust between you. Being absolutely confident that you can rely on your own trustworthiness and the trustworthiness of your partner creates unquestioned trust.

     Unquestioned trust is the bridge that carries
you from insecurity to security.

TRUST AND EXPECTATIONS

In every marriage partners have expectations of each other. What is important is the *kind* of expectations we have. When our egos take over and we relate to each other from a survival mentality we often place coercive expectations on each other. Coercive expectations are felt as demands. They imply control and cause friction between us.

For example, if I expected Evelyn to behave in a certain way (the way I prefer) or to do things in a particular fashion (the way I think is right), I would be placing coercive expectations on her. Evelyn, like most people, would object to this attempt at control. How this objection is expressed will depend on a person's personality. Some will express it directly in a head-on confrontation. Others may temporarily hide their objection only to let it out later.

For many couples coercive expectations are simply part of their relationship, unrecognized and uninterrupted. Inevitably they lead to trouble. Arthur and Kelly came for counseling because of this very problem. Arthur expected Kelly to clean house, cook the meals, and do the laundry even though she worked full-time just as he did. Arthur believed that by doing these things Kelly was taking care of him and proving her love.

Kelly objected to these expectations. She saw Arthur as selfish and felt manipulated. She wanted an equal partner, someone who would work along with her, sharing responsibilities of the home. The more Arthur insisted that if Kelly really "loved" him she would meet his expectations, the more she began feeling he "was constantly testing me" and therefore felt she could not trust his love.

Another couple, Ariel and Doug, had a similar problem. Ariel expected to be pampered. She wanted to be showered with attention and affection and indulged to an extreme, impossible degree. She wanted all this from her image of an ideal, all-perfect husband. Such a husband, she believed, would meet her inappropriate and self-centered needs to feel special.

Ariel's image of marriage was of a relationship where her expectations would be met despite her own inability to give and be loving. Doug felt used, he felt Ariel's love was a "one-way street, going only her way." He did not trust Ariel's motives for marrying him, and he resented her expectations. As a result, they fought constantly.

One kind of expectation we *do* have a right to require of each other is the expectation of *personal integrity*. Unlike survival-oriented, coercive expectations, expectations of personal integrity are not motivated by power or control. Expectations of personal integrity answer your real need to feel whole inside. They lead to peace and security by creating unquestioned trust and deepening your spiritual intimacy. These expectations are:

1. Trust that you will be sexually faithful.
2. Trust that you will not harm, reject, or control each other.
3. Trust that you will keep each other and your marriage a top priority.
4. Trust that you love each other without ulterior motives.

5. Trust that you will not abandon each other in the face of conflict, anger, or disagreements.
6. Trust in your own capacity to be trustworthy.

Living out these expectations breaks down the images you have about yourself and each other. It quiets and calms your selfish self, helping it be more willing to merge with and take direction from your spiritual self. By *earnestly* living out these six expectations of personal integrity you illuminate your marriage with the loving presence of the marriage spirit.

When unquestioned trust is established between you it serves as a daily reminder that your marriage is a reflection of your higher, spiritual self. Without unquestioned trust the basic structure supporting your entire relationship is shaky. It becomes crucial then that when trust has been damaged you take immediate action to repair and restore it. The following examples show how couples, with help and guidance, went about healing the wounds of damaged trust.

1. Trust That You Will Be Sexually Faithful

Sex is one of the ways you communicate your deepest love feelings. When making love you express your affection for each other and develop your own intensely private, personal ways of responding to each other. In your intimate moments, love blossoms and you share its fragrance. That essence is something only you two have together. It is precious, something that you trust each of you will cherish and protect.

Taking sex outside your marriage is breaking that trust. It is taking something of great value, belonging to both of you, and treating it carelessly. That is why infidelity is so painful and puts such a tremendous emotional and spiritual distance between you. Infidelity is one of the most severe traumas your marriage can suffer.

A major reason for extramarital affairs is the emotional immaturity that goes along with a survival mentality. With a survival mentality, men and women marry mainly for attachment and dependency rather than for a genuine heart-to-heart commit-ment. Their motivation to be truly intimate with any one person is not very strong. Having only superficial closeness is more to their liking. Once their need for basic security is met they feel satisfied. When this security is interrupted by stress and tension they often look for other relationships.

 Sex is one of the ways you communicate your deepest love feelings. It is precious, something that you trust each of you will cherish and protect.

Of course there are other reasons why people seek outside affairs. Often it is a way of expressing anger, of "getting even," or of getting one's partner's attention. Also, a sexual affair is one of the most available, quick-fix ways of bolstering sagging self-esteem. The excitement of someone new enables your insecure ego to lose itself in pleasure for a brief time, providing relief from feelings of confusion, boredom, and inadequacy.

 Infidelity is one of the most severe traumas your marriage can suffer.

An extramarital affair does not end most marriages. Repeated affairs, on the other hand, usually mean the marriage is over. Those couples who manage to stay together in the face of an affair usually do so by getting professional help. Unless the com-plex feelings of betrayal, hurt, rejection, and guilt triggered by an extramarital affair are dealt with fully, soon after it happens, there is a strong likelihood that they will go underground and ruin the marriage.

CAROL AND WAYNE

A CLOSER LOOK

Understanding Why: The First Step Toward Healing

We helped Wayne see that his heartfelt apology and willingness to ease Carol's pain was an essential but not a sufficient solution to their problem. We pointed out that Carol had a desperate need to understand his unfaithfulness, to make sense of it so it would not remain a mystery. That was the first step toward healing—understanding why. Wayne saw that he would have to turn himself inside out to give Carol a plausible explanation of his behavior.

As Wayne searched himself he gradually got in touch with feeling angry at Carol "for around the last four years." He said Carol was someone who was "very hard to talk to when she didn't want to hear what you had to say." There were many times, he said, when he tried to talk to Carol about things that were bothering him but she got so defensive that the issue would be dropped. Carol was afraid of criticism and did not like confrontation. Wayne felt that she placated him but never followed through on things she said she would change.

For example, Wayne felt strongly about keeping good relations with both their extended families. Carol cared less about this and often did not return phone calls from Wayne's sister or her own brother. When they did call she only reluctantly got on the phone. This bothered Wayne, and despite promising to make more of an effort to be social Carol never did. Wayne saw this as selfish and uncaring.

Wayne also said that he had tried for years to get Carol to do things with him but she always found excuses until he eventually gave up and stopped asking. For example, each spring Wayne planted a large vegetable garden. It was his pride and joy. Every year Carol would promise to do it with him but it never happened.

When Wayne told Carol he did not feel much affection from

her she offered reassurance but did not change her behavior. Wayne said he did not feel he was a top priority for Carol and had lost trust in her love.

Carol at first refused to even consider Wayne's point of view. On some level she felt that listening to Wayne's complaints meant that her pain did not count, that she somehow had brought it on herself, and that Wayne was justified in what he did. We helped her see none of this was true.

Slowly Carol acknowledged her tendency to be defensive and shut down. She said she did this to avoid confrontations. What surprised her was hearing the extent to which Wayne said he felt angered by it. And while Wayne insisted that he had made strong efforts to convey this to Carol she maintained she never heard this from him in a clear way. She did not know he was holding on to so much unfinished anger.

Carol went on to say that no matter how angry Wayne felt, he still was not justified in cheating on her. We agreed with Carol and emphasized that the only way for them to move productively forward from this point was to understand as fully as possible what had brought them to their present situation.

Holding On to Hurt for Self-Protection

Over the next few months Carol struggled with her hurt and anger, one minute feeling she could go on and forgive Wayne and in the next moment hating him all over again. "I'm always thinking about it, the thought pops into my head at different times and I start to feel hurt, angry, and depressed all over again. I'd be feeling good and something he would say or something else, a song on the radio, a TV show about someone cheating, would cause me to remember it and I'm off and running in my mind."

Counseling helped Carol see that as long as she held on to the thoughts of Wayne hurting her, trusting him would be impossible. Carol understood that she could not prevent her mind from associating some random, outside event or situation with

Wayne's infidelity. What she *could* have control over was witnessing but not actively pursuing the thoughts by dwelling on them when they did come to mind.

We showed Carol that the purpose behind her reliving the event over and over again was *self-protection*. Choosing to dwell on the thoughts was a way she reminded herself of the hurt, and this kept her guard up. It was a way she protected herself from being vulnerable and open to being hurt again. Eventually she would have to choose to let the thoughts go and take the risk of continuing with Wayne without holding back for self-protection.

Since Wayne and Carol wanted to stay together they had to learn how to rebuild their trust. This crisis in their marriage was a growth opportunity for each of them, psychologically and spiritually. Each now had a special reason to look within in a way they had never done before.

We told them that in this process of looking they would come to know themselves and each other in a new way. They would come to see how their ego-centered "me" selves, without the benefit of their spiritual selves, had made seeing, hearing, and accepting each other difficult. Giving themselves to this process would help them and their marriage heal and become stronger.

Wayne's Hidden Agenda

As Wayne cataloged the grievances he was clearly holding against Carol he seemed more and more to be justifying his affair to us and to himself. It was as if he were saying, "Look, she's been mean to me in lots of ways and I've been mean back, only I got caught." When we presented this view to him Wayne readily agreed with it. We asked him if he is a "get-even" kind of person. "Yes, I know that about myself. If someone does me wrong I'll find a way to get back at them. I've been known to do that with friends and with situations at work. I hate it when someone takes advantage of me because I trusted them."

We asked Wayne to see that the get-even response was his

selfish self reacting to being hurt and wanting revenge as a way of feeling superior. By getting even his ego felt reassured: It had been challenged but had gotten even, thereby reaffirming its power. We told Wayne that as long as his ego, with its get-even agenda, was in control he would be inviting more pain and confusion into his life. We then asked him to think about how he would handle situations in which he felt hurt and did not have a "get-even" agenda.

Wayne started off our next session by expressing a more balanced view of his "angers" at Carol. While it was true that she had avoided talking to him about issues, he said he could understand why she did it. "Carol is no match for me in an argument and when I approached her she probably heard an edge in my voice that said, 'Here comes a fight.' She knows she's not going to win with me so she probably figured there was no point in talking.

"I thought about your question of how I would respond if I didn't want to get even. I guess my whole approach would be different. With Carol I would have been more sensitive to her. I would have made sure nothing I said or did scared her off. I would have told her what was bothering me in a more loving way. I know I can do that because I do it with our son. It's a softer side of me I don't show very often. Maybe that's a mistake."

Carol's Fears

For her part Carol said that she had known for a long time that she allowed her fears to dominate how she handled certain situations. Now she saw that by allowing her ego self to run free with fear she avoided taking responsibility for her actions in the marriage. By making Wayne the "bad guy" whenever he brought up issues, she made herself the "victim."

Changing this pattern would mean becoming more honest about what she was feeling and trusting that her sacred self would help her find a way to be assertive and loving all at the same time. "What's the worst thing that could happen? If he didn't like it he would leave. If I weren't afraid of that I'd be okay. But someplace inside I know he loves me and wouldn't walk out just because I stood up for myself. I guess I would have to be more sensitive to his insecurities so I could help him see mine. I also did what you suggested. I meditated on the fact that forgiving him is as important for me as it is for him and I realize that's true."

Moving Forward

Wayne and Carol made a pledge to help each other live in the spiritual present. Carol had to use all her energy to pull herself into the *now* every time thoughts of the infidelity crossed her mind. For Wayne the major goal was getting Carol to trust him again. He resolved to do all he could to help prevent doubt and mistrust from taking hold in Carol's mind. "I've become extremely sensitive to her fears. I can literally see the doubts creep in and cross her face. I just keep talking to her, keep letting her in on everything I am feeling and thinking.

"There is no way she can doubt me. I tell her everything. Absolutely everything that's going on when I'm away from her and when I'm with her. Everything about my work, the people I work with, what I'm feeling about certain situations, where I'm going, where she can reach me at any time. I know I have to be an open book to get her trust back. A friend asked me if I feel restricted by all this. I told him no I don't. I know the most important thing to me is to get her to trust me again. And also, I've begun to listen, I mean really listen to everything she says and feels."

It took Wayne and Carol two years to get beyond the damage to their trust. They continue to be careful with each other's feelings, and the process of healing is still going on. They are working together to put their marriage on solid ground again.

2. Trust That You Will Not Hurt, Reject, or Control Each Other

JANE AND MATTHEW

Matthew called to set up an appointment to see us with Jane, with whom he has been having a four-year relationship. "We are here because of a problem I have and it has very little to do with Jane. We've been going together for four years, practically living together although we both still have our separate apartments. Jane wants to be married and I'm not able to make the commitment to do it. I love her but the thought of marriage scares me and I want to back off.

"I've had a lot of therapy earlier in my life, I know why I am the way I am, but changing this part of me doesn't seem to work. Jane wants to be married and I don't blame her. If I don't do something very soon I know I'll lose her.

"My father died when I was eight and my mother raised me and two sisters by herself. She did everything for us. She was very warm, supportive, but also very neurotic. Her whole life was devoted to her children, so much so that we were all suffocated by her. My mother was a 'saint.' We were all so afraid of doing anything wrong or anything to hurt her because she was so good, so self-sacrificing. At some point I realized that was strangling me. I felt the warmth and closeness, but I also felt the control. That's what I'm afraid of, that if Jane and I get married I'll end up feeling the same way.

"In a couple of months Jane is going away on a trip and when she gets back she wants an answer about us getting married. That's why I called, because we're facing this deadline." While Matthew talked Jane sat quietly listening, nodding in agreement. Matthew went on, "Until I met Jane I never thought I would be married. I'm very self-sufficient. But I miss her when we're apart and the time we are together is really special. She's a wonderful person. I'm closer to her than to anyone else in my life."

Caught Between Fears

Caught between the fear of closeness (which to Matthew means being controlled) and the fear of losing Jane, Matthew said he wanted to give himself an opportunity to free himself of the fear. "Whether or not Jane and I are married, I just can't go on living this way." Being able to trust was a gift he wanted to give himself. Over the next four months Matthew agreed to doing the following inner self work:

1. As soon as *any* thoughts of doubt or mistrust about Jane entered his mind he was to witness them and immediately let them go. Witnessing and letting go would keep him consciously focused in the present rather than projecting into the future.

2. He was to bring himself back to the present by reminding himself that the negative thoughts about Jane that he had just let go of were the work of his small, insecure ego self.

3. In his interactions with Jane, who was more than willing to work with him, as soon as he experienced being controlled he was to let her know without *blame, without attack, and without running away.* Jane was to be open to his feelings and then check out her behavior to see if indeed she was being controlling. If she was, she had to acknowledge it openly and honestly. If she was not, Matthew had to reevaluate his perception by stepping back and looking at it from Jane's perspective. If they reached an impasse, they would agree to let the incident go and be ready to explore the next incident as soon as it came up.

4. He was also to remind himself that any life he chose to make with Jane would be presided over by his higher spiritual self and not his ego. To help quiet his mind so that less of his energy went into creating negative thoughts about Jane and their future together, Matthew agreed to take up a daily spiritual practice such as meditation, yoga, or prayer.

We also instructed him in the use of visualization. Matthew, in the calmness following a meditation, yoga, or prayer session, was to visualize himself and Jane living happily together. With as much detail as possible he was to see himself living happily, without fear, as a married man. He was to use this visualization as often as possible to strengthen his resolve to change the direction of his life.

5. Matthew was to consciously adopt the posture of acting *as if*, that is, he was to behave as if he had no fear or doubt about marrying Jane. Very often when we act as we would if we had no fear our anticipated fear fails to materialize. Acting *as if*, to whatever extent he was able, would activate his spiritual self, which is unafraid, trusting, loving, and rooted in the *now*.

Matthew and Jane continued in counseling for a year and were then married. For the first year Jane said Matthew continued to try to push her away, distrusting, complaining, and testing her. When they started to get close, he would pull away. But Jane kept coming through. Her trustworthiness and openness helped Matthew develop a large enough trust that he finally let himself get close to her without any pushing away.

Jane told us, "We both have gained a sensitivity to what each other wants and needs. I have a great respect for his basic goodness, kindness, his humanity, I feel a sense of completeness in that. And since we've resolved the issue of mistrust and it no longer is an issue for us, I feel fulfilled and I feel loved."

3. Trust That You Will Keep Each Other and Your Marriage a Top Priority

Marriage cannot be successful without each of you wanting that success with an urgency equal to your greatest desire. Think of something that motivates your whole being with devotion and commitment. That same devotion and commitment has to be in your marriage for it to succeed.

Couples usually begin marriage counseling by describing their present situation—what each sees as going wrong in their marriage. In almost every instance the story that unfolds details how couples allow careers, children, family, friends, businesses, hobbies, and practically anything else you can think of to come before their commitment to each other.

> ❧ Marriage cannot be successful without each
> of you wanting that success with an
> urgency equal to your greatest desire.

The plain fact is that most of us do not take marriage seriously. We get so caught up in all the other demands that our marriage and the quality of our togetherness fall to the bottom of our "to do" list. The longer this benign neglect is allowed to continue the weaker our bond becomes. More and more our conversations focus on the routine and ordinary, and this dulls our sensitivity to and interest in each other. Soon we have less and less to say to each other. Under these conditions it's only a matter of time before sexual passion evaporates, and this adds to our feeling of being cut off from each other.

> ❧ The plain fact is that most of us do not take
> marriage seriously. We get so caught up in
> all the other demands that our marriage and
> the quality of our togetherness fall to the
> bottom of our "to do" list.

Keeping your marriage a priority so that you maintain your interest in and excitement for one another does not mean you close others out and create a "you and me against the world" attitude. On the contrary, establishing your marriage as a top priority frees you to become "you and me actively involved in and with the world." Your love, care, and concern for others broadens once you have the marriage spirit.

When your marriage is a top priority, being together brightens and enhances all other events and situations. You continually remind each other with a look, with a touch, with a spoken "I love you" that it is your connection at a heart-to-heart level that counts most in your life. It's this connection that infuses every other part of your life with happiness and joy. Then it becomes easier to be your best self at home, in your work, and with close friends you enjoy.

TED AND CYNTHIA

We first met Ted and Cynthia eight months after Ted was promoted to vice president. The promotion meant his long work-week got longer. He missed seeing more of his children, Sara and Andy. He also knew the promotion put more of a burden on Cynthia, who was at home full-time with the kids. But Ted had worked long and hard for this advance, it was a chance to achieve a major career goal, and he relished the opportunity. The new job also meant more travel but Ted took it in stride. For him this was the biggest challenge of his career, and Ted loved a challenge.

A Mixed Blessing

For Cynthia Ted's promotion was a mixed blessing: "Believe me, I'm happy for Ted because I know how much this means to him and I also know that we could use the money. But another part of me just hates the whole thing. I know Ted doesn't like to hear this, which is why we've been fighting so much lately, but I can't sit here and pretend its all okay with me, because its not. And, you see, this is the reaction I get [pointing to Ted, looking annoyed] so we can't talk about it without having a fight."

Ted interjected: "That's because whenever I do get home you're there with this chip on your shoulder waiting to jump all over me for the slightest thing."

Cynthia replied: "All you can see is that I'm not falling all over you because now you're a vice president. It may sound terrible but I wish he never got the promotion. He comes home most nights when I'm asleep or so tired I can't keep my eyes open. We barely talk. On Saturday he sleeps late and I don't blame him, I'd want to sleep in too if I had those hours. When he gets up I run errands and he plays with the kids. But he has very little patience for them. Maybe Saturday night we'll see friends or watch a movie. Sundays are usually horrible because by then we're picking on each other.

"I'm alone so much of the time the kids and I have our own routine. When Ted comes home he interrupts that. I almost feel like he's an intruder. He comes into my space and disrupts things. He doesn't talk, he never did. It's like he's off doing his thing and I'm doing mine but when he comes home he expects everything to revolve around him and I just can't do it."

Ted: "She's right, I can't stand hearing this stuff. It sounds almost childish to me. To listen to her you'd think I was off playing golf, which I don't do, by the way, unlike a lot of my friends. I'm not going to be working this job for the rest of my life. Now's the time when we have to pay the piper. Our time will come later. It's a sacrifice we have to make now. My job won't always be there but Cynthia will."

Cynthia: "You see, its that kind of thinking I can't go along with. How do you think that makes me feel? It's like I'm somewhere down there on your list of things to do. It's like you love me, but you're *really* in love with your job. I just won't accept that."

A New Perspective

Clearly Ted and Cynthia had become adversaries. As adversaries they lacked empathy and compassion for each other's point of view. In the face of major change and stress most of us regress. This is an important fact worth remembering: Under stress we regress.

Whenever we feel threatened, insecure, overwhelmed, and not in control our natural tendency is to withdraw, cover up, and go into a survival mode. In the Midwest when a tornado approaches people go underground, they hunker down in the root cellar until the danger blows over. We do the same thing emotionally.

   This is an important fact worth remembering: Under stress we regress.

The problem is that we frequently *overreact* to emotional stress. We act as if our lives *were* at stake. We go into a survival mode in a way that damages our connection to others. We see only our needs, our fears, our worries and ignore what our partner may be thinking and feeling. The damage to our relationship is the real threat to our security, much more than the stress we were trying to cope with in the first place.

This is what happened to Ted and Cynthia: Ted's promotion upped the stress level in their lives. Each felt like a victim of the other's indifference. In truth both were victims, not of each other, but of a joint failure to keep their marriage a priority. Their attention became more centered on how they were hurting each other than on how to work together *as a team* in the face of the changes in their lives.

Marriage counseling helped Ted and Cynthia use this crisis to grow emotionally and spiritually. Both had slipped into identifying with their small ego selves, the part of them that was feeling wounded by the other's insensitivity. Without a connection to their higher spiritual selves they held on to seeing themselves as victims of the other's narrow point of view. They were unable to recover their ability to love and come through for each other.

Becoming so upset with each other held an important lesson: The focus of their *attention* did not match their *intention*. Both claimed it was their intention to have a happy, loving marriage, yet Ted was giving almost all his attention to work, while Cynthia's attention was taken up with feeling angry and neglected. Very little conscious effort was being directed at remembering their true spiritual selves and keeping their marriage sacred. The result was disorder between them. As we helped them see this they both began to reorder their priorities. They both agreed to take responsibility for shifting their attention back to their marriage.

This perspective helped Ted become less defensive and better able to hear what Cynthia was saying. He knew he had not been giving enough importance to her and their relationship. He agreed to put his work in better balance. He said that he could do a better job at this if he knew Cynthia was more supportive of his career goals and the struggle he was going through. He missed being able to share his work with her, to talk about it together as they had done before.

For her part Cynthia realized that holding on to her anger only re-created the past and worked against empathizing with Ted. She saw that she had to let go of feeling like a victim and begin acting from the part of her that loved Ted and wanted to keep him and their marriage a top priority.

4. Trust That You Love Each Other Without Ulterior Motives

When you are not connected to your higher spiritual self you doubt the authenticity of your partner's love because you doubt that you are lovable. You doubt your own lovableness because your ego self acts in selfish ways, trying to get security for itself. Without the wisdom of your spiritual self you are unable to see that by acting in this way your ego pushes love (and real security) away. By being unloving you create your own sense of being unlovable.

DEAN AND MARGO

Dean and Margo, each of whom had been previously married, have been married for ten years. Dean has two sons from his first marriage, and Margo has a daughter about to start college. Dean is the driving force behind a large and very successful insurance agency. Margo is a former dancer and actress.

Dean and Margo do not trust each other's love. When they are not bickering or arguing they have very little to say to each other. Margo does not believe any man can truly love a woman without some kind of ulterior motive. She believes that a man's love is very conditional, that it depends on a woman being beautiful, submissive, and not at all outspoken. She sees men as emotionally weak and not trustworthy.

"Quite honestly when I met Dean and maybe for the first two years of our marriage, I thought he was different. But now I think I was wrong. He's only loving to me when I'm looking good and when I'm not saying much of anything. As soon as I express an opinion about something, his work, his ex-wife, how his kids treat him, he shuts me right up and shuts me out. You can't imagine how he speaks to me, like I was lower than low. He wants a wife he can parade around and show off, that's all."

For his part Dean said Margo gives him a hard time about everything. "She's just not easy and agreeable. She's not able to see my view about things. She thinks she's always right about everything and she has no consideration for my feelings. She tries to be helpful, like with my kids, but sometimes I think her real motive is to get at me, aggravate me, and make me wrong." Dean believes Margo loves him because of the lifestyle he can provide, because of the status and security that goes with his financial success. "In the end it all comes down to money and the material things I can provide. I'm just her security ticket through life." Hearing this, Margo quickly shot back, "You give me nothing of yourself so I might as well take what you do give me, money and the things money can buy."

Not Feeling Good Enough to Be Loved

Both Dean and Margo were struggling with strong feelings of personal insecurity. Their ego selves were full of mistrust and defensiveness. Each felt weighed down by a feeling of being unlovable. Their disappointment with each other mirrored the negative feelings they carried about themselves.

With coaching and encouragement they shared this secret with each other. Slowly and carefully, they described how they held back part of themselves, letting the other see only what each believed would be valued.

Each voiced a similar fear: that if they were truly known they would not be deeply loved. Dean grew up knowing that he could get love by being a winner, a success. For Margo, from childhood on, being beautiful brought attention and the feeling of being loved.

Now, as adults, each was yearning to be loved wholeheartedly, for who they were as real people, without pretense and conditions. Each needed the other to see and validate the inner worth they themselves doubted. The experience of being loved in this way is what each had intuitively hoped their marriage would provide.

The healing, transformative power of unselfish love is the gift we all sense marriage holds for us. Converting this possibility into a reality requires holding it consciously in as a focal point of great intention. When we hold our intention to cultivate unselfish love clearly in our awareness, our sacred self appears and shows us the way.

The Healing Power of Unselfish Love

Counseling helped Dean and Margo be clearer about what was missing in their marriage. As each became determined to be present from their higher spiritual self much of the surface bickering stopped. Now they saw this was a way they filled an awkward silence in their marriage. It was clear that a more honest dialogue needed to go on between them. Both agreed to begin risking more of themselves to make this happen.

Dean would stop pretending to always be on top of the world, with no worries or concerns. And when he was worried he would not take his frustrations out on her. He promised to share more of his real feelings with Margo, more of his doubts and fears as well as his joys and interests. He saw that it was essential that he not, under any circumstances, treat her harshly or in a demeaning manner.

He was to show her the utmost of respect and regard. In addition, he agreed not to allow day-to-day business events to consume all his attention. Now his marriage needed to become a sacred place, a top priority in his life.

Margo was to let go of overinvolving herself with Dean's affairs, be it work or kids or ex-wife problems. She clearly did not have to express her opinion on every situation that came up. If Dean did come to share his concerns she was to be a sounding board, listening carefully but making no critical comments. If Dean asked for her opinion she would express it and be as supportive as possible.

Margo needed to show Dean that she appreciated his hard work and the many pressures and responsibilities he carries. This would show her love for the "inner Dean" and reinforce her interest in having more of him beyond what he could give materially. She too had to treat their marriage as a sacred place and see that criticism, possessiveness, and hostility had nothing to do with what is sacred in and between them.

5. Trust That You Will Not Abandon Each Other in the Face of Conflict, Anger, or Disagreements

ARLENE AND JEFF

Arlene and Jeff have been married for three years. Arlene came into the marriage with a lot of survival-mentality fears. While drawn to Jeff, she was frightened of men and of intimacy. She had a strong fear of being abandoned. Because of her fears she adopted a very independent posture in her marriage. She did not want to be dependent on Jeff for anything. This "independence" was really a move for self-protection. Coming to believe Jeff's love could be trusted was a big step that took time.

"When I met Jeff I was living on my own, not needing anyone. Being independent was important to me. When we married I made sure that I pulled my own weight financially, and I know that was my not trusting. It seems crazy now, but before we came for counseling I had this fear that if something happened between us, like some terrible fight, I was afraid Jeff would walk out. There were times in the beginning, when I thought if I did the wrong thing, or said the wrong thing, he would just walk out. On a gut level I was afraid of being abandoned if I didn't live up to snuff."

Jeff said that he truly loved Arlene but he was afraid to show annoyance of any kind for fear that she would up and leave. "She's so paranoid about my walking out that with the slightest disagreement she's ready to pack up, like she's going to do the leaving first."

Fear of Abandonment

In our talks Arlene came to see how strongly identified she was with her ego self. Her ego was convinced that being abandoned would be a fate worse than death. In fact, Arlene's ego equated being left with "being worthless and having my worst fear come true, nobody else would want me." As long as she allowed her ego self to control her thoughts and feelings she would not be free to trust anyone's love.

This was the dilemma life and marriage presented to Arlene: either staying attached to her ego in fear and worry or risking letting go and trusting in the strength of a larger identity, her higher spiritual self. Consciously choosing to identify with this self would be a decision she would draw strength from. Her spiritual self had the wisdom and courage to bring her safely through any crisis.

What Arlene came to see was that what she called "independence" was based on fear and actually on a very strong dependency on Jeff. True independence is a trust in oneself. Acting from true independence would mean being able to express herself openly and freely while knowing that she had the inner strength to face what life presented without running away and avoiding disagreements.

Jeff came through for Arlene by being sensitive to her deepest fear, and no matter how angry he might have been he never used it to threaten her with. Jeff knew that any threat of abandonment would be a terrible blow to Arlene. He would encourage Arlene to express whatever it was she thought or felt about a particular situation or decision, especially when it was different from his. If he did get angry, he talked about it immediately in a non-threatening way. By continually and consistently demonstrating integrity in this way, he eventually gained Arlene's trust.

   True independence is a trust in oneself.

By choosing to identify with her spiritual self Arlene got distance from the fears that plagued her. With this new strength she began to let herself trust that Jeff loved her and that he would not abandon her. With Jeff's help she "forced" herself to express whatever feelings she had, including anger, annoyance, and disappointment. She also began to voice her opinions and views, no longer afraid of Jeff's getting angry and leaving.

Threatening to leave is a harmful way of
showing how angry you are.

When couples meet difficult times in their marriage it is often tempting to threaten divorce as an expression of anger. Such threats only add to the mistrust in a relationship. And it is this lack of trust that is the real problem—not the particular issue being argued about. Threatening to leave is a harmful way of showing how angry you are. Trust is built, supported, and kept healthy in a marriage as each of us consistently demonstrates personal integrity to the other.

6. Trust in Your Own Capacity to Be Trustworthy

It is important to remember that shared unquestioned trust begins with you. By taking full responsibility for your own trustworthiness, which *does not* depend on your partner's behavior, you demonstrate the marriage spirit.

For example, if your partner broke the trust in your marriage by having an affair, you continue to demonstrate your trustworthiness by not doing the same. If your partner speaks harshly or acts abusively, you do not retaliate by doing the same. If your partner threatens to leave, you do not come up with a threat of your own. You make sure that you do not engage in a "tit-for-tat" game. If you really value being trustworthy you begin by valuing it in yourself.

You damage the trust in your marriage when you get lost in your small self, with all its images, fears, and desires. Whenever you forget your spiritual essence you blame your partner, you focus on his or her shortcomings and not your own. You expect your partner to come through with unquestioned trust but do not hold yourself to the same standard.

HARVEY AND NINA

Harvey called saying he and Nina needed marriage counseling but that he wanted to have some sessions alone before they started together. "I hate having to admit to myself that I need to be here but I do, so here I am. I'm a freelance writer. Nina works for a big trading company here in the city. She makes all the dough, well not all, but relatively speaking what I earn doesn't come near her salary. As she's gotten more and more important in the company I've taken over a lot of the household stuff so I'm really a writer slash househusband, if the truth be known.

"Actually I love it because it gives me so much time with the kids. I enjoy it. I walk them to school most days, go on field trips, meet with the teachers, the whole nine yards. So there's no problem there, with the kids, I mean.

"But more and more, over the last two years especially, Nina and I have less and less to say to each other. Lots of nights by the time she gets home she's really fried and just wants to veg out or give the kids a bath. After that it always seems like she's in one part of the apartment and I'm in the other. I'll be writing while she's on the phone with her sister or mother.

"Sometimes I think she resents having to work so hard while I'm home so much. She'll deny it, but it's there. And I know I've been envious of her, her success and my own frustrations. So there's a lot of tension there that we don't talk about. I think we're both afraid of an explosion that might threaten everything. But it's there, we haven't had sex for the last year and a half. Why? I stopped asking and she hasn't suggested it. I know I have a lot of anger about that.

"About four months ago I met this woman at my daughter's school. We were both there to pick up the kids, who were late getting back from the zoo. We started talking. She also wants to write. I won't bore you with the details, but now we meet once a week, for coffee, and spend an hour together talking.

"I see myself becoming attracted to her, looking forward to hearing what she has to say, being interested in her week, wanting to share mine. I'm telling her stuff that I used to share with Nina. Nothing physical has happened but I feel myself getting emotionally involved with her. I'm not about to cheat on my wife but I guess I'm feeling guilty about what is going on. Something inside me is telling me to stop this, it just isn't the right thing to do.

"I guess meeting this woman, seeing my reaction to her, shows me how far apart Nina and I have drifted."

Harvey's trustworthiness in not pursuing a beginning attraction outside his marriage opened the possibility for him and Nina to get help before an affair complicated their existing problems.

If you find yourself in a vulnerable position, unsure of the right thing to do, remember an important fact: Your spiritual self is an underused resource. You could be making much greater use of it. Turn within and listen carefully to what your higher self tells you. It is always there, waiting to lend guidance, grace, and harmony to your life. Remember, by slowing down, turning within, and asking for guidance you'll avoid acting out of impulse or habit. You'll avoid going on "automatic."

Spiritual guidance is available to you. It has the clarity and wisdom to help you stay trustworthy. You can try asking for guidance in the form of a silent prayer, or in the silence of mediation. Simply say, "Show me the way to understand my present situation, grant me clarity so that I might act rightly, fairly, and with integrity."

Learning to consciously turn your attention inward for guidance through a spiritual practice can help give you the strength and courage to hold up your end of unquestioned trust.

STEP V RITUAL

CREATING MARRIAGE'S STRONGEST BOND — UNQUESTIONED TRUST

This ritual requires you to come together as a couple to explore with each other the six areas of trust we have spoken about. This ritual is to be done when you are both feeling strong and positive about yourselves and each other. It calls for an honest dialogue so it is important that neither of you is carrying any angry feelings. The ritual is an opportunity to explore feelings, it is not an opportunity to accuse and blame. Also, the ritual needs to be done when you can set aside at least an hour of *uninterrupted* time. You will each need pen and paper.

Part 1

Begin by going off by yourself and writing down the six areas of trust described in this chapter. As you read each trust area ask yourself, "Does my partner come through for me in this way?" If the answer is "No," write down one, two, or three *concrete* examples that demonstrate this. For example, if you don't trust that your partner won't harm, reject, or control you, give some incidents in which you felt harmed, rejected, or controlled.

Part 2

When you have finished going through the trust areas with your partner in mind do it again, this time about yourself. Go over each area of trust and ask yourself, "Do I come through for my partner in this way?" Write down where you think you do a good job of coming through and where you see yourself as needing to do a better job.

Part 3

When you have both completed answering parts one and two it will be time to share your observations. Before you do, it is important that you create the right setting. Begin by sitting together in quiet for a few minutes. It's a good idea to hold hands. You will need to shelve your ego and invite your witnessing capacity to be present. As you sit silently together create a safe place to share by:

- Quieting your mind. Breathe deeply and let go of any interfering thoughts. Bring your attention to this current moment.
- Activating your witnessing capacity to make sure you don't slip into blaming or judging each other.
- Letting go of images. See each other with "innocent eyes."
- Placing yourself in the spiritual *now*. Make sure your mind is not floating around somewhere in the past, or projecting into the future.
- Inviting reverence for your marriage and your partner by remembering what you love, value, and admire about your partner.

Now take turns telling each other where the trust between you needs to be made stronger. Listen to each other with an open heart and remember honesty that comes from your spiritual self is always accompanied with *kind intentions*!

BRIDGET AND DENNIS

Bridget and Dennis were able to get the most out of doing this ritual for two very important reasons. First, when making statements about how the other was not coming through, neither blamed or attacked the other. Second, as each listened to what the other had to say, they did not argue or debate what their partner was feeling, nor did they justify or make excuses for their behavior.

Bridget started with her notes. There were two areas of trust where she felt Dennis was not coming through for her. The first was number three, "Trust that you will keep each other and your marriage a top priority." "I feel I and our marriage come fourth for you. First comes your work and everything and everyone associated with it. Next comes sports, any and every kind of sport, then come the kids, especially the boys, and then comes me and our marriage. I just don't feel that I'm important to you. You don't know how much this hurts me.

"The second way I feel you don't come through is number one, 'Trust that you will be sexually faithful.' I know you have been. But no matter how many times I tell you, you still do the same thing. Every time we go out, to a restaurant, to the mall, or with friends, you always look around at other women, you flirt with them right in front of me. I hate it, it makes me feel so small. You know we've talked about this before, but every time I mention it you wave your hand at me as if to say I'm making too much about it. This makes me feel dismissed. It makes me feel that what I'm feeling doesn't count.

"These are the two places of trust I wish could change. I'd do anything if they would change."

Dennis spoke next. "Everything you just said you told me at home. I felt bad then and feel real bad about it now. I don't agree with you completely, but I'm taking your word for it. I can't argue with how you feel.

"When I did part one I realized I had trouble with number two, 'Trust that you will not harm, reject, or control each other.' I do feel rejected by you sexually. I feel you do it because you have to, not because you really want to. I also feel controlled by you. It's always *your* friends we go out with. It's always *your* family we go and visit, especially on holidays. It's always *your* family you invite to dinner or have parties for. It's like my family doesn't count with you at all, except for funerals, you come through for funerals.

"I feel controlled by you when it comes to Jessica [his daughter from a previous marriage]. It's never a good time or the right time for her to stay over or come along with us on vacations. I guess I always felt you controlled things in this way but never said much. I guess I felt it was like a trade-off, I put my work first and you controlled who we saw.

"When I did part two, I came out with the same results you did. Not with number one, about being sexually faithful, because I know I have been, but certainly with number three, about making you and the marriage a priority. I know there's a lot of truth in what you said. I feel relieved, I'm glad all this is out in the open and we have a place to start and understand it better. I feel ready and confident that we can and will work out these issues. I'm ready to commit to this."

Unquestioned trust puts your marriage on a rock-solid foundation. When you come through for each other with unquestioned trust each of you enables the other to cross the bridge from insecurity to security. As a result your ego calms down and has less hold on you. Your behavior is less influenced by your selfish self and becomes more an expression of your spiritual self. You are able to stay spiritually connected on a more consistent basis. Now the unselfish values of your higher self emerge more clearly and enhance your capacity to give each other soul-centered love.

Being Free to Do the Right Thing — Right Action

Freedom to do what one likes is really bondage, while being free to do what one must, what is right, is real freedom.

—NISARGADATTA

C H A P T E R   T E N

Truth: Acting with Personal Integrity

It is always the false that makes you
suffer, the false desires and fears,
the false values and ideas, the false
relationships between people. Abandon
the false and you are free of pain; truth
makes happy — truth liberates.

—NISARGADATTA

JOSEPH AND ANN

Joseph and Ann have been married for seventeen years and are just now beginning to be honest about sex and money. Joseph has been the keeper of money secrets, having control, making unilateral decisions, and keeping Ann in the dark about their finances so he could "manage their investments."

Meanwhile Ann held a tight rein on the quality and quantity of the sex and affection in their marriage. Neither was honest about sex and money because their marriage was really one long battle for control.

Approaching midlife and tired of their impasse they have come for counseling. Until now neither of them has been willing to look honestly at themselves. Their way of being together is dramatically different from the way of truth and honesty. Their communication is choppy and disjointed and they are awkward in each other's presence. Sexually and emotionally they are distant from each other. There is always a brittle tension between them. Slowly and carefully now they are risking being more real with each other.

When you value truth and live from personal integrity you cannot bear the daily tension Joseph and Ann live with. It would literally make you sick. Holding to the eternal value of truth puts a sense of peacefulness in your life that your ego self cannot bring. Your ego encourages self-deception, which leaves you feeling confused and with a subtle sense of shame for letting your true self down.

 When you value truth and live from personal integrity you cannot bear the daily tension Joseph and Ann live with. It would literally make you sick. Holding to the spiritual value of truth puts a sense of peacefulness in your life.

The psychologist Abraham Maslow pointed out that truth, harmony, and goodness are deep-rooted biological, psychological, and spiritual *needs*. When they go unfulfilled your happiness and peace of mind suffer greatly. Maslow said that when you ignore your higher nature you make yourself physically and spiritually ill.

For example, by betraying your need for truth, you run the risk of becoming, to varying degrees, cynical, suspicious, dishonest, and incapable of trusting yourself and others. If you ignore your need for harmony, you suffer from confusion, conflict, and a sense of frustration about your life. And ignoring your need for goodness can make you sick from being disagreeable, selfish, and unkind.

Confusion, frustration, mistrust, inner conflict, and selfishness all stress the immune system and lower your resistance to disease. They also unbalance you spiritually and cause you to become soul sick.

Throughout the ages saints and enlightened masters have urged us to lead a virtuous life by practicing spiritual values. They encouraged the core values of truth, harmony, and goodness, not because they bring you closer to a reward in the hereafter, but because spiritual values are *practical* tools that help you *now* to rise above your self-centered ego, releasing you from fear, self-doubt, and selfishness.

 Spiritual values are *practical* tools that help you to rise above your self-centered ego, releasing you from fear, self-doubt, and selfishness.

SPIRITUAL VALUES IN MARRIAGE

In marriage there is a direct connection between the values you hold and the kind of self you express to your partner. When your values come mainly from your ego self, you see your partner and other people as objects to use, and you act in selfish ways. When what's important to you comes from your higher self, you see others and especially your partner as being like yourself, wanting to be happy and needing to be loved. And it's your higher self that responds to them with caring.

For example, when truth is important to you, you are honest and act with personal integrity. When harmony is important to you, you want order inside yourself and between you and your partner. When goodness is important to you, you are kind and caring.

Spiritual values keep your marriage a sacred place because they strengthen your true self and *lead you to right action*. As we said earlier, right action is made up of behavior that is healthy and sane because it leaves no trace of guilt, shame, or regret. Your higher self, guided by spiritual values, sees "the right thing to do" and you act more spontaneously.

 In marriage there is a direct connection between the values you hold and the kind of self you express to your partner.

Truth, harmony, and goodness rearrange your consciousness and bring your spiritual self up front in your awareness. Now you are less conflicted and confused. Less of your life energy is wasted on unnecessary mental and emotional suffering. You feel less troubled by routine ups and downs. You are inwardly alive with a certain peace and less addicted to trying to satisfy your ego's endless stream of desires. When truth, harmony, and goodness are important to you, right action follows.

When truth is important to you, you are honest and act with personal integrity. When harmony is important to you, you want order inside yourself and between you and your partner. When goodness is important to you, you are kind and caring.

EMBRACING TRUTH

Once you make a conscious decision to embrace truth you act with personal integrity. Integrity means "whole," "unbroken." These are wonderfully accurate descriptions of your higher self. Acting with personal integrity means being willing to look and acknowledge when your behavior is small and petty and then make a commitment to change it. Each time you do this you rise above your ego self and strengthen your spiritual self.

The everyday give and take between you as a couple creates countless opportunities for you to practice truth. You will have a better chance of staying honest if you avoid the following:

THINGS TO AVOID FOR THE PRACTICE OF HONESTY

- **Saying "yes" when you mean "no."** Trying to avoid a conflict by agreeing with your partner (when you really don't) never works. Your real feelings eventually come through and create a bigger mess than if you had been honest in the first place.
- **Pretending to feel one way when inside you feel something else.** Faking interest, enjoyment, or enthusiasm when it's really not there only creates confusion that leads to disappointment and hurt.
- **Covering up and denying hurt feelings because you don't want to risk having more pain.** This faulty strategy may limit your pain in the short run but it ensures a bigger hurt down the road.
- **Bragging to make yourself look "big" because you feel so small.** Feeling small is the real problem. Check out your inner dialogue and zero in on any negative self-messages you find there. Refuse to repeat them to yourself, cut off their energy supply, and they will wither away.
- **Outright lying.** Measure whatever benefit you think lying will bring against this fact: Lies destroy trust, the very

foundation of your marriage. Once the trust goes you'll have even bigger problems.

When you have committed yourself to embracing truth, honesty and personal integrity will become a way of life for you. Each time you are successful in sticking to the truth your selfish self loses power. Whenever you find yourself slipping into some kind of self-deception or factual distortion just come back to your higher self. Silently tell yourself that you don't have to pretend or lie to make yourself better than you actually are. Remind yourself that by living out spiritual values you are demonstrating your true divine nature and nothing the ego has or wants is worth sacrificing that for.

WAYS TO HONOR TRUTH TOGETHER

- **Make a pact together that underscores your commitment to be honest with each other.** Make this commitment explicit by saying it out loud to each other. Publicly declaring your intention to be honest will boost your resolve and call forth your higher self.
- **Tell each other you will be kind and understanding in the face of slip-ups that are bound to occur.** Promise that neither of you will show up as a "critical parent," blaming and making the other wrong. Instead find out the thoughts and feelings that led you to be less than honest.
- **Share the process.** When your spiritual self intervenes and you see yourself about to distort the truth and you don't, share this with your partner. Keep each other informed about your successes as well as your failures. This will reinforce your togetherness and your efforts toward personal integrity.

 Each time you are successful in sticking to the truth your selfish self loses power.

The more you uphold truth the more you feel completely at ease in each other's company. There is no pretense going on, no mind games being played, no secrets kept, no "seeming" to be one way while inside thinking or feeling something else. There is no controlling, manipulating, or scheming to outsmart each other. As long as such holdouts from personal integrity are going on your marriage becomes more and more of a fiction, a make-believe story to which neither of you will feel much commitment. And without commitment leaving is very easy to do.

 The more you uphold truth the more you feel completely at ease in each other's company. There is no pretense going on, no mind games being played, no secrets kept, no "seeming" to be one way while inside thinking or feeling something else. There is no controlling, manipulating, or scheming to outsmart each other.

SPEAKING THE TRUTH

Communication is the central nervous system of your marriage. As a couple you literally talk your way through marriage. What you say and how you say it affect each unfolding moment between you. Your spiritual self makes its presence felt through *right speech*. You can limit your ego's influence by following the guidelines for right speech as taught by Buddha in his Noble Eightfold Path.

GUIDELINES FOR RIGHT SPEECH

1. **Speak the truth.** Be reliable in what you say and have no intention to deceive by what you say. Whenever you deny the truth, because of an unwillingness to share feelings or to cover up unacceptable behavior or to protect your partner's feelings, your personal integrity is being sacrificed.

Jody could not understand why Gary spent hours in the den with the door closed working at his computer until she discovered E-mail from a woman he had been corresponding with on the Internet. When she asked him about this he lied and told her it was nothing. He said he talked to lots of people through the Internet. Jody told us: "At first I believed him, but when I found a strange telephone number from Iowa on both our home and car phone bills, something told me to call. That's when I found out he had lied to me. It was like he was having an affair with this woman through the Internet. Instead of talking to me he was pouring his heart out to her on the computer. And now that they are talking on the phone, I don't even want to think of what they are planning next."

2. **Abstain from slanderous speech.** Slanderous speech denigrates and disparages another person. It creates bitterness, disharmony, and division. It alienates people from one another. The motive behind such speech is usually jealousy and anger. Often the intention is to put someone else down so that we get one up.

Richard and Ginny came for counseling because Richard said that although he loved Ginny, he was beginning not to like her because of her constant berating of his mother and sister. He agreed with Ginny that at times his mother and sister were "intrusive." He had no problem hearing and seeing the truth of some of their behavior, and even calling them on it, but what he doesn't like is "her *constant* faultfinding, criticism, and negativity about them. It makes me feel I can't tell her anything about them and makes me not like who she is as a person at times. It gets so I can't stand to listen to her voice when she talks about them. She almost never has anything good to say about them. They happen to be very generous, but she jumps right onto putting them down whenever she can."

Speaking badly about someone else through judgment and criticism cuts us off from our higher spiritual self. It betrays the personal integrity we need in order to feel good about ourselves. When our words promote friendship, kindness, and goodwill they bring us trust and affection from others, especially our partner.

3. **Abstain from harsh speech.** Harsh speech is speech motivated by anger, speech intended to cause pain. Such speech usually comes in different forms: abusive, berating, attacking, loathing, rejecting, demeaning, and disapproving. This kind of talk is insulting, hurts another's self-esteem, and tries to take away his or her dignity.

Sarcasm is a common form of harsh speech. When you're the recipient of sarcasm you feel the zinger of contempt below the seemingly "harmless" surface. When you hurt someone else by harsh speech, you damage your personal integrity. Buddha suggests: "Avoid harsh language and abstain from it. Speak such words as are gentle, soothing to the ear, loving, such words as go to the heart, and are courteous, friendly, and agreeable to many."

4. **Abstain from idle chatter.** Idle chatter is generally useless superficial talk that lacks meaning and purpose. It often leads to gossip, which could be hurtful to another person. On the other hand, idle chatter as friendly small talk could serve as an opportunity for something more meaningful later on.

These four points of right speech are excellent guidelines for you to use each day as a couple embracing the spiritual value of truth in your marriage.

TRUTH CREATES FREEDOM

Truth creates a wonderful freedom and a relaxed way of being because there is no need for defensiveness, no feeling tentative or on guard. When truth prevails there can be complete spontaneity between two people. Living from the truth of your spiritual self cracks through your blind spots and forces you to look.

"Basic integrity is just part of my makeup, that is it!" says Ava, married nineteen years. "I can't live with myself if I'm not honest. I like myself and I want to be able to live with who I am. I can't get away from myself, there's no escaping that. Knowing that I'm honest within myself holds me together, it gives me a sense of direction. That's really important to me."

Tom, her husband, said: "Self-honesty is important to me. I've gotten much less afraid to know myself in an honest, clear way. In fact, I want to learn as much as I can about myself. Of course I've known the other side of that, the hiding from myself and what that brings. Being sure about my own personal integrity, inside and outside with others, is what helps me keep my life in some kind of order. It gives me a sense of peace and wholeness."

Having the courage to look honestly at yourself, at how you behave in your marriage, is a challenge you must face if you want to grow spiritually. If there is anything on your mind, without worry you talk about it and deal with it directly. You are not afraid to be really honest with yourself and with each other, because both of you realize that this is the way you deactivate your ego and make room for your higher spiritual self.

Ellen, a career woman married for fifteen years, described her need for truth within herself and in her marriage. "Integrity is important to me. If there's anything on my mind, without any worry, I'm able to say it, to tell him, to talk to him about it, that is, to deal with it directly. I don't want to turn a blind eye to anything about myself or him, and I don't think you have to if you are really honest with yourself and you are honest with each other."

Honesty must always be motivated by kind intentions. For some couples the only truth that shows up between them comes in a blast of anger, in which the intention is to hurt rather than to heal. This is a destructive way to use honesty. It should be avoided at all costs because it creates serious damage to trust. Honesty works best when it is tied to goodwill and a desire to foster feelings of love and caring.

Personal integrity, practiced daily, upheld vigilantly, and repaired immediately is what creates truth in your marriage. Living from truth, your marriage grows, and the amount of personal joy and happiness you can experience is immeasurable.

CHAPTER ELEVEN

Harmony: Keeping Your Souls in Sync

Beauty is absent where order
is lacking.

—PHILO

MARY AND CARL

Mary and Carl began drifting apart after their second child was born. Unsure of exactly what was happening, Mary repeatedly told Carl things were not right between them. Carl had a hard time hearing her. He was listening with his "me" in the way. At first his ego made judgments about what Mary was saying and dismissed her as just being bored. Mary, to her credit, would not be put off. She kept reaching out until finally he heard her.

Mary: "My really low point was after our second child was born. That was a very bad winter for me in terms of morale. When I look back, there's no question that was the low point in my life. I had a very difficult delivery, was physically exhausted, and didn't realize what was happening. I would think over and over, what is wrong with me?

"That was a time when not much was happening between Carl and me. There wasn't a lot of conflict, but there sure wasn't much of anything else either. That was the winter we realized how bad things were for me and our relationship. We realized we could not let this kind of thing happen to us. Maybe things had to get that bad.

"I just wasn't getting cared about the way I needed to. I thought that if Carl really loved me he would know what I needed. But it didn't work that way. I had to tell him, not once in a while, but many, many times. And he finally heard me, and that's when things started to change."

Carl: "At first I tended to see Mary as bored and wanting more attention, which I was reluctant to deliver because of my own pressures. I reacted by feeling inconvenienced and hoped she would get over it. But at some point the extent of her unhappiness finally hit me—it was like her spirit was withering away. It was then that I realized that whatever else was going on in our lives, all the everyday problems of living, was of little consequence.

"I started taking her more seriously than I had been. Whatever she said we followed it through to a good, mutual conclusion. What she needed, what she was feeling, how I could help, those kinds of things. Doing that pulled us together like a magnet."

⌇ "I just wasn't getting cared about the way I needed to. I thought that if Carl really loved me he would know what I needed. But it didn't work that way. I had to tell him, not once in a while, but many, many times. And he finally heard me, and that's when things started to change."

Mary: "Once he realized how badly I was feeling about myself, he threw himself into helping me get my bearings. That was the turning point. He helped me get to express what I needed, he helped me to get out of the house for a few hours a day, he encouraged my going back to school. Seeing him respond that way made me feel so good and secure inside.

"I think the winter I'm describing, if we had not been able to handle that, I don't know what would have happened to our marriage. I could not have gone on in the marriage the way I was feeling. If we had just held on to our traditional roles, without being able to confront the situation, it would have been a disaster.

   "I started taking her more seriously than I had been. Whatever she said we followed it through to a good, mutual conclusion. What she needed, what she was feeling, how I could help, those kinds of things. Doing that pulled us together like a magnet."

"Carl showed me then that he cared for me in the way I needed to be cared for. We talked and soul-searched and explored ourselves a great deal during that hard time. It led to a whole personal reevaluation for both of us."

VALUING HARMONY

Valuing harmony brings a new perspective to your marriage: You focus more on solutions rather than problems, you are interested in cooperation instead of competing, and you carefully weigh each new decision in terms of how it will affect your togetherness.

Harmony as a spiritual value helps you wake up from the routine trance of everyday living. Most of us want peace and tranquility in our lives: We would rather have balance and order than chaos and confusion. But because we are asleep spiritually our ego pulls us along as it chases one desire after another. No wonder we end each week exhausted physically and emotionally, yearning to be on vacation. This is how we turn our lives and marriages into a tangled mess.

When you as a couple value harmony you *both* put your effort into maintaining a sense of balance and order in your daily life. Even though you may have many responsibilities, commitments, and small children running around, you guide your life in a way that brings you closest to this goal. You are able to do this because you both have a firm conviction that you will not tolerate chaos, tension, violence, or disorder in your life or in your marriage.

This conviction keeps you very sensitive to those external events and situations that could easily cause disharmony and leave you feeling distant from each other. You both keep alert and are aware of what is going on between you in your day-to-day reality. You view any sign of weakening in your closeness as a red flag.

 Valuing harmony brings a new perspective
to your marriage: You focus on solutions
rather than problems, you are more
interested in cooperation than in competing,
and you carefully weigh each new decision
in terms of how it will affect your
togetherness.

RED FLAG EVENTS

Over the life of a marriage, all couples will inevitably experience many red flag events. The most common are in-law problems, financial difficulties, buying a house, having children, changing jobs, illness, the empty nest, and retirement.

The early years of marriage are crucially important. They can either make or break a marriage. Work and career struggles, along with the stress of raising children, make these definitely red flag years. Today this stage of marriage is even more difficult than in the past because so many husbands and wives both work outside the home. For some this is by choice, but for the growing majority it is a financial necessity.

When both partners work outside the home the stress level jumps dramatically because safe child care must be arranged. Leaving small children in the care of strangers is an enormous emotional burden carried by working mothers and fathers. The worry and guilt which so often go with this situation is emotionally draining. At the end of the day there is little time and energy left to go around. But there is still shopping and laundry to be done, meals to be prepared, bills to be paid, errands to be run, and dust piling up—and that's just inside the house. Meanwhile, needs for attention, love, and affection have not gone away, both on the children's part and for the two of you.

During such stressful times valuing harmony is what reminds you to give attention to the quality of your togetherness. Otherwise, like Patrick and Jessica, you may get everything else done but lose yourselves in the process.

Patrick and Jessica both work full-time, he as a sales representative for a computer company and she as an assistant bank manager. They've been married for seven years and have two small children under four years old. They have been able to handle all their practical concerns of day care, parenting, and sharing household responsibilities. Every minute of every day is full of things to do and places to be. Weekends are no different. But they cooperate and get it all done. The trouble is that somewhere along the way, according to Jessica, they "stopped being a couple. We're really more like roommates. Sometimes it feels like brother and sister and very little like husband and wife."

Unlike some other couples in their situation, Patrick and Jessica were able to cooperate together and get household tasks done, but because harmony *between them as a couple* was not a conscious value, they drifted apart emotionally, sexually, and spiritually. Both felt the pain of their distance but were so caught up in their day-to-day responsibilities that living disconnected was the price they thought they were supposed to pay. Having waited so long to get help in reconnecting, they are now faced with the possibility of having to separate.

 During stressful times valuing harmony is what reminds you to give attention to the quality of your togetherness as a couple.

Ending up as roommates can also happen later in life. It's sad to see couples who have gotten through the difficult years of financial struggles, raising and educating children, even caring for their aging parents, and who, as they approach what could be their best years together, are little more than strangers.

HOW TO AVOID A ROOMMATE MARRIAGE

- **Take some time to step back and assess how you are doing as a couple.** All the tasks and chores may be getting done, but what is the quality of your togetherness? Are there resentments building up between you? When was the last time you went away alone? What was the last romantic moment you shared?
- **Make adjustments in your routine that make life easier for each other.** Try to cover for each other so each of you gets some quality alone time. When you do have alone time make sure you use it in a way that helps relax you.
- **Be sure to compliment each other.** Too often all partners talk about are the things that go wrong or that get overlooked. Praise each other frequently for your hard work and tell each

other how much you appreciate each other's efforts on behalf of the family.

- **Get away together.** Make it an absolute priority to get away together, whether it's for a couple of hours or a couple of days. Where you go and what you do is less important than just being together. Keep it simple and uncomplicated. If child care is necessary and there are no close relatives to call upon, work together to brainstorm suitable alternatives. Perhaps you can make a reciprocal arrangement with friends you trust to cover for each other so each of you gets away.

- **Cut each other some slack.** Don't hassle each other over little things. Both of you are probably feeling close to over-whelmed—why add the stress of nitpicking? See where and when you can let little, unimportant things go for the peace not mentioning them will bring.

- **Do not wait for your relationship to get into crisis before giving it your attention: Take steps to correct problems immediately.**

The most common mistake couples make is waiting too long before getting help. Do not allow your marriage to get so bad that it's beyond repair. Get help as soon as you see that a problem continues despite your best efforts to fix it.

If only one of you is willing to see a professional, go ahead and do it. Waiting for your partner to be ready is a mistake. Tell any marriage counselor you call that you are willing to come in alone initially but that after two or three sessions you want him or her to call your partner and invite him or her into the sessions. If the therapist you call is not willing to do this, find one who is. The patient here is your marriage and both of you need to be present for it to get the most help.

If your partner declines even after being called, continue going yourself. You may create enough curiosity that eventually he or she will want to join in. In addition, your getting help will give you some clarity on how to best handle situations on your own.

JUSTIN AND VALERIE

Keeping an eye out for red flag stresses and on what's going on between you as a couple needs to be a shared responsibility. Most often it is the wives who watch carefully to safeguard marital harmony, but husbands can also sound the alarm when things are not going well. That was the situation with Justin and Valerie. After twelve years together and three children Justin said he was almost ready to leave.

"I was sick and tired of feeling taken for granted. I just plain felt unappreciated. I don't think, at the time, Valerie had any idea or understanding of the kind of pressure most men are under. She certainly didn't have a clue about what was going on with me. And if she did I never got the benefit of it.

"And it's not like I didn't try to tell her. No matter how tired I said I was, how stressed out I told her I felt, she always turned it back to herself. What she needed done around the house, where she wanted to go on vacation, when her parents could come for a long weekend, or how much trouble the kids were giving her. Even when I would call her during the day and try to make a date for us to be alone for a few hours over dinner out, she either never could get a sitter or didn't trust a sitter or just plain didn't want to leave the kids.

"It got so that if there was a choice between the 5:46 train or the 6:56 I found myself taking the 6:56. That gave me an hour to

 Keeping an eye out for red flag stresses and on what's going on between you as a couple needs to be a shared responsibility. Most often it is the wives who watch carefully to safeguard marital harmony, but husbands can also sound the alarm when things are not going well.

myself. I'd have a drink by myself, and then head home. It was my secret time to collect myself before meeting who knows what at home. But inside I was angry about it."

Valerie: "That's what woke me up, when Justin suggested marriage counseling. I realized he was so unhappy. I knew he was always angry. No matter what we were doing or where we were going he was always in a mood, always snapping at me. He's wrong though about my not knowing that he was under a lot of stress, that I knew. What I didn't know was that he felt so unappreciated and really unloved. He never told me that and I just never made that connection.

"I was so caught up with my end, with my kids. I was so happy being home and raising them. I just loved being a mother. I just got so all wrapped up with them that I forgot about him. I figured he would take care of himself. Maybe I was angry at him for not being as involved with the children as I was.

"But I have to say he's right. The children became my life and I expected him to go along with it. I was always too tired when it came to us. I got so used to living with the tension of his anger I never thought about it having to do with us, I thought it was his job.

"It was a real wake-up call for me because I saw myself being a lot like my mother and that really scared me. She expected my father to constantly dote on her and gave him very little back. I didn't want to see myself in that light. And I would never want to see Justin the way I saw my father, weak and just taking it.

"Now I make sure he feels thought of and appreciated. I tell him often that I appreciate how hard he works for us, I make sure we get to have dinner alone, just the two of us, at least once or twice a week. I've even gotten my sister to take the kids overnight so we could be alone. It's interesting, since I am more involved with him he's gotten more involved with the children."

When we as partners are able to create harmony between us, the whole family benefits. Having parents who are in sync and connected with each other in a loving way gives children a sense of well-being and makes them feel good about themselves.

There are very few of us who do not have our partner's best interest at heart. His or her happiness is important to us. But that's just the first step. Being able to create harmony by coming through for each other is what really matters.

 When we as partners are able to create harmony between us, the whole family benefits. Having parents who are in sync and connected with each other in a loving way gives children a sense of well-being and makes them feel good about themselves.

THE TIME-MONEY TRADE-OFF: A RED FLAG THEME

It's 8:00 A.M. on a Tuesday. David sits on a couch opposite us, looking defeated. A heavy sadness seeps from him. The night before his wife asked him for a divorce. She had complained for years of being lonely and emotionally "starved," but David couldn't hear her.

Like many husbands, he was more interested in *doing* and had little patience for the *feeling* side of life. For David work and the material world were important. That's where he felt "at home." He took pride and pleasure in the financial security and comfortable lifestyle that his work provided. That was real for him. Now all that was in jeopardy. He was confused and angry.

David: "Everything I love is being taken away from me and I don't know what to do. My wife, my kids, my home. Everything I put my heart and soul into is being ripped away. I don't want to wake up in the morning in a strange place and not see my kids. I love my family. I love my home. I put my blood and sweat into that house. We're all happy there, the kids love it. My things are there. I don't want to start all over again."

When marriages end, they usually end badly. Most divorces, especially when children are involved, are gut-wrenching, bitter experiences. They continue to tear at the heart long after the legal ink has dried. Divorce is so painful because it disrupts our basic security and threatens the well-being of those we love and cherish. If you ask people what's really important to them they usually say (if they are married), "My wife [or husband], my kids, family."

While this is probably true, many husbands and wives don't practice what they preach. *What they say they value is not reflected in the everyday choices they make.* Many couples end up needing professional help because their marriage gets so little of their conscious attention.

How does this happen? The trance of everyday life, with its stress, tension, and escapes, lulls us to sleep spiritually. We over-identify with the surface dimension of our lives, with work and material possessions, and these become the measure of our value and worth. We become so caught up in our daily routines that this part of our life grabs all of our attention. When we wake up in pain we wonder, like David, how what really matters to us was left so far behind. It's a bitter irony: working so hard, giving so much of ourselves to a lifestyle, only to find it gets in the way of what we truly yearn for, loving and being loved.

Marriage, family, and love relationships are not of the material world. They emanate from a different dimension, a sacred realm of being. As we wake up to our true identity we give this non-material part of our lives more of the attention it deserves. We refuse to let our self-centered consciousness enslave us by chasing one desire after another.

When couples value harmony they begin to question just how much time they are willing to trade for money. They tend to make time the more important commodity, and some even put limits on their careers so they can be more available for family living.

In some cases this means having less materially, but spouses see the added time together as more valuable than money. Their work and careers revolve around their marriage and family rather than the other way around. They limit the negative influence job pressures have on their marriage by continually reexamining their priorities. In this way they take more control over the time-money trade-off.

 As we wake up to our true identity we give this nonmaterial part of our lives more of the attention it deserves. We refuse to let our self-centered consciousness enslave us by chasing one desire after another.

ERNIE AND ELAINE

Ernie and Elaine are both successful, he as an engineer and she as a nutritionist. As happens to many other couples, their marriage ran into trouble when Ernie's work began to take up most of his time and energy. With his promotion to vice president his career took a big step forward. Along with the increased status and salary came more responsibilities. Evenings at home became devoted to preparing for the next day's meetings. He felt as if he were always on the job, but with it all, he was enjoying himself. Inevitably, Elaine started to feel increasingly shut out. They began to argue, over little things at first, then about his work:

Ernie: "My ambitions spilled over into our marriage. I knew something was wrong but for quite some time I didn't give it any conscious attention. I was treating our relationship as an engineering problem. I wasn't allowing any feelings to surface. We hit a stalemate. We both wanted the marriage, but we didn't know how to deal with the problems we were having."

Elaine: "I was angry with him. I felt he was allowing himself to be sucked into the rat race of the business world. I feel that the establishment, the corporate business world, has almost a conspiracy against people trying to make it happily. If you're in the business world there's a great deal of pressure. I didn't care about the extra money; I wanted and needed his time and his involvement with me."

Ernie: "It's very easy to bring the job home. Whatever I didn't have a chance to express during the day, I unloaded on the family when I got home. And not by exploding. More likely it would be by just withdrawing and not being that involved with anyone. We finally had to get marriage counseling.

"Elaine wanted a trial separation. But I just wanted to slug things out no matter how painful, and it was very painful for me. The counseling really helped us. It came just at the right time. We changed a couple of things. My work and career are still very important, but I came to see that nothing is more important than our staying together and being happy. I wouldn't sacrifice that for any job, but that's what was happening. The counseling helped us get clear about what's really important to us, and that goes beyond any career.

"We've grown so much closer now, since I've been able to put things in better perspective. I've been talking more and letting her know what's on my mind. I've gotten to a place where I can tell her about my feelings. When I come home and she sees its been one of those days, we just come together and I let it out. Sometimes I can't talk right away, I need time to unwind. She gives me plenty of time, she doesn't push. I guess that's because she knows before the night's out we're going to sit down and talk.

"I can really see now what I was not able to see before. The more caring, sensitive, and aware I am of her as a person, her needs and wants, her goodness, the more aware I become of myself."

HUGH

As we discussed earlier, spiritual values have a very practical purpose. They help you find your way through the maze of "shoulds" and "wants" pulling you in every direction. Hugh, a vice president in a prominent brokerage firm, grew up in a small midwestern farming town where spiritual values were strong. Unlike Ernie, Hugh had clear ideas about balancing career and family life:

"I don't want to be so successful in my business that the only thing I live for is the business to the neglect of my wife and the boys. It's important that I try to walk a fine line between being successful enough that I am satisfied with what I am doing, satisfied with where I am, yet I am not so engrossed in my business that I live and eat and sleep it to the detriment of our relationship or what it does to my children.

"I have known too many situations where people, mostly men, have thrown themselves solely into their jobs. I can't imagine what relationship there is with their wife and children. I see a lot of this in my business and I see an awful lot of them end up in divorce.

"So to me it's important, balancing my family relationship with my own needs to succeed and be recognized and so on. Maybe this is why I seek some of this recognition in community things, because it's something more closely related to the family. Why do I serve on the school board, or run for an election, or why was I scoutmaster, or why am I involved in other things like that, why do I serve on committees in town that the town supervisor puts together? Because sure I strive to succeed, but I'm not overburdened with that desire.

"I want to succeed and I want to be successful in what I do, but I think I probably do those things because I can be successful and still receive the recognition from my wife and the children. I can have them be proud of what I have done because they can see it in the community. I can have it support me as an individual, help others, and reinforce our family life all at the same time, as opposed to a business situation where I have to take away from, rather than reinforce, our family life."

ROGER

For many years Roger, a businessman, was at the opposite end of the spectrum from Hugh. His life was run solely by his ego and his major concern was getting ahead and "becoming somebody." To him, everyone was a potential adversary to be either conquered or outwitted. After his first marriage ended in divorce he was depressed and bitter. Now, in a second marriage, his priorities have changed and he has a different outlook on life:

"My values have changed. What I valued at one time would have been much more mercenary, financial, monetary. Property, tangible things, would have been much more important. And they are not important. Relationships have become more important, and my relationship with my wife has become most important.

"Things, and numbers, and categories, all that has become less and less meaningful. It's enjoying harmony in all my relationships, especially with my wife, my family, my friends, with people, that's what counts. It just seems to make more sense that this is what life is all about, and the rest of it is so much less significant. Now I value living a more balanced life, being with my wife, being with people, above material things."

Spiritual values do not exclude interest in the material world. Both are necessary. If we make the material realm our only concern and rely upon it to fulfill *all* our needs we'll eventually come up empty. Our deeper, soul-centered needs can't be answered at the material level.

We need harmony between the material and nonmaterial aspects of our being. Most of us seem to have drifted away from knowing our inner, best self, and it's this aspect that needs to be strengthened. Adopting spiritual values helps turn your attention inward so you can receive the guidance of your more subtle spiritual intuition.

CHAPTER TWELVE

Goodness: The Miracle of Change

Care, attention, diligence, the word
good contains all that. Good means
that which is beautiful, that which is
holy. . . . Goodness is not the opposite
of that which is bad.

—J. KRISHNAMURTI

LARRY

Larry is in his first year of a second marriage and having a difficult
time. His first marriage, to Karen, was largely a custodial arrangement with very little affection. They shared interests in business
and art and very little else. Larry sometimes felt ignored but
overall he accepted their distant kind of relationship as "good
enough." Two years after he was suddenly widowed, Larry met
Alice and was immediately drawn to her warmth and her open,
unguarded way of being. They married eight months later.

Larry soon began feeling stressed by a pressure he had never
known before: holding up his end of a marriage that called upon
him to be more than just a companion. For Alice marriage meant

much more. She wanted a partner willing to be open about himself and close to her emotionally, sexually, and spiritually.

For this Larry would have to stretch himself and grow in new ways. Here he describes his dilemma: "It's the damnedest thing. I know this woman is good for me yet I see myself pulling back and fighting against her love all the time. It feels like too much work for me and, let's face it, I'm spoiled. Part of me doesn't want to work so hard. I'd like to be able to get away with doing less but I don't want to risk losing her. She's a wonderful person and I see her kindness, her goodness, and the way she loves me, I'm just not used to it, to getting it and to giving it.

"But it feels wonderful and when I do let myself go and push past my resistance, I'll give her a big hug or be really warm and affectionate when we're out with people, which is really hard for me. But when I do it I must admit I feel better about myself. I don't feel so selfish and that's good. It's almost like exercising, using new muscles. I know its good for me but if I'm not careful I'll slip back and let my old habits of being withdrawn and self-centered take over."

With counseling, Larry learned to think of his marriage as a mirror. What was reflected in that mirror was Alice's spirit of generosity and giving and his own ego-centered tendencies to withdraw and hold back. With Alice in his life he was continually faced with the choice of either "hiding" or staying in the moment and asking himself, "What's really important right now?" "What do I want to create in my life at this moment?" These questions, when taken seriously, cut through our egoism. Larry was urged to stay with these questions each time he felt his selfish self pulling on him for control, each time he wanted to withdraw and pull away from Alice. By asking himself these questions he was activating the witnessing power of his higher self.

Witnessing enabled Larry to see, from moment to moment, how he was choosing to be in his marriage. It helped him exercise his power of choice, his capacity to choose how he wanted to express himself at any moment or in any situation. The witnessing attitude became a tool Larry used to help him connect with his softer side. Being in the presence of Alice's charitable heart helped a great deal. Accepting and expressing goodness became easier for Larry. He and Alice now enjoy a closeness that brings out the best in each of them.

PASSION FOR THE PERSON

When we talk with couples who have the marriage spirit we frequently find that what initially attracted them to each other was seeing in each other "lasting personal qualities." They repeatedly used descriptions such as "goodness," "kindness," "thoughtfulness," and "concern for others" when identifying the main factors bringing them together.

Goodness is a strong aphrodisiac. There is great beauty in its innocence and simplicity. Being in its presence has a strong effect on us. We want to bask in its light. Seeing genuine goodness in another person fills us with a warm desire to be close to him or her, because that goodness pulls out the same quality in us.

When you see genuine goodness in another person it touches your soul. It creates in you a passion for the person. This kind of passion is separate and apart from sexual passion. It's a passion for the kindness, sincerity, and caring you see in another. In his or her goodness you see your own higher self reflected, so you delight in being in that person's company. This is why you hear people say, "I love being with him, I feel so good around him." When physical attraction combines with passion for the person, a powerful bond of love is created.

 Seeing genuine goodness in another person fills us with a warm desire to be close to him or her, because that goodness pulls out the same quality in us.

Gena's comment about her attraction to Craig echoes the theme of passion for the person we repeatedly hear from both husbands and wives with a strong sense of the marriage spirit: "I cared a great deal for him, but I think the love came much later. I was attracted to his seriousness, to his integrity, to his goodness. I felt deeply that I could trust him, that I could allow myself to be totally open and vulnerable. I was attracted to his genuineness. He's so real there is no pretense about him, nothing artificial. And the way he looked at me, so intense, so deeply interested. We became good friends, and from that grew tremendous physical attraction and sexual excitement."

 When physical attraction combines with passion for the person, a powerful bond of love is created.

Keeping passion for the other person alive between the two of you will depend on how you treat each other. Being good to each other is key. But goodness does not have to be sought after like one more acquisition. It will emerge naturally when you withdraw your more self-centered tendencies.

OBSTACLES TO GOODNESS

Make a commitment to goodness by letting go of the following:

- **Let go of your need to be right.** When your ego is on the scene it demands to be right because being right gives it security and control. In order to be right it will find every opportunity to make your partner wrong. Letting go of needing to be right unplugs the power from your ego.
- **Let go of your need to feel superior.** Because your selfish self is basically insecure it is always searching for ways to be one

up in order to feel "better than." It is hard to be connected to someone you feel is either beneath you or above you.

- **Be genuine.** Once you accept yourself as your best spiritual self you will not need anyone's praise nor will you fear anyone's disapproval. If being genuine causes friction between you and your partner, choose to see it as part of a process of mutual self-transformation. Use the friction as grist for your marital mill. Everything that seems negative can be put to a higher purpose. It can be used to better yourselves and your marriage; nothing gets wasted.

- **Let go of consistently putting your needs first.** Goodness is generous and giving, it makes no demands. Make it a practice to be just as interested in your partner's needs as you are in your own.

- **Let go of any images you are carrying about yourself or your partner.** Remember, when you project ahead you create fear, when you dwell in the past you create depression. Be in the moment, without images, fully present and unpreoccupied. Only then are you able to *accurately* "read" and come through for one another.

- **Let go of a "me first" mind-set that sees and reacts to every situation from only your point of view.** Without empathy how can there be love? It is essential that you be able to put yourself in your partner's shoes. Adopt the practice of asking yourself, "What meaning does this situation have for my partner? What is he or she thinking and feeling right now?"

When you both act with compassionate goodness you create a deep and caring friendship. You integrate goodness into your life by daily acts of thoughtfulness, consideration, caring, and concern. At first, if you're not used to doing this, making an effort to do it might feel mechanical. You may even question, "Is this what I should do if I'm a good person?" Don't be put off by feeling awkward—eventually your caring will flow easily and spontaneously because you have taken valuing goodness seriously.

Every day, through small acts of loving kindness, demonstrate consideration and caring for each other.

Welcoming Goodness

Some of us have been conditioned to shy away from goodness, to be skeptical of it, or feel we are not equal to giving and receiving it. We feel awkward in its presence and do not welcome it into our lives. Consequently, we miss the benefits of an important growth and healing tonic. Goodness soothes the soul. It grounds us in what is worthwhile and genuine when so much around us is calculated and temporary. All of us would do well to check our resistance to goodness so that it flows more freely within and between us.

 Goodness soothes the soul. It grounds us in what is worthwhile and genuine when so much around us is calculated and temporary.

How Do We Begin?

Goodness begins with being kind to yourself—not self-centered pampering, but real caring, especially for the parts of yourself that you are unhappy with. Maybe you have doubts about how lovable you are, or you are not happy with how you look, or you see that you lack confidence, or that you have a tendency to be selfish or to overreact in certain situations. It is not self-pity that you need, and it's not blaming or criticizing yourself, either.

What you need is kindness and compassion. Where will it come from?

Goodness, kindness, and compassion are your true nature. At the center of your being you are pure goodness. Your true spiritual self radiates goodness. Every spiritual tradition known to us emphasizes the purity of your essential nature. What is to be gained from believing otherwise?

Spiritual masters urge you to practice goodness, to hold it as a value that shapes your thoughts and behavior, because they know it will point you back to your true identity. Tapping your innate goodness requires cutting through the smoke screen your ego throws up to keep you confused about who and what you really are.

HELPING GOODNESS TO FLOWER

Goodness will flower in you as you keep the following pointers alive in your awareness:

- **Remember your true identity as a spiritual being.** Remind yourself frequently, "I am spiritual energy in a physical form." Living from this awareness will bring joy into your life. Do not allow your ego to convince you that you are anything else.
- **Keep in mind that most, if not all, of your suffering and presumed shortcomings belong to the false self of your ego.** When doubts, fears, and insecurities arise, hold to the truth of your being. Take your stand in the witness, silently observe them, and let them pass.
- **Edit your inner self talk.** Know that your small ego self always works toward the same goal: having more and more control over your consciousness. It wants to be the only voice you hear. Notice when it has a strong negative message or when you're puffing yourself up, and how often you are lost in the past or projecting into the future.
- **When angry feelings arise, stand back, observe them, and be still.** Let them pass through you like a cool breeze. If

you don't act on angry feelings, if you don't give them life by getting involved with them, they will eventually pass.

- **Be your own loving parent.** If you never had a loving parent, act as a loving parent would, by doing what you would do for any hurt or injured child. You comfort, reassure, and when necessary, forgive. Be patient with yourself. Keep at it, speak to your ego as if it were a frightened child. With a loving, kind voice, say: "Calm down, it's all right, everything is going to be fine. You are not alone."

 Tapping your innate goodness requires cutting through the smoke screen your ego throws up to keep you confused about who and what you really are.

Following these pointers takes energy away from your ego self. Whatever energy your selfish self does not have becomes available to your higher self and can be used to extend kindness and compassion to yourself. Once you are able to be good to yourself, you can easily and effortlessly extend compassion to your partner and other people as well.

CARING ABOUT OTHERS

Many marriages self-destruct because the partners in them cannot go past themselves to make the other an important priority. So many of us identify only with our ego that being number one is all we care about. Present-day society caters to and reinforces the ego's selfishness. Having more and the best of everything seem to be all that matters. Have you seen the bumper sticker that says, "He who dies with the most toys wins"?

Marriages built solely on the ego's self-centeredness are flimsy and superficial. The partners in them do not have a sense of meaning about their lives that goes beyond "me thinking." In his wonderful book *Learned Optimism* Martin Seligman, Ph.D., offers the view, supported by research, that depression abounds today partly because our expanded sense of self-importance hides an emptiness inside ourselves. The ego tries to fill that emptiness with more and more self-interest.

This is the same self, Seligman says, that has lost a larger sense of meaning because of a weakened belief in God, family, and country. In former times such beliefs were supports we relied upon for comfort and security. Today, however, when defeats and disappointments come, as they inevitably they do for everyone, the grandiosity of the ego backfires on us. We blame ourselves for not being adequate and, according to Seligman, "have no spiritual furniture" to fall back on. Without a sense of meaning beyond mere self-interest, when adversity strikes the self is "set up for depression."

Goodness, on the other hand, is an effective antidote for the selfishness of a "me first" mentality. Why? Because goodness requires empathy and commitment, the ability to invest yourself, your time, energy, and interest in a larger purpose beyond self-interest. It means being less concerned about yourself so you can be more concerned about others.

Reaching Out

Couples with the marriage spirit who actively value goodness are doing just that, making a contribution to the larger common good. Victor, married for twenty-five years, is a successful writer and reporter for a major newspaper. The creative challenge he faces each day brings him a sense of pride and satisfaction. But when asked what it is that is really important to him, he said:

"On a day-to-day basis, the nature of my profession demands a great deal of creativity. It's constantly coming out, so one of the things that I have to hold to is being able to continually do this. But that is not the God I live for. The God I live for is really to serve people. I love people and I enjoy being with them.

"The day-to-day thing in our life that governs both my wife and myself is to serve people. Wherever we are needed we go. I feel a joy in working with people, using my time professionally and otherwise in seeing that I can do something for others. And my wife is very much the same way, we see this very closely."

Martin, a retired executive, makes this observation: "I have become much more interested in and concerned about other people. My relationships with people are much better than they ever were. I think my wife has had a strong influence in this area because she's a very people-oriented, kind person. And I've become that way myself.

"I have grown since I retired because working in business, in a corporate structure, leaves very little time for personal development except as it relates to your job. Now I have time to devote not only to myself but to my wife, my family, and other people. Prior to that my growth was related to making money and moving up in the corporate structure.

"In the corporate world you get paid for your mind and your hands, your feelings are worth nothing. Your feelings are a detriment to you, so if you don't get paid for them, you're not going to use them. But I've learned to see people as people and not as objects that I can use. It's a whole different way of life, to look at a person as a person, to see their value, their worth, regardless of whether they can do anything for you or not."

When goodness is important you feel more compassionate and look for opportunities to help others, to volunteer and become involved in social problems. The Golden Rule becomes reality for you. Marion and her husband, Joseph, also share a conscious commitment to helping others. Joseph told us that because they so totally agree on this basic value there is never any conflict over how to spend their time or where to spend their money. A good part of their efforts, both emotionally and financially, are devoted to serving others.

Marion: "I like to do things with people, be of service to people. I don't like to call myself a compulsive do-gooder, I'm really not that. But if something I'm doing doesn't really serve someone else or something other than just myself, it's, I don't like to say waste, but it's something like that. My motto to myself is, 'Don't waste this day without doing something for someone else.' "

Holding to spiritual values changes how you, as a couple, approach life itself. Crisis, conflicts, and difficult transitions are lived through with less frustration, bitterness, and resentment. This basic change in outlook helps you meet life with less inner turmoil. You stop fighting against its natural current, not by being passive, but by seeing life's challenges as opportunities for expressing your best self. You give up obsessing about results and put all your energy into doing what is needed now. You allow life to unfold and let happen whatever will happen. Gwen saw her spiritual growth in these terms:

"After I got married and had children, one of whom was born with a severe disability, I began to realize that you have to come to terms with life. Life won't dish everything out on your terms so you have to come to terms with it. And I think that is a real growth. It mellows you and makes you feel more at peace. Otherwise you're always fighting, wanting things to happen just the way you want or else. So, I know I've grown in patience, understanding, and compassion. And because of that I'm a better person, more fulfilled, much more happy, more of a good, open person."

 Holding to spiritual values changes how you, as a couple, approach life itself. Crisis, conflicts, and difficult transitions are lived through with less frustration, bitterness, and resentment.

More than any other factor it is living out the spiritual values of truth, harmony, and goodness that expands your love beyond a survival mentality. Wayne Muller in his book *How Then Shall We*

Live? makes this same observation when he states: "Loving kindness, sympathetic joy, compassion, mercy: these are the unmistakable footprints of our spiritual life."

 More than any other factor it is living out the spiritual values of truth, harmony, and goodness that expands your love beyond a survival mentality.

Once spiritual values become your new guiding life principle, your ego is merged into and is directed by your sacred self. Then your marriage, sharing each day together, celebrates and amplifies your love. No matter what life presents, being together feels like a blessing.

STEP VI RITUAL

BEING FREE TO DO THE RIGHT THING — RIGHT ACTION

Part I: Virtuous Stocktaking

Taking time to reflect on the ways spiritual values operate in your life can be helpful. The following questions will help you in the process of looking within. By yourself, with a journal to record your thoughts, make time to be in a quiet place where you can open to yourself without interruption.

1. Rate your level of honesty, using the following scale: (1) Sometimes honest, (2) Honest 50 percent of the time, (3) Almost always honest, (4) Always honest.
   A. With yourself.
   B. With your husband or wife.
   C. With close friends.
   D. With your parents.
   E. With your siblings.
2. Why are you less than honest with any of those above, especially your partner?
3. What are the thoughts and beliefs that you hold about yourself that influence how honest you are? For example, do you have a strong need for approval? Are you afraid of conflict?
4. With regard to your partner are there specific topics or issues about which you feel you cannot be fully open? What are they?
5. What is your bottom-line fear about honestly sharing these issues with your partner?
6. Imagine having a greater level of honesty between you and your partner. What effect do you think it would have on the overall quality of your marriage? (Little or none? Moderate effect? Greatly improved?)
7. What effect would more honesty have on your sexual relationship? On the issues you most often fight about? On how you relax and play together?
8. How well are you able to "read" your partner, to know what he or she is thinking and feeling by how you see him or her acting? (Not good? Fairly good? Very good?)
9. Do you offer these observations to your partner or do they stay unspoken?
10. Write down some examples of when and how you demonstrate goodness to your partner.
11. When and how do you see goodness flowing to you from your partner?

12. When there's not much goodness flowing from you, what gets in the way?

We spiritualize our everyday life by practicing the values of truth, harmony, and goodness. Personal integrity, psychological order, and compassion open our hearts and free us from a limited, self-centered ego. Prayer, meditation, and the beauty of nature help us hold on to spiritual values and the right actions they naturally guide us to.

It is worthwhile to make a daily or at least weekly stocktaking of how successful you have been in rising above your ego while going about the mundane activities of life. The following questions can help in your assessment. They are not a pass/fail quiz, but a guide to support you in your value awareness. Answer them (and any additional ones you can think of) in a straightforward fashion. You may or may not share the results with your partner. This is only a guide for you. Here are the questions:

Was I able to rise above my ego self in my thoughts and attitudes today?

Was I able to rise above my ego self in how I spoke and what I spoke about today?

Was I able to rise above my ego self in what and how I ate and drank today?

Was I able to rise above my ego self in how I spent money today?

Was I able to rise above my ego self in my actions at work today?

Was I able to rise above my ego self in my relationships today?

Was I able to rise above my ego self in my treatment toward myself today?

Part 2: Sharing Spiritual Inspiration

Paul and I spend some time each day, at least one hour, meditating together on some spiritual reading. We take turns reading out loud. At a certain point we agree to stop and quietly meditate on what we heard. Then we talk about it, each of us sharing the particular meaning the passage had for us. Usually this brings new insights or clarifies or confirms an awareness we may have intuitively felt or been struggling to understand.

In addition, we often get together with friends who are also interested in expanding their spiritual consciousness. A small group setting in which people share readings and spiritual insights is extremely uplifting. There is a spirit of participation as each person reads or speaks about what is spiritually important for him or her. No effort is made to "push" a particular spiritual view, but rather the focus is on being open, on learning and sharing meanings in order to grow.

We strongly urge you as a couple to share time together in this way. Begin by putting aside uninterrupted time for meditation on a passage from the Bible, the Koran, the Upanishads, a Buddhist text, the Kabbalah, or any other book, poem, painting, story, or piece of music that sends a *spiritual* message to you. Take turns either reading to each other or by yourselves and then share and contemplate what you heard.

Part 3: Merging with Beauty

We've spoken before about the importance of incorporating the beauty of nature in the rituals you practice. Once again in this ritual we stress getting away from the routine of daily living and merging with nature's beauty as primary to the path of the marriage spirit.

When the mind falls into mechanical routines it could get stuck there for years. When you arrange to be by yourselves, as a couple, in the beauty of nature you literally give your mind a rest. Whether it's for an hour, a day, or a weekend (the longer the better), make arrangements to be in some place of natural beauty. This in and of itself is a ritual couples need to practice for the well-being of their marriage.

Part 4: Reaching Out to Others

Volunteering your time and energy reinforces the oneness that we all share as living beings on this Earth and strengthens your togetherness as a couple, because it opens your heart to compassion and takes you away from yourself. Look to see where, when, and how you as a couple (you might even include children) can be of service to someone else. This could be a family member needing some help or assistance, it could also be a neighbor, friend, or organization. Somewhere close by you there are people (or animals) who are suffering or in distress who will benefit from your compassion. Make giving to others a continual ritual in your life, be it once a day, week, month, or year. Teach your children to do the same by modeling compassion, showing them it is important and something you care about.

Embracing the values of truth, harmony, and goodness has two important benefits. The first benefit is that transcendent values bring out the presence of your higher self and send your ego to the sidelines for a much-needed rest. The result is a clearer sense of life as more joyful and less of a struggle.

Second, these values help you as a couple spiritualize the ordinary occurrences of everyday life. With personal integrity, inner order, and a sense of empathy and generosity daily events become free from contradictions and conflicts. Routine stress is minimized in the presence of greater peace of mind and clarity of thinking. Spiritual values also help you, as a couple, appreciate that love and lovemaking emerge not from the body, but from the soul.

Soul-Centered Love

*I have loved thee with
an everlasting love:
therefore with loving-kindness have I
drawn thee.*

—THE PROPHET JEREMIAH

In love is found the secret of divine unity.

—THE ZOHAR

Nurturing Love

The love in your heart wasn't put there
to stay —
Love isn't love until it's given away.

—ANONYMOUS

Soul-centered love
is your heart's true desire. Everything else is a substitute. Deep
down we all want to know that we are fully loved, accepted, and
cherished in the heart of another. We don't question that children
need and deserve such love, but as adults we try to fool ourselves
and pretend we've outgrown it or that we can do without it.

As your spiritual intimacy deepens, the love you share becomes soul-centered. With soul-centered love you give each
other physical, emotional, and spiritual nurturing, you purposely
and deliberately help each other grow, and you feel fully known,
deeply loved, and profoundly valued.

Through our work with couples who are moving with the
marriage spirit we discovered three dimensions of soul-centered
love: nurturing, intentional, and revering love. While each dimension has specific qualities, they overlap and support each
other. They are intertwined like a single thread woven into the
strongest marriages. Study them, practice them, and we guarantee

you will share a love that transcends anything you've previously experienced together.

~ With soul-centered love you give each other physical, emotional, and spiritual nurturing, you purposely and deliberately help each other grow, and you feel fully known, deeply loved, and profoundly valued.

Nurturing Love

Nurturing love is made up of all the behavior, large and small, that satisfies your need for giving and receiving attention, affection, understanding, empathy, and unselfish involvement. It is the way you nourish each other physically, emotionally, and spiritually. The word nurture means "to nourish, to feed, to give sustenance," and sustenance means "to strengthen." Nurturing love is essential because it is the love that sustains and strengthens you, individually and as a couple.

This kind of love sends a strong, clear message. It says, "I'm here for you, you are a major priority, you can count on me. Your happiness and well-being are just as important to me as my own."

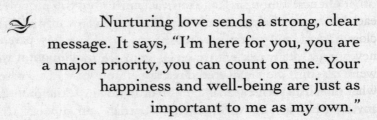

~   Nurturing love sends a strong, clear message. It says, "I'm here for you, you are a major priority, you can count on me. Your happiness and well-being are just as important to me as my own."

Nurturing love comes alive in actions, not just in words. It cannot be known only on an intellectual level; it must be deeply felt as well.

ATTENTION: THE ART OF LISTENING AND SEEING

Nurturing love is the willingness to take the time to listen to each other with full attention. The root meaning of the word attention is "to stretch." Giving attention—being attentive—requires stretching past yourself to your partner. As we said earlier, you do this by shelving your ego, putting aside your own agenda, and seriously tuning in to what your partner is saying.

When you truly listen you are "all ears," *listening with your whole being.* It is your interest and attention that nourish your partner when she or he shares her- or himself so intimately with you. Opening up to each other in this way, "self-sharing" and truly listening, *on a daily basis,* creates a deep and genuine love.

Claudia is a twenty-nine-year-old physical therapist with a strong sense of the marriage spirit. Here she describes "staying in touch" with her husband, Christopher, through self-sharing. "We both work and have a lot on our minds, but we make the effort to stay in tune with each other. We always talk at least once a day on the phone, but that's just to touch base. Usually in the morning before we leave for work we check each other out, we find out what's on each other's mind, and if there's anything we need to talk about we find out then.

"It's like getting a reading on each other so we know where each other is emotionally and physically. It starts us off feeling close and I think that's important for a marriage. My parents never did it, really talk on that level, and I always thought it was weird that they didn't. It seemed like they didn't have a clue about what each other felt from one moment to the next. I don't want anything like that between me and Chris."

Listening and self-sharing is the part of nurturing love that husbands find most difficult to do. Listening takes time; it is not a quick fix. Men more than women, are conditioned to be goal-directed. They equate being strong and capable with getting results as quickly as possible. Giving the time and attention that real listening requires is something that many men are not used to doing.

Self-sharing is also difficult for men because they do not routinely talk about their feelings. They are more in touch with their thoughts than they are with their feelings. In fact, when you ask most men what they are feeling they will tell you what they are thinking and not see the difference until it's pointed out to them.

These two traits, not listening and not sharing inner thoughts or feelings, are the major handicaps men carry into marriage. They approach their relationship almost exclusively through their task-oriented ego. As a result, wives unanimously feel ignored and taken for granted. While many husbands think their marriages are going along fine, their wives feel poorly loved.

Many wives, on the other hand, when faced with husbands who have trouble listening, too often in their frustration leap to a damaging conclusion: "If he won't listen he doesn't love me." They withdraw, holding back warmth and affection, which then triggers an angry reaction from husbands who feel misunderstood and unappreciated for all the other things they do.

Having the marriage spirit means cooperating to do a better job of communicating. Take time to reread Listening While Shelving Your Ego in Chapter Eight. As with any skill, practice is what counts. As a husband you need to remember that listening and sharing thoughts *and feelings* is within your conscious control. Listening is not a genetically determined trait. It's a learned behavior. The more you take the time to slow down and practice listening and self-sharing the better you'll be at creating emotional closeness, which is what most wives crave.

As a way of encouraging wives to be patient and not jump to premature conclusions, Paul frequently tells them that when it

Self-sharing is difficult for men because
they do not routinely talk about their
feelings. They are more in touch with their
thoughts than they are with their feelings.
Ask most men what they are feeling and
they will tell you what they are thinking
and not see the difference until it's
pointed out to them.

comes to communicating feelings they should think of their
husbands as being "emotionally challenged." He also thinks it is
a good idea to set up conversations with a clear introduction of
what is required. For example, *"I really need you to listen and hear
me out,"* or, *"I see you're preoccupied about something, this is one of
those times that I'm feeling shut out, please share with me what is on your
mind."*

This gives husbands an opportunity to shift mental and emotional gears so they can do a better job of responding. Be sure to
reinforce all efforts with an accepting, noncritical response. Let
him be able to see, by the way you respond, how important
understanding him and being understood is to you.

Wives, when faced with husbands who have
trouble listening, too often in their
frustration leap to a damaging conclusion:
"If he won't listen he doesn't love me."

Warren and Molly have been married for six years. It is a
second marriage for both, Molly's two young children live with

them, and on weekends Warren's two teenagers stay over. Keeping everyone happy and on good terms can get taxing at times.

Meeting the situation successfully means Warren and Molly have to be clear with each other about how they see things developing with the children. They know tension can easily spill over into their relationship. Warren talks about how they stay on track together. "Every night before we go to bed, we open up our thoughts and feelings to each other so we know exactly where we are. We know if we didn't do that on a daily basis we would soon be drifting apart.

"Doing it on the weekends when the kids are all here is a must. It's amazing how we really need to bring out these things. Assuming that you know how the other feels is really very misleading."

Nurturing love means practicing the art of listening and seeing. The art in both is being able to *get your ego out of the way*. Then you will not be so tied up with your wants and needs that it is impossible to fully understand your partner. Listening is easier because you are not wasting a lot of attention distorting what you hear by filtering it through the needs of your ego.

It is the same with the art of seeing. Whenever your ego is out of the way your perception of reality is clearer. You will make fewer mistakes both in life and in your marriage. For example, when you remove your selfish self with its need to be right, its need to protect itself, and its need to control everything from your marriage two important things happen:

- First, your ability to be sensitive to and read each other is much stronger because you are not preoccupied with yourself, and you are not judging and blaming each other.
- Second, because you are better able to read each other you know when to reassure and encourage each other, when to give each other time alone, and when it's vital to reinforce trust and commitment.

When your ego is out of the way, you are
better able to read each other, to know
when to reassure and encourage each other,
when to give one another time alone,
and when it's vital to reinforce trust
and commitment.

AFFECTION AND LOVEMAKING

The concept of a man is a restriction. The concept of a woman is a restriction. A man is more than a man, and a woman is more than a woman. Before the woman appears, there is the divine. Before the man appears, there is the divine.

—JEAN KLEIN

Affection and lovemaking are important ways you nurture each other, but the quality of that nurturing depends on the degree of consciousness you bring to each other. Affection and sexual love from your ego self are very different from affection and sexual love that come from your spiritual self.

With spiritual intimacy, a couple do not just "have sex," they make and create love not only physically but verbally, emotionally, and spiritually as well. Making love is richer, deeper, more transcendent; it transforms the entire environment you inhabit as a couple. Nurturing love moves you from having sex to lovemaking as a mystical union.

Sex from your ego is object-to-object sex. It's something we "do to" each other. It takes place from your small self with its limited sensitivity and awareness. Lovemaking becomes a mechanical satisfaction of a physical need. The ego self is so caught up in what "should be," with achieving some particular result or performance, that we miss staying open, relaxed, and receptive to each other. We have a script in our mind and that's what we follow. We are so focused on the act itself, on our expectations and performance, that making love becomes just one more way we measure and judge each other.

A good example of object–to–object sex happens when a couple has infertility problems and they *must* "make love," whether they feel like it or not, at specific times. This kind of on-demand sex can have a disastrous effect on a couple's genuine lovemaking. When your ego is there between you in the bedroom you fall into this mechanical, passionless kind of sex even when you do not have infertility problems. You can avoid dulling the passion of your lovemaking by doing the following:

KEEPING PASSION ALIVE

- **Be relaxed by emptying your mind.** The only way you can be receptive and attentive as a lover is by being fully and completely in the *now*. Remember, when making love there is no "you" watching and judging, there is no routine to follow, and there is no performance to rate.

- **Remember that lovemaking from your higher self does not begin and end in the bedroom.** It is the result of the loving you do in each and every moment outside the bedroom. It is this larger connection that gives lovemaking a "being with" quality rather than a "doing to" or "getting from" feeling.

- **Do not fall prey to media-hyped versions of "great sex."** These are always exaggerated and make you feel inadequate. Your lovemaking is unique to you as a couple. Stay with making it as free and enjoyable as possible.

- **Be on the lookout for when your ego self begins to make judgments about what's happening between you sexually.** Do not give energy to self-talk that criticizes either your or your partner's sexual behavior. When these thoughts come up witness them and then let them go. If, however, a consistent pattern of dissatisfaction develops, talk it through. If it persists do not wait too long before you get some professional help.

> ❧   When there is spiritual intimacy, a couple
> do not just "have sex," they make and create
> love not only physically but verbally,
> emotionally, and spiritually as well.

As a contributing editor to the *Ladies' Home Journal* magazine column *Can This Marriage Be Saved?* Paul was once asked to moderate a discussion among husbands about what they really expected sexually from their wives. A group of husbands from different parts of the country, with different backgrounds and different jobs, were flown in to New York City to explore the issue.

A major point they all agreed on was that what gave them the most pleasure was seeing their wives freely enjoying their *own* uninhibited sexual passion. For these husbands seeing their wives "turned on" was their biggest turn-on.

The problem is that many husbands don't understand what it takes to produce this kind of free-flowing sexual expressiveness. Most of the time it has nothing to do with sexual technique. It has so much more to do with what goes on outside the bedroom. As we said earlier, because men tend to be task-oriented in their thinking they compartmentalize their feelings. Almost without realizing it they reserve their most tender affection for the bedroom. Wives, on the other hand, want that affection throughout the day, because this helps them feel connected emotionally. And with that emotional connection in place they can feel freer sexually.

Eve, looking back over a marriage of seventeen years, says a "good enough" sex life would have been fine with her. However, Liam's affection both inside and outside the bedroom helped Eve overcome her inhibitions: "He was very gentle with me in overcoming many inhibitions I had. He helped free me. I would say more than just in a sexual sense because I was always an inhibited person, always observing society's rules to the letter of the law. He never pushed, he always helped. He helped make me more aware of myself in a physical way, in the way I looked, my attractiveness, and so on. He always liked the way I looked, he always felt I was pretty and I never did.

"He lets me know always that he thinks I'm beautiful. He's always kissing me, hugging me, loving me, physically and verbally. He's always telling me he loves me, how great I am."

 Men tend to be task-oriented and compartmentalize their feelings. They reserve their most tender affection for the bedroom. Wives, on the other hand, want that affection throughout the day, because this helps them feel connected emotionally. And with that emotional connection in place they can feel freer sexually.

For women, especially, feeling free sexually comes as a result of emotional closeness. Feeling strongly desired, understood, cared about, listened to, and included in their husband's inner thoughts and feelings is what frees the passion husbands so look forward to.

Men often see sex as a way of getting close, while women more often want to feel close before lovemaking begins. It's very easy for these differences to divide a couple. Each views the other as uncooperative and a power struggle ensues. Keeping communication clear so that you are connected *emotionally* outside the bedroom is essential.

RICHARD AND SYLVIA

Richard and Sylvia have been married for fifteen years. He comments: "There was a time early in our marriage when I wanted sex more often than she did and this caused us some problems in the beginning. She wanted to have more togetherness, more closeness."

Sylvia: "I tended to see sexual intercourse coming after we feel close; Richard tended to view it as a way of getting close. We finally were able to recognize this for what it was, but it took time. There were times when I would say, 'Oh, here it comes again.' He would be wanting to have sex and either I couldn't or wasn't interested or something."

Richard: "Looking back it was almost as if I didn't know there was anything else except intercourse. So if she wanted closeness, I translated this as sex. I would start getting sexual and she would say, 'Hey, wait a minute.' That's where our problem would begin. I didn't understand what was going on and would react badly."

Sylvia: "He would start to get angry and then, of course, that would just repel me and it would just defeat the whole process. We would get into cycles with that where you begin to ask yourself, 'How do we get out of this?' He is feeling uptight and angry and I need to feel close before we do this otherwise I feel kind of used."

Richard: "But eventually, after many, many talks about it, it finally became clear to me. I became more sensitive to her needs for this presexual, emotional closeness; this freed her, in a sense, to initiate being sexual. It was that I was coming on so strong, that she didn't even have a chance."

Sylvia: "His being warm and affectionate generally, unrelated to sex, helped. I used to have the feeling that I would never have sex unless I was really turned on, and I don't feel that anymore. It's okay if it's primarily his need, I can enjoy it, that's all right. It doesn't have to be fireworks every time, so I'm more relaxed about this. But that theme of differences in how we viewed it had been the area in our sexual relationship that had really gotten us into difficulty sometimes. Even though in the overall picture our sexual relationship has been very good and very important to us."

Sexual passion does not happen in a vacuum. It is created by the many acts of caring, thoughtfulness, and loving attention we show each other. Certainly kissing, holding, hugging, and touching each other affectionately are part of this. But so are kind words and expressions of praise, admiration, appreciation, and love. This is what sustains warm, positive feelings of closeness and leads to free-flowing sexual passion.

Nurturing Love Is Monogamous

When you have the marriage spirit you are monogamous by choice. One of the reasons you can keep this commitment is the deep sexual satisfaction you experience with each other. Being attracted to other men and women is not a threat because each of you knows you will not act on that attraction.

With unquestioned trust between you it is easy to acknowledge when you see an attractive man or woman whom you find appealing. When you feel secure inside yourself and between you, hearing such information becomes an innocent, light-hearted event rather than something to be kept hidden. Being open in this way defuses such attractions and adds to the passion in your marriage.

Bennett, who works in the film industry, told us: "Certainly I find other women attractive. I like women a great deal and enjoy being in their company. If I'm with my wife and I see an attractive woman I'll mention it, just like I'd mention seeing an attractive car or house or a beautiful tree or whatever. It gets talked about and that's good. But while I may find other women attractive, I'm continually discovering my wife, sexually as well as personally, and in every other way. There is a joy in that.

"I could never be unfaithful to her. That would be dishonest, it would hurt me as well as her. It would be a short-lived thing, it would be sexual, and I would feel terrible afterward. It would be a betraying of trust. It would be giving to someone else something that is very important to both of us."

When you view your marriage as a sacred place, not only would you not betray your trust, but in addition you value and look forward, as Bennett does, to the *continuing discovery* of each other. With spiritual intimacy you know there is no limit to the extent to which your hearts can open, no limit to the passion that intensifies between you, no limit to how high you can reach in transcending your "me," and no limit to how deeply you feel about each other.

ENDLESS DESIRE

Soul-centered nurturing love contradicts the widely held notion that sexual attraction falls off as a couple spends year after year together. This is not true when your consciousness is liberated from making images. Images dull your passion because they stereotype and dehumanize your uniqueness. Without images partners stay open to each other's inner and outer beauty. While the sexual pace of some couples slows as they grow older, sensual excitement and attraction for each other does not diminish. In fact, with nurturing love lovemaking keeps getting better.

 With spiritual intimacy you know there is no limit to the extent to which your hearts can open, no limit to the passion that intensifies between you, no limit to how high you can reach in transcending your ego, and no limit to how deeply you feel about each other.

Even after many years together, partners who have the marriage spirit make it very clear that the excitement of their early attraction to each other is still strongly present. After fifty-two years of marriage to Andrew, Bernice finishes her day wanting only him:

"I just love him and I was always attracted to him, physically, emotionally, and spiritually. That's the only way I know to explain it, and it's still there. In the evening when it's time for him to come home from the office, I'm all ready. I told him I was going to have to hook another rug for the hall, because I wear it out walking to the door to see if he's coming. I really just want him!"

 When you make love from nurturing love you merge heart and soul. Free of your ego self, you float beyond space and time.

When you are imbued with the marriage spirit lovemaking can range from merely touching and holding each other to strong, uninhibited sensuality. At its height it includes a deep, transcendent exchange of energy, a "cosmic unity" carrying you beyond your ego and your body as well. What unfolds contains a feeling of "oneness," a feeling of unity with something much larger and beyond yourselves.

When you merge body, mind, and senses making love from nurturing love you do it selflessly. Without "me first" constraints, you float free, beyond space and time. This joining leaves the *familiar you* behind. It is a self-transcendent experience, a *celebration* on the physical plane of the mystical oneness you share.

EMPATHY AND UNDERSTANDING

Empathy operates as an understanding, a benevolent perception that makes it possible to see and feel another's hurt and pain. Empathy means feeling with and for another. It is being able to put yourself in your partner's place so you sense and understand his or her pain, confusion, and upset.

JACK AND ANITA

By the time Jack, Anita, and their three children went on vacation Jack and Anita were feeling totally burnt out. They made plans to stay at a resort, where they would have their own cabin with activities for the children and themselves. Anita was dreading the first morning after their arrival. Half the day would be spent shopping, stocking the cabin with food, cleaning supplies, and all the other things necessary for an eight-day stay.

When they arrived she discovered that Jack, by going through their own house, had carefully and painstakingly made a detailed list of everything they would need. He had called ahead to the resort staff and arranged for them to do the shopping before the family arrived. Anita walked in to a cabin completely stocked with everything they needed. She was thrilled and delighted.

Jack demonstrated nurturing love by being understanding and empathizing with Anita, wanting to ease her burden. His sensitivity to what she was feeling came through in his behavior, which showed Anita that her happiness was important to him.

Nurturing love means being interested in the details of each other's life, without being forceful or intrusive. It is being sensitive to changes in each other's mood or attitude and wanting to go that extra distance to do things that help and bring each other a sense of well-being.

BEN AND NANCY

Ben has achieved a good measure of success as a writer. But there were many lean years before recognition came. Here he and Nancy talk about the love they felt from each other during those difficult times. What they are each describing is the empathy, understanding, and support of nurturing love:

"I could always talk to her, always, always, always talk to her about anything. And she listened, and she helped, and she was interested, and she understood. She was always there, never complained, always was very supportive even when it meant at times shutting her out. And even while I was writing and she wasn't following her creative interests, she wouldn't complain. I would get up very early on Saturday and Sunday mornings to write and she would never object.

"She knows that my work is very important to me and she will do everything to see the conditions I'm working under are the best. She'll be very quiet, she'll cook me breakfast, she'll give me support, she'll ask me how I'm doing, she's extremely helpful. When I have a problem and I talk about the problem there is no hesitation, she will just give up what she is doing to talk about the problem with me. If she sees that I'm upset, she'll try very much to alleviate that upset. I feel very loved, very supported, I feel extremely close to her, I love her deeply, I just feel extremely fortunate."

Nancy: "Then and now, he is completely interested in the details of my life, and accepting of my shortcomings. He is very sensitive to who I am. He just completely understands me, more so than anybody else in my life, more than I've ever felt. He has a thorough understanding of who I am. His total involvement with me makes me feel absolute security, a sense of completeness and lack of fear. Lack of certainty about the future used to cause me a lot of fear. This kind of security that I'm talking about diminished that feeling. I feel so complete in it."

 Nurturing love means being interested in the details of each other's life and being sensitive to changes in each other's mood or attitude. It's wanting to go that extra distance to do things that help and bring each other a sense of well-being.

The feeling, so common today, of men and women not under-standing one another, of seeing the other sex as a mysterious bundle of contradictions or as insensitive, uncaring, and superficial doesn't hold for couples with the marriage spirit. That's because nurturing love leaves you feeling that you are deeply understood.

With nurturing love there is no hiding how you feel or what you're thinking, no deception or pretending. You don't short-change yourself just to please your partner. This is the mistake Stacey made in her marriage with Jim. She believed loving Jim meant putting her own feelings aside. Stacey: "I don't know half the time what I really feel. I don't let myself count. I know that what Jim wants, at times, makes me feel uncomfortable, but I go along with it because I want so much to please him. But I know I lose myself in my marriage. I feel like I can't win because then he gets angry with me because he says I'm not being real in what I'm saying."

Jim: "I don't want her just to go along, I want to hear her point of view, I want a full partner, not a 'yes person.' And when I confront her with her not telling me what she really feels, she denies it, skips around it, and then starts to cry. I just can't get through to her."

Stacey's "selflessness" was generated by fear. She was operating from the belief that if she doesn't please Jim by going along with him, she is not being a good wife, and that eventually he will leave her.

Nurturing love has no fear in it. It leaves you feeling thoroughly at ease with each other because you know that you can be completely natural and open and that you'll be accepted. Your everyday behavior with each other reinforces feelings of honesty, goodwill, and kind intentions. And this leads to a daily self-sharing.

UNSELFISH INVOLVEMENT

So often we hear one partner say, "I know he [or she] loves me. I just don't feel it the way I need to." Unselfish involvement is the antidote to this situation because it promotes a dialogue that keeps you aware of and sensitive to each other's needs. There is a consistent awareness of what is going in each of you, from the superficial to the deepest level. Love must be expressed or it does little good. With unselfish involvement feelings of love are turned into concrete, loving actions.

The Talmud says, "The highest form of wisdom is kindness." Kindness is a natural outcome of unselfish involvement. Loving kindness, which unselfish involvement brings, flows naturally from your sacred self as nectar flows from a ripe fruit. Kindness is part of your true nature, only you do not realize it because you are so distracted by the desires, problems, and fears of your narrow self. As you draw closer to your true divine nature, kindness returns in your words of caring and tenderness and in the things you do to help and support each other.

 Acts of kindness rarely fail to move and inspire us. They always gain respect and admiration. They are a needed reminder of life's true purpose — the generation of unselfish love.

Small acts of kindness speak volumes of nurturing love. Cooking a good, healthy meal, doing household chores and keeping up with repairs, and creating a comfortable, pleasing home are all loving deeds and ways you nurture each other. So is showing kindness in acts of consideration and thoughtfulness.

Paul, knowing I do not enjoy shopping and seeing that I needed a winter jacket to wear around the barn, ordered one for me (without my asking) that he thought I would like. *Acts of kindness rarely fail to move and inspire us. They always gain respect and admiration. They are a needed reminder of life's true purpose—the generation of unselfish love.*

LUCILLE AND PHILIP

When life surprises us with difficulties and hardships little comforts mean a great deal. At those times the caring of nurturing love helps us feel strong within so we can carry on. Lucille and Philip, a couple we mentioned earlier, have been married for thirty-five years. They have known the worst and best of times. They grew up poor in the rural South, and their early life was made more painful by racism and bigotry.

At age twenty, Lucille had a miscarriage and was sterilized without her consent. She and Philip came north hoping for better times but found years of struggle instead. Jobs were hard to come by and never lasted long enough to put them out of debt. Gradually, despite all the obstacles, they were able to make a life together. They adopted two sons, started doing well financially, and never stopped supporting and caring for each other. Here each describes the very essence of nurturing love.

Lucille: "He helped make me more confident in myself, by him being there, by us being together, someone I could rely on and depend on. I've always been a very shy person, always a step back kind of person. He's more go-getting and outgoing and he pulled that out of me. I just wouldn't talk much, only if it was something very important. I have to say thanks to my husband, he has brought me out of a lot of depressed stages by getting me to talk. I am grateful to him for that, he helped a need in me by telling me what I had to say was important.

"He cares for me in lots of different ways. The way he acts, for instance. I'm a beautician and I have very long hours—from eight in the morning till eight, nine, ten at night. He always has my food ready when I come in, and even if he's not in he'll have the food in the oven nice and warm. Or sometimes, when I come in he takes my shoes off and rubs my feet, sometimes he'll run my bath. If, at times, I want something or need something, he'll give and share with me. I know he loves me. I have no doubts about that at all.

"I feel very secure in our relationship. He just seems to have a lot of love not only for me but for humanity. Sometimes out of the clear blue sky when I think of our life and how far we have come, I tell him, 'You're a special person.' His loving and caring freed me to grow."

Philip: "Lucille has helped me become more reasonable, more tolerant, more understanding. I guess because she loved me and through patience, a lot of patience, and through respect for me, she just stuck to her guns. It seems that my life was somewhat molded more as a strong man through her tenderness in dealing with me.

"She used to do domestic work years ago and when I came in the evening to pick her up, the lady would say, 'Could you fix this thing in my house? Your wife said you can do it.' She always had that confidence in me, she'd say, 'My husband can do it, my husband can do it,' and I'd say, 'I don't know if I can do it or not,' but when I tried I could do it because she built up my confidence. She believed in me, she believed I could do it and I would tackle it. Because she said I could, I could, and I did it.

"Our relationship is good and she never tries to do anything to hurt me or harm me. She's always looking out for my interest. Helping me to pay the bills, sharing her money, there's no division between us where I have my own bankbook and she has hers. Our position has never been this is mine and this is yours. It's always been what's mine is yours and what's yours is mine. We just say 'we' instead of 'I.' She's unselfish, that's the word.

"Being loved by her makes me feel good, it makes me feel very important, very proud, very successful, very thankful. Her caring about me had a lot to do with my growth. As a matter of fact, it had all to do with it."

Nurturing love is the first basic way you must come through for each other to have the marriage spirit. The following is a list of attitudes and behavior that convey nurturing love.

Nurturing Love Is Conveyed By:
Attention

a. Looking to *actually* see.
b. Listening to *actually* hear.
c. Talking to openly share your fears, sorrows, angers, preoccupations, as well as your joys and pleasures.
d. Giving freely and willingly your time and interest.

A Frequent Verbal Display of Affection

a. Frequently saying "I love you," while looking into each other's eyes.
b. Frequently praising, complimenting, giving recognition to each other's efforts.
c. Frequently making statements of appreciation, gratitude, and thankfulness to your partner for his or her goodness, kindness, and thoughtfulness.
d. Acknowledging each other's accomplishments to friends and family.
e. Never using put-downs, sarcasm, or ridicule to make a point.
f. Consciously using a kind and tender tone of voice and demeanor.

Frequent Physical Display of Affection

a. Touching, holding, hugging, kissing, outside the bedroom, apart from sexual desire.
b. Clear yet *subtle* messages, by a look or a touch (which only the two of you would understand) of sexual desire and responsiveness outside the bedroom.
c. Free, uninhibited expressions of your physical love for each other inside the bedroom.

Empathy and Understanding

a. Being able to feel along with your partner, "seeing with the eyes of another."
b. Sensing your partner's moods and feelings, wanting to understand them, "hearing with the ears of another, feeling with the heart of another."
c. Being positive, offering goodwill.
d. Anticipating needs. Taking over *willingly* when the other is ill. Looking to see what needs to be done in situations before being asked. When your partner looks overwhelmed suggest the two of you do something that will be relaxing, or suggest that he or she get out alone for a while.

Unselfish Involvement

a. Being helpful and cooperative rather than being competitive.
b. Being honest and open, not holding secrets.
c. Showing genuine interest in the *details* of your partner's life, without being forceful or intrusive.
d. Honoring commitments, being reliable and dependable.
e. Being able to sacrifice without regret.
f. Discouraging self-destructive behavior.
g. Having a supportive and uncritical attitude.
h. Demonstrating loving kindness.

Feelings Created by Nurturing Love

You know you are giving and receiving nurturing love when you *feel* understood and deeply cared about, "warm" inside, happy, sexually responsive, stable, secure, trusting, able to face problems, self-confident, capable of reaching out to others.

CHAPTER FOURTEEN

Intentional Love

The most empowering relationships
are those in which each partner lifts
the other to a higher possession of
their own being.

—TEILHARD DE CHARDIN

Intentional love is
what makes you grow individually and as a couple. It's the way
you foster each other's self-expression and creativity. Intentional
love means deliberately doing everything you can to help your
partner express his or her particular talent and potential. It is an
unconditional willingness to help your partner fulfill him- or
herself in his or her own unique way.

In marriage you demonstrate intentional love by giving your
partner freedom to grow, by being a sounding board, and by
modeling growth through your own attitudes and behavior.

This giving, so that the one you love grows, does not feel like
sacrifice or an imposed burden. It is done freely when each of
you realizes how important it is to express your particular
potential. When you both understand this kind of growth as a
vital need that must be fulfilled you watch for it, encourage it,
and respect it as essential. Your joint commitment to mutual

growth through intentional love adds tremendous strength to your relationship.

Everyone accepts that the parent-child relationship is devoted to creating a positive environment for children to grow and develop in. What we have not as yet clearly recognized and given enough attention to is that marriage, our most intimate adult relationship, can serve a similar purpose.

PROVIDING FREEDOM TO GROW

Partners who grow together stay very much in love, while those who don't usually end up divorced. Unfortunately, some people believe that by encouraging their partner's individuality distance will develop in their marriage and their togetherness will be threatened. This is a mistake.

Healthy individuality is never a threat to marriage. In fact, the root meaning of the word individual is "undivided, inseparable, indivisible." It means being whole and connected. When each of you helps the other grow to feel this way you create a powerful bond of love and admiration between you.

 ✌ Partners who grow together stay very much
in love, while those who don't usually
end up divorced.

On the other hand, where intentional loving is missing partners complain of feeling trapped and controlled. To them marriage feels like having to sacrifice their individuality. By the time Brett and Louise came for counseling Brett had already made up his mind to leave. He said his marriage felt like "a vise squeezing the life out of me."

Brett: "For the past twenty years I've lived Louise's life, not mine. And I realize that it's partly my fault for allowing it to get that way. But Louise has convinced me by her behavior that she really doesn't want an equal partner, she wants someone who will do for her, take care of her, put her on a pedestal, have everything her way, and not have to reciprocate by doing any of those things for anyone else. She's not able to give support, encouragement, or praise unless in some way it directly benefits her."

May and Alan came to speak with us when they were already legally separated. Both were having doubts about having moved too quickly in splitting up. Now they were looking back to see what they could learn and perhaps to consider getting back together. We asked them why they had separated. In May's answer we find a good description of feeling trapped.

May: "Alan works very hard and is a very good provider but he is also a very rigid, inflexible type of person. He always has to have his own way. He wants me around him all the time. He wants to know that I'm here working for him like he has to work for us. All he cares about is that his clothes get washed and his meals are cooked. My doing things for me, things that make me feel happy and good about myself he has no tolerance for. If I can do them without any inconvenience to him, fine, if not he wants me to drop them and stay home. I feel trapped, I can't live like that."

BARRY AND LAUREN

By contrast we see in the following example what intentional loving looks like. Barry is an aerospace engineer who heads up a research and development team. Lauren had been a top honors student at college but had put off having a career to raise a family. After two children and watching Barry steadily advance in his company, she decided she needed to get back to her own professional development. With Barry's encouragement she applied and was accepted to medical school.

Over the next six years Barry, in addition to his own job, became a constant source of strength and encouragement for her. While Lauren took courses and did clinical work and an internship, Barry, with the help of baby-sitters, had to take over the lion's share of child rearing, car pooling, arranging for play dates, and running a household. It also meant being there for emotional support when Lauren became overwhelmed by the stress and was ready to quit. Barry's behavior illuminates important aspects of intentional love:

- *He was a strong encourager,* urging Lauren to apply to medical school despite her doubt and fear.
- *He was willing to take on the extra household responsibilities* that would fall to him once Lauren began full-time studies.
- *He was flexible and cooperative,* often going out of his way to adjust his own schedule so it fit into Lauren's frequently changing class and study schedule.
- *He was willing to change roles* and become a "househusband," being both mother and father to their two children.
- *He offered his help freely* without complaints or resentment.
- *He was willing to do with fewer material comforts, so that he could provide financially.*

Another example of intentional love is when either one or both of you makes lifestyle changes that create opportunities for growing. Hope and Howard, to foster each other's spiritual development, adopted a policy of being "materially undemanding." In order to follow this policy they agreed to carefully watch their egos' need to want and to acquire. Each time they said "no" to something they actually did not need they created the possi-

---

 Unfortunately, some people believe that by encouraging their partner's individuality a distance will develop in their marriage and their togetherness will be threatened. This is a mistake.

---

bility of working less. Whatever time was then freed they used to follow spiritual interests, such as going on retreat and finding ways to serve others.

BEING A SOUNDING BOARD

Intentional love is the kind of love that carries you through periods of personal doubt, anxiety, and depression. When your partner is feeling down or upset you can be a sounding board by putting your own feelings aside and fully hearing him or her out. This kind of help can only be offered—it *cannot be forced* or pushed onto your partner. You can only reach out, invite, and make yourself available. It is up to your partner to accept. When he or she does accept you can help your partner sort out conflicted thoughts and feelings in the following ways:

- *Draw him or her out.* Ask open-ended questions that call for more than a "yes" or "no" answer. For example, "What thoughts are going through your mind right now?" Or, "I see that you are upset, what are you feeling right now?" These "door openers" create conversation, they are a way of saying, "Tell me more."
- *Listen without analyzing, forming quick opinions, or rushing in with solutions.*
- *Reflect to your partner what you hear him or her saying. This will help your partner be clear about what he or she is thinking and feeling.*
- *Offer support and reassurance while discouraging negative thinking.*
- *When asked, describe your view of the situation.* Highlight for your partner what you see as the ego at work in his or her self-defeating attitudes and behavior.
- *Remind your partner to look at his or her upset or troubling situation from the spiritual self and not the ego.* This means asking, "If you had no fears or desires of any kind, what would you be doing differently in this situation?"

By being a good sounding board you meet a major responsibility of a loving partner: creating a marital safety zone where each of you can talk comfortably about upsetting feelings or issues. *This requires letting go of your need to fix things.* Remember, listening does not mean you must have answers and solutions.

Neil runs his own business. He says that he avoids talking to his wife about company problems because it inevitably leads to a fight. Neil: "She doesn't understand the scope of the issues involved yet she always insists on giving me advice that I can't really follow or take that seriously. That's not being helpful. If I disagree with what she says, we end up fighting. When I don't share what's going on she feels shut out and there's a tension between us. Either way I lose. All she needs to do is just listen and be understanding."

The other side of being a good sounding board is the willingness to share feelings honestly. When either of you is feeling troubled and conflicted, you grow emotionally and spiritually by taking the risk of allowing yourself to be fully known to your partner. When you do you will be exposing your ego's private logic, with all its fears, worries, and doubts, to a new light of awareness. Shining a spotlight of attention on your ego reveals its hold on you and at the same time frees you, by opening a space for your spiritual self to return.

No matter how vague you may seem or how confused and illogical you may sound, making the effort of putting your confused thoughts and feelings into words is crucial. By doing so you make yourself transparent, so your partner knows what is on your mind and in your heart.

Often partners tell us they are reluctant to share what they are feeling for fear they will either hurt or anger the other. If your partner becomes hurt or angry these feelings must then be handled in a constructive fashion. Here is where listening and sharing become crucial. Difficult feelings such as hurt, anger, disappointment, and embarrassment are spiritual stretch points, opportunities for you to shed your selfish self and demonstrate that you can listen, empathize, and support one another. Use the guidelines we discussed in Chapter Eight.

 Being a good sounding board requires
letting go of your need to fix things.
Listening does not mean having answers
and solutions.

When you share your innermost thoughts and feelings you are giving your partner a genuine gesture of love. Your sharing says: "I trust you and welcome you into my inner world," and this creates an immediate bond of closeness. With intentional love you understand that helping each other sort out troublesome thoughts and feelings is a natural part of marriage. It doesn't seem inappropriate or excessive. When your partner feels down, for whatever reason, help is freely offered.

In survival-mentality marriages, in which soul-centered, intentional love is practically nonexistent, partners will frequently complain about "having to be a therapist" for each other. Both are reluctant to be caring helpers because they have not experienced their partner as caring for them in a reciprocal way. Then any effort made to help, whether it comes by way of guilt or compulsion, will not go well.

 By being a good sounding board you meet a
major responsibility of a loving partner:
creating a marital safety zone where each of
you can talk comfortably about upsetting
feelings or issues.

---

274   SOUL-CENTERED LOVE

Here Steven describes the kind of intentional love Joyce gave him in their marriage. Before they married he was worried that when his insecurities came out between them she would turn these against him. Instead she offered the kind of help that makes up intentional love. "I could never add up all the hours Joyce spent listening to me, talking to me, encouraging me, being supportive of me. She never criticized or was mean. I never felt ashamed with her and that was one of my biggest fears, that she might use it all against me.

"But that never happened. She helped me look at the worst parts of myself without feeling humiliated. She was always there, helping me out of whatever trouble I created for myself, real or imagined. She helped me see myself, to understand my feelings and my actions. I just know I'm a lot better off emotionally because of her."

By suggesting that you use intentional love to help each other during times of personal stress and upset, we are not suggesting that you do the work of a mental health professional. If your partner is in serious or prolonged emotional distress you will need the help of a professional person outside the relationship.

MODELING GROWTH FOR YOUR PARTNER

Another way you show intentional love is by demonstrating attitudes and behavior you would like to see your partner change or adapt. For example, if you want your partner to be more optimistic and less of a worrier, make sure you display a positive, optimistic outlook yourself. If you want him or her to eat differently or exercise more frequently model that behavior yourself. Modeling is a powerful nonverbal way to shape behavior because it eliminates lecturing and "nagging."

Years ago Evelyn began using the time from 5:00 to 6:30 each morning for spiritual reading and contemplation. Each morning, with rare exceptions, she would pop out of bed and begin her routine. Her discipline made a distinct impression on me and soon I was also getting up early. Now both of us use this early morning time to do spiritual reading, share inspirational passages we come across, exercise, and meditate. Modeling is not forcing or coercing, it is simply demonstrating by your own behavior what you value and consider important.

Modeling also includes taking risks for and with your partner. Deena sang in both her high-school and college choirs. Marriage and children had put her love of singing on a back burner. When a local theater group announced they were putting on her favorite musical she thought about trying out but quickly talked herself out of it.

Her husband, Al, knew how much she loved music and urged her to go for it. Deena agreed to go on Saturday morning to the audition, but when the time came she could not bring herself to do it. Al suggested they go together, which helped Deena find that extra courage she needed. She tried out and got a part. Al continued going with her twice more, and when it was clear that Deena no longer needed his support, he happily dropped out.

Another kind of modeling is trying on new activities or joining our partner in activities that we would not typically engage in ourselves. When Paul began pursuing an interest in horses by reading about them, visiting farms, going to shows, and taking riding lessons, I went along with him. After trying a few lessons the fear of being up so high on a horse discouraged me. Paul continued and invited me along each time he went. Sometimes I joined him and sometimes I didn't.

When he told me about a smaller horse that was easy to ride (the Paso Fino), I tried taking lessons again. Since Paul was getting more serious about riding I thought it would be fun if we could do it together. This time, determined to conquer my fear, I stayed with the lessons. Now my love of horses is a true joy. Each of us owns one—he the smaller one and I the larger one.

Another way you help each other grow and stay interesting to each other is by sharing an intellectual intimacy. This means sharing ideas, information, and learning. One of you may be interested in philosophy, the other in architecture, or it might be that one of you loves to cook while the other is passionate about photography, old cars, or carpentry. The interests themselves matter less, it's sharing these interests that keeps you connected. If only one of us has such an interest, sharing it in a way that will stimulate a dialogue helps our partner grow.

When Michael went back to school for a master's degree, Marge was home with the kids, but she credits her husband with helping her grow right along with him: "All through his education he made sure that I knew about the books that he was reading. I went to some seminars and courses with him, which meant getting baby-sitters and all that. He never left me behind while he was meeting new people and learning about new things. And I of course jumped on the opportunity. Since then we have a contract where one year is continuing education for him and one year is for me and we cover for each other while that happens. This is my year."

Intentional love draws you together in the pursuit of expanding your horizons. Helping each other grow endears you to each other. It is the second basic way partners with the marriage spirit demonstrate soul-centered love. Here is a list of attitudes and behavior that convey intentional love.

Intentional Love Is Conveyed By:
Providing Freedom to Grow

a. Provide security. Be willing to support each other financially and emotionally.
b. Be flexible and cooperative. Rigidity is not a sign of strength of character.
c. Share responsibilities. Do not hold rigidly to fixed roles.
d. Be materialistically undemanding.
e. Encourage each other's independence.

Being a Sounding Board

a. Show interest in your partner's inner world of thoughts and feelings.

b. Listen carefully without analyzing, forming quick opinions, or rushing in with solutions.

c. Clarify what you've heard before offering a different perspective.

d. Offer reassurance and discourage giving in to negative feelings.

Modeling Growth

a. Demonstrate behavior and attitudes you would like your partner to adopt.

b. Take risks for and with your partner. When one of you is hesitant or feels too stuck to make a growth move, make that move together. Help your partner break new ground, and then when he or she feels safe, back off.

c. Encourage and support each other by expressing strong *belief* in each other's ability.

d. Try on your partner's interests by joining him or her in activities.

e. Share ideas, readings, and learning.

Feelings Created by Intentional Love

You know you are giving and receiving intentional love when you *feel* less afraid and more courageous, adequate, optimistic, liberated, eager to invest your energy and enthusiasm, capable of accomplishing your goals and reaching your potential.

CHAPTER FIFTEEN

Revering Love

> In marriage you are neither the
> husband nor the wife; you are
> the love between the two.
>
> —NISARGADATTA

Revering love is the third dimension of soul-centered love. It combines with nurturing love and intentional love to create a powerful force of romantic passion inside your marriage. This kind of romantic passion becomes a reality when you end the habit of letting your small ego self have complete control over the amount of love you invite into your life.

With revering love you are fully known, deeply loved, and profoundly valued. You treat each other as precious and do not take each other for granted. You consistently show respect and devotion by valuing each other's uniqueness and holding each other in high esteem.

By assigning your ego a minor rather than a major role in your life you bring your spiritual self forward. Your spiritual self *can* create revering love because it does not blame, judge, attack, or defend. Your higher self sees, cherishes, and values all the positive traits that initially attracted you to each other: the kindness, strength of character, sense of humor, beauty, caring, sensitivity, intelligence, generosity, and warm, good nature. When your spiritual self guides your awareness these qualities stay ever clear to you. The goodness you see in each other stays fresh because as you notice and respond to these qualities you call them out more strongly in each other.

 With revering love you are fully known, deeply loved, and profoundly valued. You treat each other as precious and do not take each other for granted. You consistently show respect and devotion by valuing each other's uniqueness and holding each other in high esteem.

THE ROMANTIC PASSION OF REVERING LOVE

For many couples, romantic passion is something they share only in the early stages of being together. This experience is so common that diminished passion has come to be expected as couples pass more and more years together. How can we understand this from the point of view of the marriage spirit? Since ancient times mystics have described the height of never-ending passion and love as the soul's desire for unity with the divine. They tell us that the intense passion of a spiritual consciousness is the result of the soul being on fire with a sincere desire to know God.

As married partners our passion wanes when we fail to realize that the love that flows between us represents, at the earthly level, our soul's intense yearning to know and connect with its own divinity. The romantic passion we share is our humble effort to know and express our inner godlike qualities, our true divine nature.

 For most of us love's passion slips away. The ego with all its fears and desires rushes back in and we allow it free rein. Why? Because we have not understood that *romantic passion is spiritual in nature.*

Revering love helps us make this "divine connection" happen because it sweeps away all the fears of intimacy that your small ego self harbors. In the romantic passion of revering love your ego falls away and you are there, innocent, unguarded, unselfish, and connected soul to soul. Nothing else seems to matter. Your soul is rescued from an isolated separateness. The joy of mutually unfolding your lives together lies outstretched before you.

Yet, for most of us love's passion slips away. Our ego with all its fears and desires rushes back in and we allow it free rein. Why? Because we have not understood that *romantic passion is spiritual in nature. And because it is spiritual in nature, it can only live and thrive when your selfish self is not acting on its own, but is guided by your spiritual self.*

 Passionate romance comes alive in each look of admiration, each touch of fondness, each word of tenderness. Every gesture sends the message, "I love you, I value and cherish you, and long to make love with you."

Revering love, coming as it does from your higher spiritual self, continually rekindles romantic passion between you. Each time you demonstrate that you respect, value, and hold each other in high esteem you express revering love. As this quality of love continually moves between you, you directly perceive ever more clearly the divine core of your partner's being. What you see there thrills you because it reflects an *intuitive sensing* of your own divine essence.

An intuitive sensing is a way of knowing that is different from the usual way we know things. Intuition means "knowing without the use of rational processes, immediate knowing." It's this sense of immediate knowing that signals an intuitive awareness. It's a kind of feeling/knowledge that bypasses logical thinking. Where the rational mind says, "Prove it, show me how," intuitive perception says, "I understand."

When your skeptical ego tries to convince you that revering love and in fact all of soul-centered love is "too idealized and unattainable," the intuition of your higher self, with a clear, peaceful certainty, says, "Yes, it is possible." It immediately grasps a more subtle, basic reality operating beyond outer appearances.

The meeting of your souls in revering love happens in "loving stillness," when the ego mind is absent. In that silent sacred space there is freedom for you to look at your partner, at his or her essence, *not his or her body-mind,* seeing directly into the divine in him or her. With such a profound looking your partner's awareness expands and he or she feels his or her own divinity. Your partner is so strongly attracted to and affected by the depth of your looking, that he or she spontaneously looks back at you, *past your body-mind* into the divine in you. This depth of looking moves you and you feel your own divinity.

 The meeting of your souls in revering love happens in "loving stillness," when the ego mind is absent.

Without a word spoken, in the sacred place of your marriage, you have through your love created a direct experience of your spiritual oneness, your true divine nature. Passionate romance comes alive in each look of admiration, each touch of fondness, each word of tenderness. Every gesture sends the message, "I love you, I value and cherish you, and long to make love with you." This is the living romance of revering love.

Revering love closes a giant cosmic circle. Beyond the differences of male and female, of likes and dislikes, beyond the petty squabbles of your egos, you share the sacred oneness behind all creation. It is this divine oneness which is cherished in revering love. By intuitively sensing the divine in each other your souls touch and feel joyously, passionately at home together.

  When your skeptical ego tries to convince you that revering love and, in fact, all of soul-centered love is "too idealized and unattainable," the intuition of your higher self, with a clear, peaceful certainty, says, "Yes, it is possible."

VALUING AND HOLDING EACH OTHER IN HIGH ESTEEM

It is important to understand that romantic love and passion get renewed each and every day by the quality of thoughts and beliefs you hold about each other. Your thoughts create your reality; they produce the feelings that color your mood and influence what and how you communicate with each other. So for the health of your relationship it is essential to let go of negative thinking.

By negative thinking we do not mean thoughts that only pertain to your partner. Negative thinking is any thought of

Revering love closes a giant cosmic circle.
Beyond the differences of male and
female, of likes and dislikes, beyond the
petty squabbles of your egos, you share
the sacred oneness behind
all creation.

failure, disappointment, or discouragement. It is thinking that
puts yourself or someone else down. It is thoughts that carry
spitefulness, jealousy, and envy. Negative thinking feeds on fears
and worries, on misfortunes of one kind or another.

All of us are susceptible to this kind of thinking because events
that foster it come to us every day on the evening news. Negative
thinking can also come to us totally by chance, triggered by some
random cue or association our mind makes to one thing or
another. Fortunately, while we may not be able to prevent negative associations, we do have the power to limit their influence.
This is where witnessing is so helpful.

As we have said earlier, witnessing negative thoughts takes
away their power to upset our emotions. Rather than dwell on
them and get swept away on a rising tide of bad feelings, either
about oneself or about another, witnessing enables us to let such

 You build your love anew each and every
day based on the quality of thoughts and
beliefs you hold about each other. Thoughts
do not occur in a vacuum. They produce the
feelings that color your mood and influence
how and what you communicate.

thoughts rise up and pass away. If we do not hold on to them they will come and they will go.

With your minds free of negativity and full of positive thoughts of each other you create passion because you revere each other. You pull out each other's best self when you value and hold each other in high esteem.

It is only from a clear mind, free of negativity, that revering love is possible. And it is revering the highest in *each of you* that links you and your partner as kindred souls. Always think the best of yourself and your partner, offer goodwill and never hold a grudge or nurse bitter feelings.

When you are loved and valued in this way you develop a sense of self-worth that is unshakeable. This comes from seeing that your partner has taken the time and made the effort to know you through and through. He or she has listened to your stories, heard your complaints, shared painful memories and precious moments, cheered your highest victories, and cried for your sorrows. He or she has seen the best and worst of you, and, in the face of it all, has said, "Yes, I love *you,* you and none other do I want in my life as friend, lover, and life partner."

Rebecca and Clint have been married for eighteen years. Rebecca talks about his valuing her and the feeling of self-worth and love it "ignites" in her:

"First of all, I respect him, I have great respect for his integrity. That gives my love a very basic foundation. And I think his continually letting me know how important I am to him—his continually doing that ignites a deep feeling of self-worth that only he, my husband, could bestow on me. Other people could tell me and it just doesn't mean the same thing. And I could read it as many times as I want in all the woman's magazines and it still doesn't mean the same thing. Knowing that he values me ignites a sense of caring and passion and love that is overflowing."

Hilary, married eleven years, explains in detail the many ways she feels respected and valued by her husband and what this has meant to her in terms of her own personal growth:

"His loving comes to me easily because he tells me a lot of

how he feels about me. I recognize that would be empty if it weren't followed by actions. It's in his thoughtfulness and a lot of other different ways that he makes me feel that I am very important to him. It comes out in terms of decisions he makes, his taking my feelings into account. He shares himself with me and I have a strong sense from him that he values my thinking, he values how I feel about things. He values my body, not only sexually but also in terms of my being healthy. I just have a really deep sense of care and thoughtfulness from him.

"It has a definite effect on me, it's just terribly freeing. It's the kind of thing that just releases me to have a lot of energy to invest in other things. I don't have to have a lot of energy tied up in being concerned about whether he really cares for me; that frees me to invest myself in a lot of different things.

 "It's in his thoughtfulness and a lot of other different ways that he makes me feel that I am very important to him. It comes out in terms of decisions he makes, his taking my feelings into account."

"His caring for me is very basic to me in terms of my well-being: to feel cared for, to feel important to him. I think I could function without it, but God, life would be meager. His loving has made a richness of living and a richness of relationship that I am grateful to have. Also, I feel a very strong sense of acceptance from my husband. Now that doesn't mean agreement. In fact, I think it has been harder for me to accept some things about myself than it has been for him to accept. There are times that I have done something bitchy and he had a real sense of forgiveness and that is powerful. That kind of valuing me, my very soul, that I don't experience anywhere else, I experience with him."

We asked David Mace, one of our early mentors, mentioned in

Chapter Eight, about feeling loved and valued in his marriage. David's comment vividly captures the essence of revering love and underscores how important it is to feel that your partner knows you through and through and still loves you:

"I know my sense of identity is continually reinforced by her understanding of me and her acceptance of me. What I mean is that I think that nobody has a secure sense of identity until he or she is in a relationship of being fully known and deeply loved. That, for me, is the definition of a completely secure sense of identity.

"I am fully known and I am deeply loved. If I were not fully known, I could always have the fear that if people knew things about me that they don't know they would reject me. If I were known and rejected that would be awful, but to be fully known and deeply loved is the only way to a secure identity. There is no way, I think, to a secure identity in isolation. I know my wife knows me through and through, and I know she loves me, and I know I'm OK. That is where the loving finds its completion."

LAUGHING AND PLAYING TOGETHER

A Japanese proverb says, "Time spent laughing is time spent with the gods." Ancient wisdom tells us that playfulness, humor, and laughter are basic qualities of your higher self. When you love deeply and are connected emotionally and spiritually there is a general feeling of lighthearted gaiety and playfulness. Couples living out the marriage spirit laugh a lot. They enjoy a good sense of humor and take time to play together. Laughter, humor, and playfulness are a large part of revering love.

Playing brings out your natural innocence and creative imagination. When you are lost in play and creativity you are fully absorbed in the present, spiritual *now*. Here your ego has no foothold to establish itself. Your selfish self comes in only when play becomes a means to an end, such as winning. Winning is about competition, not play. Play is an end in itself, it calms rather than agitates. Playing, laughing, creating, sharing in and cultivating beauty together lift our spirits, massage our soul, and deepen the bond between us. So it is essential for couples to balance their life together with a healthy amount of wholesome play.

 Playing, laughing, creating, sharing in and cultivating beauty together lift our spirits, massage our soul, and deepen the bond between us. So it is essential for couples to balance their life together with a healthy amount of wholesome play.

It doesn't matter how you play as long as you are both able to find the beauty and joy in it. It can be the beauty and joy of creating or participating in art, music, literature, or dance. It might be the joy that comes from working out physically or playing tennis or jogging. Some couples enjoy the beauty of nature, hiking, walking on the beach, or camping.

One of the favorite ways Paul and I play, aside from being with our friends, is by grooming, feeding, and riding our horses. For us, riding through quiet woods and over mountains is wonderfully relaxing. Beauty, play, laughter, and creativity all point you back to your sacred ground of being, your sacred self. Sharing in this strengthens and reinforces revering love.

LAURA AND JERRY

Laura and Jerry, married for ten years, talk about the *reciprocal* nature of soul-centered loving in their marriage.

Laura: "I think the main thing is that he believes in me and respects me, and makes me feel I am a very worthy person. He talks to me, he tells me he loves me, and there's a daily kind of closeness, there's a lot of talking and sharing between us. I realized that he thought I was a very nice person and that I had a lot to give, and he made me believe it, too.

"He values me as an individual, and I don't feel he expects things of me I can't do or be. He doesn't have any images about me. I guess I always enforced an image about myself. I would have been a happier person had I just been myself, but I couldn't know that until I was with him. He was secure and stable, and he valued me as I really was. I mean, he allowed me to be myself, and he let me allow myself to be."

Jerry: "I guess I learned to love from her love. I've always felt that being a recipient of her love makes me larger somehow inside. I learned that love causes you to expand. That's how I think of it. Knowing that you can trust someone to love you just as you are helps free you."

 "He talks to me, he tells me he loves me, and there's a daily kind of closeness, there's a lot of talking and sharing between us. I realized that he thought I was a very nice person and that I had a lot to give, and he made me believe it, too."

LOVING EACH OTHER FROM YOUR SPIRITUAL SELVES

You know that you are loving each other from your spiritual selves when:

- You often experience a clear, direct perception of newness as if you are meeting for the first time.
- You feel flooded with a feeling of goodness coming from your partner through you and back from you to your partner.

- You feel a complete ease of being. You can be totally yourself.
- You experience a feeling of acceptance surrounding you, acceptance coming from you to your partner and vice versa.
- You experience a quality of focused attention between you that feels effortless.
- You feel a joyous excitement, which brings out a feeling of happiness in you.
- You are acutely aware of your partner's interest, care, and concern about you. And those same feelings are moving through you to your partner.
- You intuitively sense that in a *larger reality* you and your partner are not just body, mind, senses, thoughts, or feelings, but are indeed sacred spiritual beings.

The spirit of never-ending, unselfish love is within you. You do not have to search for it; it is already yours. Rediscover it within you, demonstrate it through your words and deeds, and like a beacon, it will draw love back to you. Love begets love. Love is your natural state, your true divine nature. All you need do is remember this and look for every opportunity to bring it forth. When you do this as a couple you express the marriage spirit and your marriage becomes a sacred place.

ANDREW AND BERNICE

Bernice and Andrew are still very much in love after fifty-two years of marriage. Theirs is a wonderful example of how all three dimensions of soul-centered love blend to create a lasting, loving marriage. We first mentioned them briefly when we spoke about nurturing love. They have carved out a loving life together despite a very common problem: Andrew's business stole away precious time and energy from their marriage.

As the owner of a large company doing business here and in Europe, Andrew had to work long hours and make frequent trips out of the country. Early on he and Bernice discussed this and came to an understanding that for Andrew work needed to be a priority.

For many couples this would have led to a marriage full of conflict. Bernice and Andrew do not fall into this category. Their marriage is sound through and through, conflict minimal, and their passion for each other undiminished. In their comments we can see the important ways they came through for each other and understand why their love has stayed so strong.

Bernice: "He helped foster my growth completely. He always wanted and encouraged me to do the things that I enjoyed doing. And he would do things with me I enjoyed doing, whether he had selected them or not. He always gave me freedom. He's never said, 'Where have you been?' or, 'Why did you do that?' and certainly never, 'What did you spend the money for?' Never. He's always encouraged me. He encouraged me to join a women's group and would go with me to things they had when we'd bring husbands and things like that.

"He always talked things over with me. Even when we had a house full of children and I was worn out at night, I would go to bed but the minute I heard him come in I knew he would have something interesting to tell me. He always told me about his work and things that had happened. Whenever he discussed difficult problems that came up he would ask me what I thought about them. I didn't always expect him to take my advice, and he knew I didn't.

"I was a sounding board for him. I would listen because I was interested and he loved to talk things over with me. That kept me feeling that I was a part of his work and that he respected my opinion. It helped me feel important and that I had worth. I grew because he stimulated my growth, he promoted it by making me feel that whatever I wanted to do, whatever I felt, and whatever I had to say was important.

"He was not a very demonstrative person because his mother and father were not, but I taught him to be because I need it. I told him I need attention and loving more than I need food. And

I think just by being loving to him I taught him to be more openly affectionate.

"I guess the principal thing that lets me know he loves me is that he always includes me in. He's always been rather important in the circles we've been in and I know that people know me if I'm with him and that they are friendly with me because of him. But he has always made me feel that I am of importance, that I have a personal value."

Andrew: "First of all, to say that she has been understanding and cooperative is too light a word, though that expresses it. She's been willing to sacrifice, which had to be done during many of the early years of our marriage, so I could do what needed to be done for our business to flourish.

"I like to travel more than she does but she has been a good traveling companion. If there was some business meeting she was always glad to be with me, or when she could not, she was willing—and I mean that, I don't mean she tolerated—she was willing to stay with the children while I was away. While she was here with small children, I would be on some meeting in Europe. I never felt she resented that. There were times I was wrapped up so in my work that it brought problems. But we always made sure they never got out of hand. Together we each did whatever was necessary to solve them.

"I've learned a great deal from her. She's helped me by sharing things she has learned. She's an avid reader and she always shared her reading with me. Also, she has always encouraged me to talk to her about my frustrations. She listens to me, if I have some frustration at the end of the day, and I'm about to climb walls, she hears me out. I have not expected her to be my therapist but she did hear me out, and it was a tremendous help to me.

"There are so many ways she shows her love: by being a good companion without any feeling of force or make-believe, by doing things that would make life comfortable for me, that can be anything from good cooking, which she likes to do, to wanting to be with me in what I was doing, sensing times when my needs would be more than that of any others of the family at the moment.

"For example, there was one time at work when I was too tired to go on and I felt I couldn't take another day, but as usual I had two meetings that night. I called her over the phone and said, 'I feel like I've got to get out of town—not far, but I just feel I've got to, just for one night and I'll be all right. I need a good night's sleep. I've got two meetings but I can get someone else to take my place.' She said, 'How soon could you go?' I said, 'I could be ready within an hour.' She said, 'Well, I could be ready in thirty minutes.'

"She came, picked me up at my office, asked me where I wanted to go. I said, 'I don't want to have to decide. I'm too tired. Just someplace fifty miles away, get a motel, go out to dinner, have the evening together.' And we did. I came back to my work rested, and it was three or four days later before I even thought to ask her what she did about our four children! That expresses love. I never had any doubt about her love. Being loved by her makes me feel warm, it gives me a desire to reciprocate, and a feeling of self-worth, comfort, gratitude, I could go on and on."

In what ways was this couple able to blend all the dimensions of soul-centered love? We'll briefly review it for you as follows:

Andrew

1. He included Bernice in all areas of his life, including telling her all about his business and their entire financial status. (revering love)
2. He helped her feel important by making sure she knew everyone he worked with and by introducing her to all the influential people he came in contact with. (revering love)
3. He talked things over with her, sharing himself by talking about his feelings and the things that meant a lot to him. (nurturing love)
4. Andrew was interested in the details of Bernice's life. He involved himself in her world and would clear his calendar

to go to functions that were important to her. (nurturing love)

5. He supported her growth by encouraging her to try new things and went with her to meetings and events of interest to her. (intentional love)

6. He recognized Bernice's need for affection and his own difficulty with it. He developed his ability to be more giving to her by being physically and verbally affectionate, by letting her know he desired her, by being kind, generous, and giving of himself. (nurturing love)

7. He encouraged her independence. (intentional love)

Bernice

1. She was understanding and cooperative. She accepted being alone a great deal with the children so Andrew could pursue his career. She was willing to sacrifice without resentment. (intentional love)

2. She was a sounding board for Andrew. She listened to his problems without projecting her needs and opinions. (intentional love)

3. She was a good companion, doing things that he enjoyed, and she made sure they played together. (revering love)

4. She made life comfortable by anticipating and meeting his needs. (nurturing love)

5. She shared her readings and interests with him. (intentional love)

6. She was warm and affectionate and she let him know she desired him. (nurturing love)

7. She structured her life and time in ways that let Andrew know clearly he was a priority. (revering love)

Through revering love you actively demonstrate your devotion to and reverence for each other. It is the third and final dimension of soul-centered love. The following lists of attitudes and behavior show how revering love is conveyed.

Revering Love Is Conveyed By:
Valuing Your Partner's Uniqueness

a. Allow your partner to be him- or herself, do not saddle your partner with preconceived images of how he or she "should be."

b. Avoid comparing your partner to anyone else.

c. Make it a priority to know what is important to your partner. Do not try fitting him or her into a mold.

d. Offer your partner an abundance of acceptance and approval.

e. Speak highly of your partner. Express admiration, appreciation, and gratitude directly to your partner and about him or her to others.

Holding Your Partner in High Esteem

a. Show your partner the utmost respect and regard through attitudes and behavior that reflect consideration, thoughtfulness, adoration, honor, and esteem.

b. Give your partner importance. Include him or her in your world of thoughts, feelings, and plans.

c. Make decisions that take your partner's needs and interests into account.

d. Structure your life and time in ways that let your partner know he or she is a priority.

Laughing and Playing Together

a. Develop a sense of humor and be able to laugh at yourself.

b. Cultivate an optimistic, pleasant, uplifting attitude toward life and each other.

c. Learn to have fun together. Find things you both enjoy. Stick with it, brainstorm ideas, you are bound to come up with more things than you ever thought possible.

d. Get outdoors, share the joy and beauty of nature.

e. Remember happiness is your true nature, there is no greater delight than sharing laughter and fun.

Subjective Feelings

You know you are giving and receiving revering love when you *feel* valued, able to see your shortcomings, accepting of yourself, peaceful, happy, grateful, fortunate, connected to your partner and in love, awake to your own spirituality and compassion for other living beings.

STEP VII RITUAL

SOUL-CENTERED LOVE

Soul-centered love is so important to the marriage spirit that having a way to gauge it is essential. Look over the lists of attitudes and behavior at the end of the chapters on Nurturing Love (Chapter 13), Intentional Love (Chapter 14), and Revering Love (above). Place a (+) next to those things you think you do a good job of and a (−) after those where you think you need improvement. Use a (?) for those items you are not sure about. Do this alone and then go over your responses together. See if you agree with each other's assessment. Give particular attention to areas that need improvement.

Next, each of you pick at least one attitude or behavior in either nurturing, intentional, or revering love that you would like your partner to refine and strengthen. Give each other a gift by agreeing that you will consciously work at changing whatever attitude or behavior your partner indicates is important to him or her.

ANDREA AND VINCENT

When Andrea and Vincent did this ritual together Andrea asked Vincent to make more of an effort at revering love, specifically at holding her in high esteem and showing her more respect and regard, especially when she approached him with concerns important to her. She gave as an example what happened when they were house hunting. Andrea wanted desperately to have a house of their own, while Vincent was content to look more casually.

She turned to him and said, "I begged you to give me an hour of your time to just look at a house with me. I didn't ask you to buy it, just to look. You couldn't be bothered, you barely looked up from the computer. I kept coming back to you, I pleaded with you to give me some time and look at the house with me. And this didn't happen just once, this happened each time I found a house I liked. I would beg you to look with me, you wouldn't. It got to a point where I felt so dismissed, so degraded, so humiliated at having to beg and plead. I didn't feel valued or important to you. I need you to love me with revering love."

Vincent acknowledged that this was true. He apologized and told Andrea he had been angry with her and was wrong for showing his anger this way. He said he loved her and could and would show her revering love. He added that he never intended to hurt her and could see and feel her pain.

When it was Vincent's turn, he said, "My anger got in the way. It was wrong and I'm not offering it as an excuse. It won't happen again. What I need from you is nurturing love. It seems like I'm the one who always goes to you with a hug or a kiss and most of the time it seems like you couldn't care less. It would feel a lot better if I had more affection coming from you to me. Then it wouldn't feel so one-sided the way it does now. I'd like to feel that you desire me as much as I desire you. Don't get me wrong, I'm not talking only about sex, just some affection, feeling loved and wanted would be nice." Andrea acknowledged the truth in Vince's observations: "You're right about that. I know I can do better there and I will."

Remember, when your partner makes a request do not feel compelled to defend, explain, or justify your past behavior. Just listen so you are clear about how your partner needs to be loved by you. Give a strong statement agreeing to come through for him or her. Then do it! As you go forward be sure to acknowledge and praise each other for coming through.

The Marriage Spirit

Living with the Marriage Spirit

What we usually call human evolution
is the awakening of the divine nature
within us.

—PEACE PILGRIM

As we come to the
end of our conversation we hope that the information presented
has encouraged you to move your marriage to a new level of
intimacy. This kind of movement, so important and beneficial to
you, has even wider ramifications.

The soul-centered love you share is part of an eternal current
of unselfish love in the ocean of human consciousness. And, in
the same way that we have evolved physically, our consciousness
is also changing and evolving. The transforming power of divine
love is moving all of us steadfastly toward higher and higher levels
of spiritual integrity. If this were not the case our world would
have self-destructed long ago. As a part of this current of unselfish
love, when you change, the world changes with you.

By now you know that marriage is much more than a physical and emotional love affair. Marriage is, most importantly, an

opportunity to recognize your true identity in each other. It is a spiritual exercise designed to help you transcend your self-centered ego. When it serves this purpose marriage becomes a sacred place. It nurtures your deepest yearnings to believe in something larger than yourselves, something more important than your usual "me-first" agenda.

We hope that the path of the marriage spirit has changed your understanding of yourself. You have used the everyday give-and-take of being together as a rare opportunity to self-correct your identity. Now, you no longer see yourselves as isolated egos hemmed in by the narrow conditioning of a survival mentality. Rather, you have learned that at the spirit level your individual identities merge and become one. This is the ground of the divine. Getting there is your life's real journey.

   Marriage, much more than a physical and emotional love affair, is a spiritual exercise designed to help you transcend your self-centered ego.

An essential requirement for this journey is being conscious of what is truly important in your life. For this you need the wisdom of your spiritual self and not your ego. Your spiritual self can guide you to what is important because it is not motivated by self-interest. You rediscover your higher self by rising above your ego and shifting your attention and your identity to the background, the larger sacred awareness that observes all the workings of your smaller self.

Witnessing makes this shift in identity possible. Witnessing is the precious instrument essential for the liberation of your true self. With its neutral observation you see your ego self's tendency to cut off love from flowing in and between you. Chief among these tendencies are the images you have formed about yourself and each other. It is these images that stand in the way of love and fight against the marriage spirit. You cut through images by developing imageless perception. This way of looking allows you to let each other be "new" by releasing past hurts and helping you live in the spiritual now.

Life, for most of us, is often difficult and filled with pressures. But when you re-envison your marriage as a sacred place you no longer use it as a dumping ground for everyday stress. You don't allow anger to accumulate between you because now you understand that accumulated anger kills love. It disconnects you spiritually, you are no longer "in communion," and this causes your communication to break down. By treating anger as a spiritual warning signal you give it the attention it requires and you keep love and passion alive. Defusing anger enables you to communicate clearly and solve conflicts without damaging your relationship.

Handling anger skillfully is part of working together to establish unquestioned trust between you. Unquestioned trust puts a rock-solid foundation under your marriage. It underscores how essential it is to never underestimate this crucial part of your marriage. The six dimensions of unquestioned trust we describe gives you a guideline for measuring and improving the quality of your trust. Make good use of it.

 You rise above your ego by shifting your attention and your identity to the background, the larger sacred awareness in you that observes all the workings of your smaller self.

As you become more in tune with your spiritual self, the values of truth, harmony, and goodness take on greater meaning. These values come from your spiritual self and not your ego.

The nonmaterial dimension of life becomes most important to you. People and relationships get top priority, all the rest comes second. It is your ego's veil of separateness which distances you from those most dear to you. Making money, being successful, raising children can all become overwhelming when only your ego is involved. It is the spiritual values of truth, harmony, and goodness that keep you anchored on the path of the marriage spirit.

We know that many people feel diminished by marriage. They believe that marriage means sacrificing their individuality. This is true of survival-mentality marriages, which lack soul-centered loving. Soul-centered loving is self-transcendent. It makes marriage a vehicle for personal and spiritual growth. It enriches, fulfills, and keeps you growing so that you have the best opportunity to be all you can be. This is a cornerstone characteristic of the marriage spirit: It lifts you beyond your ego self's limiting beliefs and expectations.

 The unselfish love of the marriage spirit comes from your higher self and not your ego, because your higher self expresses the values of truth, harmony, and goodness.

We have described three kinds of soul-centered loving for you. Please put them to good use. They give you a new vocabulary to use so you can talk about your unmet needs in a clear, descriptive way. And they give each of you a blueprint to follow so you can come through for each other. Remember that old patterns die hard. Not many of us have had good role models when it comes to love and marriage. You are starting over with an entirely new vision of your relationship. Go slowly and be easy with each other. Welcome your mistakes and difficult moments for what they really are, spiritual opportunities for rising above your ego self.

Helping each other grow in this way releases a new wave of love inside your marriage. The spiritual power of unselfish love has no boundaries and no limits. It finds its completion in a much wider circle. When you, as a couple, follow the marriage spirit and enrich your love and caring for each other, you transcend your individual well-being and contribute to the well-being of the entire human family.

Many couples today are searching for ways to put greater love and meaning in their lives. Without the marriage spirit you risk endlessly pursuing random cures and escapes. In doing so you overlook that which lies dormant within you: your capacity for soul-centered loving. Unselfish soul-centered love is the spiritual balm needed to soothe your survival mentality.

 When you, as a couple, follow the marriage spirit and enrich your love and caring for each other, you transcend your individual well-being and contribute to the well-being of the entire human family.

We wish you the very best. Stay with the marriage spirit, take time together to do the rituals provided, encourage and be good to each other and you will master the key paradox of marriage— being a strong independent individual while at the very same time being passionately connected, heart and soul as one.

Index

314 INDEX

nurturing love (*cont.*)
  unselfish involvement in, 261–64,
    266

observation, silent, 120–21
overcompensation, 143–44

pain, of anger, 130–31
parents:
  being your own, 234
  disapproval from, 90
  enjoying the role of, 220
  and images, 93–94, 142
  loss of, 106
  praise withheld by, 51
  and reliving the past, 110–11, 178
passion:
  as celebration, 258
  creation of, 284
  as dulled by images, 257
  erosion of, 279–80
  keeping alive, 252–56
  for the person, 48, 229–32
  physical display of affection, 265
  and reverence, 47, 49
  romantic, 278, 279–82
  sources of, 256
passivity, and control, 43
past:
  clinging to, 105
  and depression, 231
  as distraction, 108–9, 121, 160
  early recollections of, 118–19
  hurts of, 112–13
  images of, 102–3
  reliving of, 110–12, 178
  vivid moments of, 118
perception:
  direct, 103
  imageless, *see* imageless perception
  and seeing, 250
perfectionism, and control, 58
Philo, 212
planning:
  need for, 104–5
  vs. projecting, 104

play, 286–88, 294–95
power, *see* control
Practical Mysticism (Underhill), 31
prayer:
  benefits of, 30
  daily practice of, 46
  role of, 45–46
  spiritual energy restored in, 46
  for spiritual guidance, 193
projecting, vs. planning, 104
projection, of anger, 129, 130
Proust, Marcel, 89
psychology, and spirituality, 13

readings, inspirational, 31
reality:
  as if, 84
  as created by your thoughts, 282
  larger, 289
red flag events, 215–26
  being taken for granted, 219–20
  roommate marriage, 216–18
  time-money trade-off, 221–23
  work-career, 216
reinforcement, positive, 38
renewing reverence, 19–54
  choosing capacity for, 49
  marriage as sacred place, 37–54
  spiritual intimacy, 21–36
  Step I ritual, 50–54
reverence:
  exchange of feelings of, 48
  and falling in love, 47–48
  longing for, 48
  renewing, *see* renewing reverence
  and spiritual self, 48
revering love, 278–95
  Andrea and Vincent, 296–97
  Andrew and Bernice, 289–93
  conveying, 294–95
  and divine connection, 280
  giant cosmic circle closed in, 282
  laughing and playing together in,
    286–88, 294–95
  Laura and Jerry, 287–88
  reciprocity in, 287

About the Authors

EVELYN and PAUL MOSCHETTA are a husband-and-wife marriage-counseling team happily married for twenty-three years. As ambassadors for strong, healthy marriages they have been helping other couples solve relationship problems since 1972. Since 1990, in addition to a full-time clinical practice based in Manhattan and Huntington, New York, the Moschettas have been contributing editors at *The Ladies' Home Journal*. They collaborate on the monthly feature, "Can This Marriage Be Saved?" which is the most popular and longest-running column in that magazine.